Superman
vs.
Hollywood

How Fiendish Producers, Devious Directors,
and Warring Writers Grounded an American Icon

Jake Rossen

CHICAGO
REVIEW
PRESS

An A Cappella Book

Library of Congress Cataloging-in-Publication Data

Rossen, Jake.
Superman vs. Hollywood : how fiendish producers, devious directors, and warring writers grounded an American icon / Jake Rossen.—1st ed.
    p. cm.
Includes bibliographical references and index.
ISBN 978-1-55652-731-9
1. Superman films—History and criticism. I. Title.

PN1995.9.S77R67 2008
791.43'651—dc22

                                2007036527

Cover and interior design: Visible Logic, www.visiblelogic.com
Cover illustration: Paul Fricke, www.paulfricke.com

Published by Chicago Review Press, Incorporated
814 North Franklin Street
Chicago, Illinois 60610
ISBN 978-1-55652-731-9
Printed in the United States of America
5 4 3 2 1

Contents

Foreword

Don't talk to me about Superman, son. I know Superman.

From the Golden Age comics secured behind my sophisticated laser death traps to the Christopher Reeve cape hanging in my hall, I have lived and breathed Clark Kent's alter ego since I was four years old. As I've mentioned elsewhere to the point of tedium, I grew up thinking that Kal-El of Kryptonopolis was as real as Santa Claus and the Easter Bunny, and was crushed at age seven to discover that he wasn't part of America's rich history but merely the most famous fictional character of all time. So began a love affair that has lasted my entire life, and that surely reached a new nadir recently when I outbid all others for the sadly deceased Frisky the cat from *Superman: The Movie*. Frisky is now stuffed and mounted on top of my piano, where he stares at guests every time we have a dinner party.

You see, I know all about Marlon Brando suggesting he play Jor-El as a bleeping green suitcase. Kevin Smith already told me Jon Peters wanted Lex Luthor to have a gay alien dog in the aborted *Superman Lives*. And I'm fully aware that Kryptonite was created for the Superman radio show because the producers felt he was a little too indestructible. So this book held little allure for me at first. Like a jaded old hooker, I had seen it all as far as Superman was concerned, collecting every scrap of gossip, from the David Michael Petrou movie companion to the Internet fan sites calling for director's cuts of *Superman II* and even *Supergirl*. I knew it all.

Or so I thought.

I will readily admit that this manuscript lay on my desk for close to two weeks before I cracked it open. Originally, I just saw it as a favor to a guy whose journalism I liked and got ready to go through the motions with a typical five-hundred-word endorsement. I opened it up at a random page on a tea break one afternoon, my senses dulled, expecting to read the same old anecdotes recycled in a hundred ways already. But here was something I didn't know. Followed by *another* arcane fact. And another. And another. By the time I looked up an hour had passed and I was halfway through it. Switching the phone off, blanking out my deadlines, and making another monster cup of tea, I took the rest of the day off, chilled out on my sofa, and read this mutha in a single sitting. In Superman terms, I was Like a Virgin reading this. Touched for the very first time. So much of this material is so good and so new I felt like I was eavesdropping on a private conversation in a Pinewood pub. I have since loaned the manuscript to three friends who all agreed that they can't imagine this ever seeing print without big legal pens cutting out all the best bits. And yet here it is, untouched and in your hands, the definitive guide to the Superman movies and genuinely the most impressive tome on a character I love like Osama loves Muhammad.

This is no fantasy. No careless product of wild imagination. This is the real deal, and Jake Rossen compiles it all so effortlessly and with such an endearing pace you will not be able to put it down, not even if a loved one is screaming and burning and begging for help in the next room. Any man who can take the backstory of *Lois & Clark* and make it a page-turner must surely win some kind of prize. Couple that with everything you need to know about Bud Collyer, Bruce Timm, and the Salkinds and you have a book I want to read more than that enormous secret diary Superman keeps in his Fortress of Solitude. In some parallel universe, for example, Warner Brothers agreed to a *Superman III* that didn't replace Brainiac with Richard Pryor, Mr. Mxyzptlk with Robert Vaughn, and Supergirl with Billy Connolly's psychologist wife. There's a tidbit like this on every page and a lot of pages here to enjoy in bed or in the bath or in the bookstore, reading it for free.

Those who know me know that I'm a Superman snob. I've been trained in this mythology like a geek Bruce Lee, so believe me when I say I can give this book no higher recommendation.

Stick the kettle on, find a comfy chair, and enjoy.

MARK MILLAR
Scotland
Earth Prime
August 6, 2007

Mark Millar is an award-winning comic book writer who has penned Superman: Red Son *and* Superman Adventures *for DC Comics. His other works include* The Ultimates, Ultimate Fantastic Four, The Authority, Civil War, *and* Wanted. *For more details see www.millarworld.tv.*

Prologue

The Klansmen were furious.

Dozens of them were congregated in a nondescript room in Atlanta, shaking cloaked heads at the worrisome news that their sect leader had just shared: an act of gross subterfuge had transpired over the airwaves. Millions of Americans had now become privy to their passwords, their rankings, their closely guarded methods of organized hatred.

All of it fodder for some goddamn comic book radio show. Their mission had been compromised, sacrificed at the altar of popular culture. Kids, one Klansman sighed. His kids were in the streets playing Superman vs. the Klan. Some of them tied red towels around their necks; others pranced around in white sheets. Their struggle for racial purity had been reduced to a recess role-play.

Stetson Kennedy listened, doing his best to give off irate body language. He scowled. He nodded. He railed.

The covert activist waited patiently for the Klan to settle on new passwords, bizarre handshakes, fresh methods of clandestine communication. When they did, he would call radio journalists Walter Winchell and Drew Pearson, offering the results of his infiltration into the group for public consumption.

He'd also contact Robert Maxwell, producer of the *Superman* radio serial. Maxwell, eager to aid the humanitarian mission of the Anti-Defamation League, would promptly insert the leaked information into his show's scripts. In between fisticuffs, his cast would mock the KKK's infrastructure, the group's loathsome attitudes rendered impotent by the juvenilia.

The Klan roared, demanding revenge on their traitor. "Show me the rat," their leader said, "and I'll show you some action."

Kennedy cheered, just as they all did. He was buoyed not by hatred but by the idea that the group's contemptible secrets would once again be publicized. Superman's influence would go far beyond the comics pages, into the realm of political performance art.

It was one of the precious few times the superhero's mythology would be done justice by those in the world of show business—a measure of respect that would eventually prove to be as rare as Kryptonite itself.

This is not a book about Superman.

Not exactly, anyway.

Those expecting a dissertation on the Man of Steel's endless comic book escapades will be well served by a litany of other offerings, the most comprehensive of which is probably Les Daniels's agreeably titled *Superman: The Complete History*. If you're desperate to find out when Krypto the Superdog first barked, I highly recommend it.

This volume concerns itself instead with Superman's myriad Hollywood travails, those television and film and even radio incarnations that intended to translate his four-color fantasy world into living, breathing action. It's a daunting task, in many cases so difficult that Superman productions can often be described as torturous, painful, or heart attack inducing—literally.

While I have the greatest respect for the comics medium and its unique method of telling stories, most Superman fans are admirers because of Christopher Reeve, Dean Cain, Tom Welling, or George Reeves. The pervasiveness of film and television allowed the character to be seared into the national psyche, his rich mythology becoming household currency. Long before Hollywood would sink its talons into the concept of "synergy" and capitalize on existing brand awareness, Superman was a multimedia force.

(Which is not to say the originating medium had little influence. During World War II, Superman's comic book incarnation was required military shipping, deemed an "essential supply" to the Marine garrisons at Midway Islands. His titles enjoyed a circulation of 1.5 million copies monthly, and 25 million readers eyed his truncated comic strip adventures daily.)

Superman has marched to the drums of the latest technology with regularity: When radio boomed, so did he. When movie serials were in vogue, he was packing the houses. When television was installed in millions of homes, there he was. I would not be shocked to visit an entertainment hub twenty years from now and observe patrons dangling from the ceiling, immersed in the illusion that they're flying over Metropolis.

There are the highs: Bruce Timm's lyrical animated series, or Christopher Reeve's impeccable, earnest performance that remains the most indelible portrait of the Man of Steel. And the lows: Superman prancing on Broadway, or at the mercy of low-budget syndicated television.

At his finest, he is under the care of respected filmmakers like Richard Donner; at his worst, he's subject to the tantrum whims of producer Jon Peters, who took the reins of the film franchise in 1994 and promptly announced a deep hatred for his costume and power of flight. The proclamation marked the beginning of a decadelong development process for a new Superman feature, one that wound up costing tens of millions of dollars before a single frame was ever shot.

Superman is the avatar for all that is good and bad in Hollywood. Handled with care, he becomes a fantastic science fiction figure, an icon of nobility, and a testament to the power of the filmed imagination. Dismissed as a soulless commodity, his image is stamped on toothbrushes or made to play second fiddle to a misplaced comedian, the originating narrative for such pursuits a mere afterthought.

Most egregiously, there is Warner Bros.' treatment of Jerry Siegel and Joe Shuster, the cocreators of Superman. By the late 1970s, the company bragged it had made over a billion dollars on the character's licensing alone.

At the same time in Queens, New York, Shuster, legally blind, slept on a cot next to a broken window. Siegel made $7,500 a year as a clerk.

There is more—much more. "Enough to fill a book," I once told an editor who had assigned me a retrospective piece on the Superman film franchise. There are car accidents and fistfights; lawsuits and threats; incompetent stunt people and fatal accidents; hurt feelings and broken friendships. To embark on a Superman adaptation is to practically invite stress levels that would fell ordinary men.

Superman vs. Hollywood is as much a cautionary tale of Hollywood excess as it is a history of one of our modern mythological figures. The great Harlan Ellison is fond of saying that only five fictional creations resonate all across the world, regardless of language or locale: Mickey Mouse, Tarzan, Robin Hood, Sherlock Holmes, and Superman.

Of those, only the Man of Steel can boast of dropping actors from wires.

———

Studio-approved retrospectives on their films aspire to be little more than treacle, and Superman historians are often muzzled in their attempts to accurately portray the character's valleys. (Ilya Salkind once told me he made an offhand remark about *Superman IV* being "the end of the franchise" to a Warner-sanctioned documentarian. It didn't make the cut.) I have done everything in my power to obtain the plain truth, though history can become muddled in the eyes of witnesses, and I must apologize in advance for any errors or omissions.

I am indebted to the people who graciously gave their time to offer insight into Superman's storied multimedia history, including those who shared memories of their tenures as Superman caretakers, even when those recollections were not always pleasant. My thanks go out to Stetson Kennedy, Leslie Cabarga, Ray Pointer, Noel Neill, Jack Larson, Bob Holiday, Neal Adams, Peter Lupus, Ilya Salkind, Tom Mankiewicz, Jack O'Halloran, Jeannot Szwarc, Marv Wolfman, Gerard Christopher, Bryce

Zabel, Kevin Smith, Sylvain Despretz, George Newbern, Dan Riba, Butch Lukic, Bruce Timm, Dan Gilroy, Keith Giffen, Kevin Burns, and Paul Bernbaum.

Equally knowledgeable about all things Superman are the numerous webmasters who, via their online efforts, helped organize and sort out the endless archives of his screen journeys. I'm indebted to aintitcool.com, chud.com, supermancinema.co.uk, redboots.net, capedwonder.com, supermanhomepage.com, theages.superman.ws, jimnolt.com, and dcmegasite.com. This saga is ongoing, and I'm sure these sites will be on top of all future developments.

Appreciation also goes out to the staff of *Wizard* magazine, particularly Mel Caylo, whose freelance assignment was the impetus for this book; Jeremy Wright, who provided valuable insight for a first-time proposal; Alison Jo Rigney at Everett, who met my abrupt demand for photos with valuable advice and attention; Yuval Taylor and Devon Freeny, two very patient editors at Chicago Review Press; Mark Millar, for a ringing endorsement; my parents, Tim and Jane, for their encouraging words; my sisters Lisa, Dawn, and Susie and my brother Brandon for the same; and my friends Donna and Anne, who were both just as excited as I was by the prospect of telling Superman's celluloid story but who didn't keep nearly the same hours.

Unlike most victims of the Hollywood mulcher, Superman can't vent his frustrations by entering rehab, getting arrested, or spilling his sordid tale to Barbara Walters. This book is intended to give him a voice, an ironic reward for one of the most powerful characters in fiction. Enjoy.

Test Patterns

In Des Moines, Iowa, an eight-year-old Superman fan, James Henderson, put on a Superman suit, jumped off the second-story landing and crashed. Said he, with a sprained ankle, "The darned thing wouldn't work."
—*TIME* magazine, August 10, 1942

Almost immediately following his debut in *Action Comics* #1 (June 1938), Superman's publisher—known for years as National Periodical Publications before settling on the more familiar moniker of DC Comics—charged press agents Allen Ducovny and Robert Maxwell with tailoring the character to radio. The airwaves remained the premiere comfort media of the nation, spinning science fiction and fantasy tales for a youthful demographic yet to be weaned on video games and sensory-assault summer blockbusters.

Unlike today's creator-owned comics properties, Superman belonged solely to the publishers; his true fathers, writer Jerry Siegel and artist Joe Shuster, were therefore entitled to no recompense when their character appeared in another medium. If National felt the urge to prostitute him in wildly unfaithful incarnations, the duo could do little but sigh. Fortunately, their employer's respect for Superman had yet to devolve.

Ducovny and Maxwell orchestrated a sample track that featured raucous sound effects and the "Look, up in the sky!" mantra that would later become an embraceable cliché of the character. The now-archaic Hecker H-O Oats cereal company liked what it heard and signed on to sponsor the

Radio personality Bud Collyer in a publicity photo from the 1950s. Collyer portrayed Superman in over two thousand episodes of the radio drama, making him the most prolific actor in the character's history.

(Everett Collection)

series, funneling it a budget and then petitioning stations for airtime.

The duality of Superman and his alter ego Clark Kent—one an alpha male of the highest order, the other drenched in faux meekness—initially convinced Maxwell he would have to hire two actors to play the bipolar title role. Radio veteran Clayton "Bud" Collyer's audition assured him otherwise: Collyer's Kent was a high-pitched milquetoast, but after dashing into a phone booth, his Superman came from the diaphragm, possessed of a guttural growl that would prompt any two-bit hood to rethink his ill-gotten acquisitions.

Collyer, who had made his name on such radio swashbucklers as *Terry and the Pirates*, brayed resistance to the role. Like the many actors to come after him, he feared that portraying such a broad, well-known character would rob him of opportunities to branch out in the future.

National offered a compromise: since they wanted to maintain the illusion that Superman was a real entity, and since Collyer feared typecasting, they would agree not to credit him with the role. While many actors would've found the idea of anonymous performing repugnant, Collyer was enthused. He signed on.

The performer had little to do when the fifteen-minute series *The Adventures of Superman* premiered on February 12, 1940. Superman's infantile origins were detailed, and it wasn't until the labored exposition expired in episode 2 that Collyer was able to don the tights in the theater of the mind.

More than eighty-five stations transmitted Superman's robot-smashing exploits to the masses. The syndicated program's 5:15 P.M. time slot was conducive to the youth of the country's school obligations; they could watch the show to either avoid homework or reward themselves for having done it. Ten weeks in, it had become the highest rated of any thrice-weekly entertainment series on the air.

Producers figured Superman would need some downtime in between bouts of saving his adopted home. As in the comics, the *Daily Planet* was his place of employment. Perry White emerged as his gruff, leather-voiced boss, and cub reporter Jimmy Olsen made himself readily available for regularly scheduled kidnappings and mortal peril. Both supporting characters were inventions of the radio producers, though Siegel had earlier devised an anonymous copyboy in the comics who bore a resemblance to Olsen.

Over the course of the series, several different actors assumed the role of Lois Lane. Rolly Bester and Helen Choate each contributed performances as the mischievous feminist, but eventually the part fell to Joan Alexander, an accomplished radio performer. Producers, unhappy with her delivery, canned her; she won the role back during a blind audition. Of the three actors to portray Lane, she tallied the most performances, though Rolly claims the more impressive trivia credit by being wed to *Green Lantern* comics scribe Alfred Bester.

Some time into his employment, Collyer demanded his two-week vacation. Not wishing to interrupt the program, Maxwell and his writing staff created the idea of Kryptonite, long-lost remnants of Superman's home world that would prompt an extreme allergic reaction in the Man of Steel. During Collyer's break, listeners sat in rapt attention as Superman did little more than moan in the background, felled by the noxious mineral. Later, Collyer's sabbaticals would be hidden by the arrival of Batman and Robin, fellow National crime fighters who guarded Metropolis in his absence.

In 1946, Maxwell embraced the offer by civil rights activist and counterfeit Klansmen Stetson Kennedy, proffering a two-piece narrative that had Superman scolding the racial divisiveness of the Klan and airing their dirty laundry to a squealing audience.

"The law offices, state, county, FBI, House Un-American Committee, they were all sympathetic with the Klan," Kennedy would later remember. "The lawmen were, ideologically at least, close with the Klansmen. The court of public opinion was all that was left."

Ostensibly aimed at children, Superman's radio dramas were often broadcast to assembled nuclear families; one phone poll showed that 35 percent of their audience was composed of adults. But regardless of whether parents listened, the activist believed the younger demographic was worth attending to. "Even back in the '40s, they had kids in the Klan, little girls dressed up in Klan robes at the cross burnings. I have photos of an infant in a cradle with a complete Klan robe on. It seemed like a good place to do some educating."

Kennedy infiltrated the group and served up its secrets to *Superman*, then watched as Klan morale dipped and membership enrollment ebbed. Desperate, the Klan tried calling for a boycott of Kellogg's, a new sponsor of the show, but racial intolerance was no match for the appetites of post–World War II homes. Rice Krispies and Corn Flakes remained breakfast-table staples, and Superman's battles with the close-minded continued.

Emboldened by his success against the Klan, Superman took aim at Communism, a favorite target of the anti-Red Collyer. When infidels threatened to blow up a synagogue in a symbol of religious persecution, Superman laid their plans to waste. The story line caught the attention of *TIME*, which finally coerced Collyer into disclosing his identity to the masses. (His alter ego had already been revealed to his local religious community: his Sunday school classes were populated by children eager to hear the testimony of Superman.)

In 1949, Collyer begged off any future obligations to the character. (Michael Fitzmaurice would take over the role for the show's final year.) By then, Collyer had invested nearly a decade and two thousand episodes into the mythology, which makes him the most prolific actor ever to have assumed the mantle, though not the first to don the suit. That honor goes to Ray Middleton, who appeared in costume during the 1940 World's Fair for "Superman Day."

"He was a resplendent figure," gushed the *New York Times* of his modeling, "attired in his tight-fitting blue pants, red boots, red cape and helmet to match."

Close enough.

Contrary to public assumption, Walt Disney was not the first person to produce a cartoon featuring sound. Archaically charming as 1928's *Steamboat Willie* is, 1924's *My Old Kentucky Home* gets due honors for being the first animated subject to have a soundtrack. The short's producers also included a sing-along bouncing ball, which they had developed during the silent film era to entice viewers to aid and abet the communal theater experience.

The ball and the sound cartoon were just two of many innovations pioneered by Fleischer Studios, an oft-forgotten contributor to the animation industry. While Disney's empire swelled with the success of feature-length animated films like *Snow White and the Seven Dwarfs*, Max and Dave Fleischer saw little of the recognition historians would later feel they were due.

Born in Vienna, Austria, in 1883, Max had been an art editor for *Popular Science Monthly* and a cartoonist for the *Brooklyn Daily Eagle* newspaper. He and brother Dave formed their animation studio in 1921, drawing on a shared interest in engineering to propagate a series of revolutionary advances in the animation business. (Brother Charles, interestingly, had devised the infuriating claw arcade game that has frustrated millions of people—including the government: he had to destroy hundreds of machines when they labeled it a gambling device and came after him.) Max had perfected the art of rotoscoping, which allowed artists to trace the movements of live-action models. The result was a startlingly realistic physical cadence for their trademark animated clown, Koko.

In the 1930s, cartoons were still primarily the realm of funny animals; animators used the medium to create fantastic imagery not yet possible on film. Fleischer stepped away from that model when he introduced Betty Boop in the early part of the decade. Boop had originally been cast as a literal dog—an inauspicious origin for a woman who prided herself on her sexual charms—but time and thought morphed her into a full-fledged femme fatale, her curves and batting eyelashes serving as innocuous sexual fodder for audiences. Artists had fun flirting with her excesses: a breast popped out of Betty's dress for a fraction of a second in *Betty Boop's Rise to Fame*. In other entries, Betty had to deal with the veiled sexual advances of potential employers. In a "stag" film intended only for distribution to the military, Betty herself made advances on a wary Popeye.

In 1934, Boop's popularity emboldened nightclub siren Helen Kane to sue the Fleischers and their distributor, Paramount, alleging that they had based the character on her onstage persona without permission and thus adversely affected her earning potential. (One would imagine the reverse would be true, that an ersatz Boop appearing live would entrance club-goers.) Lawyers for both sides argued ceaselessly over the provenance of Betty's "boop-oop-a-doop" catchphrase. The judge eventually found on behalf of Paramount, due in part to their deeper legal resources.

The character's good-natured sexuality was extinguished that same year, when Mae West's real-life pout prompted Hollywood to institute the Hays Code. The edict governed "good taste" in theaters: gone were Betty's curves and dripping sexual subtext. She eked out a smothered existence until 1939. Disenchanted, the Fleischers refocused their attention on their license of King Features' *Popeye* strip. The barely intelligible sailor proved popular with audiences, particularly the cinematic device of having him imbibe spinach when he needed extra strength to ward off nemesis Bluto.

By that time, Paramount had acquired the screen rights to Superman, after Republic Pictures let their option from National expire. Republic had figured on producing a film serial but found the task of making the character fly an impenetrable roadblock.

Paramount had no such concerns—if they were to have Fleischer Studios animate the character, no valuable actor would have to be strung up on Peter Pan's rented wires. The studio approached Max with the offer, figuring he would leap at the chance to work on such a prized property.

They were wrong.

"Doing something like Superman required a great deal more realistic study than what they had been doing with the cartoon animals," said Fleischer historian Ray Pointer. "Cartoon human figures like Popeye and Betty Boop had been their foundation." Superman would require a more involved commitment to human anatomy.

Animator Max Fleischer in Gulliver City, Florida, in 1939. Fleischer and his studio are credited with pioneering several advances in the industry, as well as producing nine lavish Superman theatrical cartoons in the 1940s. The shorts influenced later incarnations, including *Superman Returns*.

(Everett Collection)

The Fleischers had attempted "realistic" human animation only once before, with their feature *Gulliver's Travels*. Intended to usurp Disney's dominance in animation, it was only a modest success, damaged in no small part by their truncated eighteen-month production schedule. (Disney had spent four years perfecting *Snow White*.) Dismayed by the reception, Max wasn't enthused about tackling such a formidable license as Superman. He quoted Paramount a budget of $100,000 per episode, astronomical for any medium at the time.

To Fleischer's surprise, Paramount accepted his proposal, inadvertently forcing the animation studio to mature. "Paramount did them a favor by moving them forward into an arena that no one else was doing, which was an animated science fiction series with realistic characters," Pointer said. "In that respect, they wouldn't be saddled with doing bad imitations of Warner Bros. and MGM cartoons, which is what they had been trying to do."

Max and Dave used the generous funds to develop pencil tests for their animation, then a luxury in the medium. Dave sketched out the art deco–inspired look of the series, with buildings seemingly influenced by Fritz Lang's *Metropolis*. Joe Shuster's Superman model, prepared as a reference for the animators, was a broad-shouldered Adonis, his villains as menacing as they appeared in the comics series. All told, the Fleischers wound up spending $50,000 for the debut episode. Compared to the $14,000 spent on an average Popeye cartoon, *Superman* clearly benefited from the new standards in the industry. (Subsequent episodes saved money by reusing the same intro segment, and were brought in at a more reasonable $30,000.)

Likely at the urging of National, Paramount enlisted both Collyer and Joan Alexander to reprise their radio performances for the animated series.

(All voice actors went uncredited.) In the first installment, simply titled "Superman," Collyer's Kent was at his most prepubescent, the better to contrast the hero's booming baritone. He would deepen the reporter's timbre in later shorts.

With no worries on the soundtrack front, the Fleischers nonetheless became embittered by the ideosyncrasies of the production. The brothers had recently abandoned their studio in New York City for the more inviting climate of Miami. They professed the need to expand to handle the workload, but Pointer believed the motive was less noble. "Max and Dave had summer homes in Miami and they loved it. They thought they could just go down there and make a big production center. Plus, Miami gave them a tremendous tax incentive." Paramount was eager to have them commence work on *Gulliver's Travels*—and to avoid the New York labor strikes that had plagued Fleischer Studios in 1937—so the distributor funded the move.

"But from a logical standpoint, it doesn't make sense," Pointer argued. "There weren't any lab facilities down there, so they had to ship back and forth to New York. In the case of the *Superman*s, they had to send them to Technicolor in Hollywood. You're sending that stuff thirteen hundred miles, and you're running the risk of the plane going down and the negative being lost in a fire."

No such tragedy occurred, but the byzantine shipping schedule resulted in several delays. The third installment, "Billion Dollar Limited," was scheduled for a December 17, 1941, release. Memos from the studio to Paramount estimated its completion at December 19; the studio implored its distributor to "lean" on Technicolor to deliver the print sooner. "It certainly is swell of you," Fleischer employee Charles West wrote.

Regarding the segment "The Bulleteers," West wrote complaining that the DuPont sound recording stock was flaking off and harming the film. Worse, the Fleischers' insistence on their own homegrown ingenuity came back to bite them. "Their cameras were self-built," said Pointer. "The thing that's interesting is that mechanized animation cameras started to come into being in the 1930s, but the Fleischers had built their own equipment, so everything they did was jerry-rigged. If you really know where to look, even in the first *Superman* cartoon, there are camera abrasions due to a flaw in the equipment."

Despite the pitfalls, the first short was ready for a September 1941 bow. Teaser trailers ran for Superman's screen debut, a first for the animation business. Children previously raised on the character's comic book and radio exploits would now be able to see him in full motion, a streaking blur of red and blue across the sky. There would be additions to the mythology they had come to know, including the indelible "Up, up, and away" mantra, which was written by an uncredited Jay Morton, one of Fleischer's scribes.

The shorts themselves were almost eerily devoid of any dialogue. Superman and his peers were portrayed in only the most superficial light possible; many of his adversaries went unnamed. But what the series lacked in character development it more than made up for in sheer visceral beauty. Superman's city was awash in stylized buildings and sensational colors. A myriad of camera angles gave the proceedings a dynamic quality not normally found in the cartoons of the era; shadows loomed in frame, breathing conventions of real life into the fantastic scenarios.

After a cursory intro detailing Superman's alien origins, the inaugural episode presents twelve minutes of action: a mad scientist threatens the populace with a dangerous beam weapon. Far more resourceful than her later incarnations, Lois jumps into (and flies) an airplane to investigate. Preparing for her inevitable need for rescue, Clark changes in a stockroom in silhouette, the likely result of animators finding the removal of his suit too tedious a task for animation. Not willing to totally abandon the anthropomorphic animals that were a hallmark of cartoons at the time, the filmmakers gave the villain a rambunctious pet parrot.

The initial short was held in high enough regard to merit an Academy Award nomination for Best Short Subject (Cartoon) of 1941; to Max's chagrin, it lost to a Disney production, *Lend a Paw*.

In "Billion Dollar Limited," Fleischer's more fragile portrayal of Superman contrasts with the imperviousness of later renditions. Tear gas hurled by desperate train robbers makes him cough and gag; the act of pulling a train uphill prompts him to strain every muscle fiber in his animated form, expelling the same effort one might see in a gym-lashed power lifter. "Arctic Giant" is notable for presenting an unfrozen beast that bears more than a passing resemblance to Godzilla, predating the debut of that character by nearly twenty years.

The Fleischer shorts, nine in all, present Superman as little more than a strongman with aerial abilities. His contentious relationship with Lois is often reduced to her chastising Clark for not being in the middle of the action, at which the feeble newsman and the audience share a smirk.

Because the serials aired alongside feature presentations, it's virtually impossible to gauge their popularity, though the character was sufficiently ingrained in the public consciousness to garner hospice with projectors in over seven thousand movie houses. As of 1942, Paramount had dubbed it the most profitable cartoon in the company's history.

The success of the shorts belied the cancer growing in the Fleischer camp. Max, the businessman, and Dave, the creative head, were straining to understand each other. Both men had problem marriages: Max's wife had once attempted to take her own life by swallowing iodine. Dave's home life was unsatisfying to the point that he sought out extramarital company, as did his brother. When Max learned of Dave's infidelity, he was aghast. The moral hypocrisy was too much for Dave; the two turned mute toward one another, communicating only via interoffice memo or through secretaries.

The brothers' hedonism manifested itself in other ways as well: Dave, an ardent gambler, actually kept a bookie on call in the studio offices. Whatever funds weren't being bet on horses were risked in the stock market.

Though more *Superman* shorts were still to come, the Fleischers were not to be involved with any of them. In 1941, Paramount's attitude suddenly turned insolent. Three years earlier, they had loaned the brothers $100,000 to help fund their transplant to Miami. Without warning, they were calling in their marker. If the brothers could not pay in full—and they surely couldn't—the studio and all its visual and physical property would revert to Paramount.

Paramount's tactics were patently illegal: all parties had signed a contract assuring the brothers that they had ten years to reconcile the money owed. If such documentation were presented in court, the Fleischers' burden would be eased. But when Max was called away to New York to meet with Paramount executives, the Miami offices were ransacked, and vital records were purged. Max's nephew Ozzie would later confirm that he bore witness to scores of boxes being emptied from their offices and tossed into a bonfire.

Max Fleischer now had no legal leg to stand on. Paramount threatened to withhold the studio's payroll, which would force him into bankruptcy. The social stigma of the threatened financial collapse was enough of a deterrent for Max to finally give in.

In giving his oral history to a journalist in the 1970s, Dave Fleischer claimed Paramount cronies had taken him out on a boat and threatened to sink it unless he relinquished his stake in the studio. Given Dave's advanced age at the time of the interview, his credibility is called into question; what is known is that when presented with the formal papers, Dave signed them and returned them to Max in less than five minutes, hardly a reasonable amount of time to absorb the details of such an important document.

Paramount was granted full ownership of the animation house. Renaming it Famous Studios, the new owners coerced Max into signing a letter of resignation that they kept on file. Some months later, they pulled it out and "accepted" his departure.

Paramount's methodology, which resembled nothing so much as organized crime, had roots in that institution's primary motive: obtaining money, and lots of it. Their ultimate goal may have been to nullify the 1932 agreement signed by Paramount and Fleischer to adapt King Features' *Popeye*. According to a provision in that contract, all negatives featuring the character would be destroyed in ten years' time, an agreeably nominal stretch during which to circulate the footage in theaters. But few people had considered the prospect of television, which would eventually prove to be a medium full of endless recycling potential.

By the early 1940s, cathode tubes were rolling off assembly lines with ominous regularity. Paramount needed to be able to not only breach the original contract but also avoid cutting Fleischer in on the revenue promised by fledgling TV stations. "It would make sense to Paramount if they could get the Fleischers out as the middleman," Pointer explained. "They would have everything to gain. But the thing that doesn't make sense is the fact that King Features is also a party to Fleischer and therefore should've had a copy of that agreement as well."

If King Features did indeed keep a copy on file, they weren't quick to present it. With the Fleischers out of the way, both King and Paramount were free to make use of *Popeye* however they pleased; his seaside travails would become a staple of television for the next six decades—and produce a hefty corresponding profit.

Despite its unflattering removal of the brothers, Paramount maintained a working relationship with their animators, many of whom wound up toiling for Famous. Eager to continue with the Superman license, the studio rolled out eight more shorts through 1943. Though similar in style, these installments presented the Man of Steel with different obstacles. Gone were the more sensational science fiction elements: Superman now opposed embarrassing German and Japanese stereotypes, his gross intolerance fueled by the raucous patriotism of a nation mired in war.

"Japs are stealing the dive bomber," Lois is heard to exclaim. "OK, little man," Superman says, patronizing a foreign adversary. The tonal change came courtesy of wartime rationing. "It was to film companies' advantage if they could say they were producing films for the war effort in order for them to get film," said Pointer. "If it had some sort of a propaganda message to it, and they could justify they could distribute it to the armed forces in order to contribute to the morale of the war, then they could qualify."

(Animated Superman's military movements were in sharp contrast to the actions of his illustrated doppelganger. National had long struggled with how best to portray a nigh-invulnerable metahuman during wartime without making a mockery of the real soldiers who were sacrificing their lives. The solution was simple: in the comic strip, Superman tried to enlist, but his X-ray vision accidentally read the eye chart in the adjoining exam room, flunking him out of military contention.)

Despite some inventive dissolves—a cigarette burning a newspaper, which reveals a new scene; Clark adjusting a necktie, then his bowtie during a formal soiree—the Famous entries in the *Superman* cartoon mythology of the 1940s are a relative disappointment. Paramount began to scrimp on budgets, easing up on complex sequences and fanciful camera movements.

By the time the episode "Secret Agent" was released in July 1943, Paramount felt Superman had worn out his welcome. With their exorbitant budgets, the comic book shorts didn't do enough business to justify their cost. The rights dissipated without any attempt of renewal; Paramount figured it would be more economical to pursue the *Little Lulu* license, another brand name that dangled a more attractive price tag in front of them.

Max's legal complaints against Paramount wouldn't materialize until several years later; his son-in-law, plagued by heart problems, was heading Famous, and paternal concern prompted Fleischer not to make waves and potentially aggravate his condition. When he finally did bring action, it was too late: the statute of limitations was up. Disillusioned, Max went back to work for the Handy Corporation, a production house that made educational films, for which he had toiled in the 1920s. Attempts to resurrect Koko the Clown died on the vine in 1964, signaling the end of Max's involvement in animation.

Superman's animated fate, as Paramount had anticipated, did indeed lie in television. In 1955, the studio announced the sale of all their animated shorts, including 661 Fleischer creations, to television distributors for an impressive $4.5 million. Max and Dave saw none of the money. Worse, their names had been barred from appearing in the credits.

In a move that would prove impenetrably frustrating to future Superman rights holder Warner Bros. years later, the transactions made it incumbent upon the buyer to renew any applicable copyrights for their shorts. Distributors like Flamingo Sales would eventually go out of business; National, which should've had ownership of the cartoons revert back to it, found itself with a scattered paper trail. By the latter part of the century, Max Fleischer's *Superman* cartoons had fallen into the public domain, where they were subject to all manner of ignoble treatment by third-rate video distributors. An Amazon.com search brings up more than seventeen permutations of the series, with wildly varying degrees of presentation quality.

Despite the personal turmoil that accompanied the production, cartoon historian Leslie Cabarga argued that the Fleischers turned a creative corner with *Superman*. "I think it was the first time you were really seeing science fiction in animation, with somewhat of a noir approach. It was subject matter that cartoons had never ventured into before.

"They really took cartoons in a whole new direction. And it's one that almost foreshadowed the anime and Japanimation movement. *Superman* called for it."

By 1948, Superman had logged thousands of entries on radio. The seventeen Fleischer/Famous shorts had enraptured audiences eager to see him take flight. Radio staff writer George Lowther handled the character in prose with his full-length origin novel *The Adventures of Superman*. All mediums considered, his exploits had been exposed to more than fifty million people—many of whom considered a night at the movies to be the zenith of escapism.

In the bowels of Columbia Pictures, a costumer was commissioned to begin stitching a gray wool suit and a flowing cape. Superman was to take flight under the constraints of real-world gravity—which would present all the accompanying real-world problems.

———

Republic Pictures had snapped up the rights to Superman virtually at the moment of his comics debut in 1938; for a time, they even began braying about his pending arrival as a flesh-and-blood superpower, causing no end of hyperactive behavior among impatient fans.

Purveyors of live-action film serials had long been attracted to pulp heroes; their staccato bursts of activity, broadly drawn personas, and high public profiles made them perfect for studios looking to shepherd children into movie houses week after week. The serials were often known as "cliff-hangers," because episodes would usually end with the protagonist being placed in inescapable mortal danger. To see how he'd cheat certain death, audiences would be forced to view the following week's vignette. (In many cases, the resolution would be an outright cheat: the vigilante who was seen going over a cliff in his vehicle would then be revealed jumping out of it—though it was clear he hadn't done so in the previous chapter.)

Unlike the Lone Ranger or Flash Gordon, however, Superman's primary appeal was his gift of flight. And if kids spent their dime on a chapter of something labeled *Superman*, consumers railed, he'd damn well better fly. But reality was quick to set in: the late 1930s were not a time of special effects ingenuity for film studios, especially those producing cheap and dirty serials under the budgetary gun. Worse, National was proving to be entirely too meddlesome to deal with; the company wanted to exert more influence than Republic was willing to concede. Eventually, the studio opted not to renew the expensive license, allowing Paramount to pick up the film rights for their animated serial.

(Ironically, Republic then staged the exploits of Fawcett Comics' Superman knockoff, Captain Marvel, in 1941; mannequins on wires were used to simulate his aerial daring.)

When Paramount absolved themselves of the Superman business in the mid-1940s, Columbia Pictures was confident enough of its optical abilities to snap up the rights from National. The studio had already engorged itself on other attractions from the four-color world: comics icons like Brenda Starr and the Phantom grabbed the majority of its market share.

Columbia's go-to serial maven was Sam Katzman, a producer renowned for his ability to get things done as quickly and as cheaply as humanly possible. He was a pleasant man, so "miser" isn't an apt description, though he was known to question even the loose change of the cast and crew. He was equally stringent regarding the narratives. During rewrites, Katzman would often poll his fifteen-year-old son; if the boy could guess how a suspense sequence was going to be resolved, it would be revised.

Under the Katzman regime, films would sometimes be shot, edited, and scored within twenty days, a breakneck pace that even those accus-

First screen Superman Kirk Alyn in a publicity photo from 1948. Alyn was said to be distressed he was not invited back to the role when the character moved to television in 1951.

(Everett Collection)

tomed to today's episodic television schedules would find abhorrent. Once, when a studio executive made an offhand comment about needing a picture to tie in to the Korean War, Katzman had *A Yank in Korea* ready for distribution in six weeks.

"If you were to X-ray every Oscar," Katzman told *TIME* in 1952 of Hollywood's more laborious efforts, "you'd find every one of them has an ulcer inside."

For *Superman*, Katzman evaluated dozens of circus strongmen, professional wrestlers, and amateur boxers; while some possessed the barrel chest expected of the hero, none offered any appreciable screen presence. He eventually sought out Kirk Alyn, a fit day player who had been employed on numerous Katzman serials. Alyn was Americana animate, with dark good looks and broad shoulders. His performance career had origins in vaudeville and dance; the athletics required wouldn't be a problem.

Katzman summoned Alyn to an impromptu audition and barked at him to strip down to his briefs so his physique could be examined. Satisfied his star wasn't hiding any excess flub, he told Alyn to report to work in a few days.

Casting Lois was less traumatic. Noel Neill, a Paramount contract girl, received a phone call from her agent. A succinct offer had come in from Katzman, no audition required. "My agent said, 'Well, I've got you a job in a serial playing Lois Lane,'" Neill recalled. "So I dashed out and bought a *Lois Lane* comic book. I had never been into comics. It had been a boys' thing in that day. I wanted to see how Lois Lane looked, get a vague idea of what she was like."

Shooting commenced in late 1947. Alyn had been fitted for a Superman costume in dull gray and brown to better simulate bright colors on black-

and-white film. Initially, producers figured they could string Alyn up on wires and then edit out the incriminating evidence of the illusion later on. The tactic didn't work; reels of footage with Alyn painfully dangling from a harness had to be scrapped. Mindful of the financial constraints, Katzman ordered that the shots of Superman flying be accomplished in animation, a jarring transition that nonetheless would likely be forgiven in that era of primitive effects.

Alyn took performance cues from radio's Collyer, altering the pitch of his voice so his Clark was testosterone deficient and his Superman was a booming orator. His dance training afforded him an appreciable degree of muscular endurance, which came in handy when he was forced to cart around unconscious damsels in his arms for a good portion of the day. No stuntmen were used to substitute for him, which was of particular concern when he found himself eighteen inches from a speeding train during one shot.

While Neill found Alyn generally pleasant to work with, the two had virtually no time to chat. Katzman would oversee upward of 120 setups a day, which might equal twenty minutes of screen time. In contrast, a major studio picture would be fortunate to log two minutes during the same shift. "Katzman planned everything ahead of time very well," Neill said. "He always hired people he knew were dependable, the heavies and such. He knew they could do it in one take, or two at the most." When Neill would flub lines and exceed her allotment of takes, Katzman would rant and rave.

Despite Katzman's thriftiness, the serial came in at a then-staggering $350,000; it was the most expensive cliffhanger ever produced at the time. With fifteen chapters averaging fifteen minutes each, however, Katzman had essentially shot a four-hour film for a fraction of the cost of an A-list studio release.

The first episode of *Superman* was released in January 1948, courting the some ninety million patrons of the more than seventeen thousand movie houses in operation at that time. The serial was even innocuous enough to be screened in public schools to reward students for a job well done, and perhaps to provide a symbol of nobility to be emulated. By the time the fifteen chapters completed their run in April, Columbia had rung up $1 million in grosses, which makes the Man of Steel's inaugural live-action exploits one of the most successful serials ever made. His adventures even translated to foreign countries: impatient South Americans sat down for the entire four-hour narrative in one marathon screening.

Despite its mammoth overall running time, directors Spencer Bennet and Thomas Carr left precious little time for introspective characters or complicated twists. As was the norm for the serial era, *Superman* was a gleefully efficient actioner, capable of leaping over large plot holes in a single bound. The most substantial exposition comes in the first chapter, where wheezing special effects depict the fall of Krypton—complete with an animated explosion—and the journey of young Kal-El to his new home. Only during the last thirty seconds of the reel does Superman make his appearance in full costume, ready to save a train from a pending stretch of broken rail.

Ensuing chapters kept his feats at manageable levels: Lois becomes trapped in a cave; Lois hovers near live electrical wire; Lois is ready to drive over a cliff. (Has any other reporter endured the kind of mortal peril that the steel-nerved Lane faces on an hourly basis?) Jimmy Olsen suffers his requisite kidnappings. Perry White emerges as the lone supporting character who's not a total submissive; in chapter seven, he even gets into a fistfight with a heavy (and wins).

The MacGuffin of the piece is the Spider Lady, woodenly portrayed by Carol Forman, who seeks possession of a ray gun the government has perfected. Although her character wasn't inspired by a comic book counterpart, the femme fatale is still typical of the flavorful rogues that serial heroes were accustomed to thwarting. In a clumsy bit of irony, she winds up being electrocuted in her fetishistic spider web apparatus.

The success of the film wasn't lost on Siegel and Shuster, the character's creators. National had been more than generous with them in the decade following Superman's debut, signing over more than $400,000 in cumulative salary to the duo. But as Superman's popularity grew, so did Siegel and Shuster's discomfort over how much control National exerted—their names had not even appeared in the credits of the serial. In many people's estimations, the character could become a multi-million-dollar multimedia force in the coming years. Superman's fathers would see little of it unless they pursued legal action.

And so they did. The duo sued National for $5 million, demanding ownership be turned over to them and claiming damages for profits not duly shared. Manhattan news broker Albert Zugsmith acted as a liaison between the parties and cut a weak deal: writer and artist combined would receive a meager $100,000 in total gratuities. In exchange for that paltry sum, National obtained the rights to their 1944 ancillary character Superboy. In essence, Siegel and Shuster wound up with even less legal claim to their creation than they had before. A spiteful National even removed their names from the credits of the comics. The two fell into an emotional malaise that would linger for the next several decades.

Katzman, meanwhile, was busy plotting his next Superman series. "The serial made good money for Columbia," Neill said. "So Katzman called everyone's agent and said, 'We want to do another fifteen chapters.' So, fine, fine. Back to work."

Atom Man vs. Superman lensed in 1949 for a 1950 release. Thanks to the strong reception of the first serial, Katzman and Columbia splurged and staged live-action flying sequences with Alyn, which ultilized some none-too-convincing camera tilts. The film would also introduce to the screen a key part of Superman lore: the villainous Lex Luthor, portrayed with effective manic glee by Lyle Talbot. (Another crucial piece of mythology was discarded when Katzman vetoed the iconic phone booth costume change; he felt the booth would be too expensive to shuttle around sets.)

Unlike Collyer, Alyn was displeased that he had received no on-screen notice for his performance in the first Superman serial; the character was listed in the credits as though he were playing himself. The edict came from National's offices in an attempt to perpetuate the notion the hero was an alien Santa Claus, as real as a child's imagination allowed him to be.

The snub was alleviated in part by the hefty $10,000 check Alyn got for the sequel, double his pay for the initial installment. At first Katzman balked at the demand for a pay hike, but he realized it was a small concession to the peace of mind afforded by Alyn's presence. The kids liked him, and there was little point in starting a new search that would have to weed out the endless stiffs that showed up for employment as the hero. (Once, an aspiring actor in a Los Angeles theater uprooted seats and tore down doors to "prove" he would be perfect for the role.)

Alyn was even agreeable to performing the kind of publicity stunt that would surely offend the egos of latter-day thespians: he showed up for an all-star charity baseball game in full Superman regalia, fielding hits from Bob Hope and Hopalong Cassidy. When it was his time for an at-bat, Alyn was lobbed a baseball rigged to explode, the better to invest fans in Superman's mighty swing. Unfortunately, Alyn struck out. The pitcher genially kept tossing it until Alyn connected.

Atom Man vs. Superman was released in summer 1950 to vacationing children ravenous for the Man of Steel's further adventures. As with the Spider Lady's ray gun, the ancillary evil here is technological, a teleportation ray that mad genius Luthor has created. In order to mask his identity, Luthor doubles as Atom Man, a helmeted foe with designs on destroying the Man of Steel. In a device that echoes through 1983's *Superman III*, the villain attempts to produce artificial Kryptonite. Fortunately, the synthesized variation doesn't hold up well when exposed to air.

True to Katzman's penny-pinching, *Atom Man* makes considerable use of stock footage: Kent darts into a storage room to change his clothing in a scene repurposed four times over; shots of rockets and earthquakes were pulled from Columbia's archives.

Despite the economy of some scenes, a portion of the budget does wind up on-screen. Trapped in the realm of the "empty doom," to which Luthor has banished him, Superman maintains a convincing ethereal presence. (To convince Lois he's still alive, his spirit self composes messages on her typewriter.) To coerce a criminal into talking, he tosses him fifty feet in the air like a child might toss a ball.

Though it was superior to its predecessor, *Atom Man* screened to slightly diminished returns. Film serials were becoming creaky, nearing expiration due to the increasing pervasiveness of television. After a nominal investment in the equipment and antenna, households could enjoy a myriad of episodic TV programs for free. The ramifications were not lost on National, which began eyeing the upstart medium with the voracious scrutiny of the profit-minded.

Katzman considered producing a third Superman serial, but Columbia was beginning to shy away from the outmoded genre. The news was disappointing to Alyn, who had found work already beginning to dry up. He returned to New York stages, but not before railing at Katzman that Superman had pigeonholed him. Katzman's sympathy prompted him to call Alyn when Columbia acquired the film rights to the comic book character Blackhawk in 1952. The excitable World War II pilot had been a staple of the propoganda movement in years past, and *Blackhawk* was one of the last comics-branded serials to make it to screens. Alyn portrayed the titular character, though business didn't warrant a sequel.

The comics themselves, that endless wellspring of inspiration for all media big and small, were facing their own forced evolution. Critics were becoming more vociferous in their claims that the stories were little more than training manuals for lurid, irresponsible behavior. In 1948, a Los Angeles County boy was apprehended after poisoning a fifty-year-old woman; he informed police that the offense and its methodology had been derived from a crime comic. Another impressionable youth was found hanging from his garage rafters, a comic depicting a hanging figure at his feet. In hysterics, the Los Angeles County Board of Supervisors passed a law banning the sale of such sensational titles to anyone under eighteen. The ordinance never made it out of rural areas.

National's upright civil servicemen were largely exempt from such histrionics. Their heroes, they argued, were fine role models for youth. This was by and large the truth, though some hotheaded op-ed columnists did remind readers of 1942 weird-news avatar James Henderson, the boy who had donned a makeshift Superman costume and dived off his second-story landing, spraining his ankle.

The moral movement wasn't of sufficient force to dissuade National, who in 1951 saw an opportunity to take their star character to an entirely new medium, one that was quickly becoming the dominant media force in millions of American homes.

Superman would fly again, and this time children wouldn't have to leave their homes to see it.

The Monkey Suit

I flew to the coast where Superman's ghost / Lay shot on the bedroom floor. / He said, "Watch out for TV; it crucified me. / But it can't crucify me no more."
—Don McLean, "Superman's Ghost"

In the 1950s, the comics medium offered little hospice for the costumed adventurers who had soothed juvenile wartime spirits during the previous decade. Of the dozens of heroes who had populated newsstands during those more tumultuous times, only Superman, Batman, and Wonder Woman survived the increasingly prurient tastes of the market.

Gone were the escapades of the Human Torch and Captain America, now seen as stuffy relics of a more gee-whiz era. Taking their place were horror and crime anthologies; each issue of *Tales from the Crypt* or *Crime Does Not Pay* contained at least three lurid tales of karma delivered with all the subtlety of an anvil. If you were a cheating louse of a husband, you could expect to be served as dinner before Charles Atlas made his compulsory appearance on the back cover. Such comics used the guise of the morality play to justify extreme bloodletting, their covers enticing readers with gloriously imagined severed heads, gore dripping down and out of the borders.

Fawcett Comics, which had enjoyed massive success with its faux Superman, Captain Marvel, attempted to reconcile the two disparate genres by injecting horror elements into its premier hero's escapades. It was to little avail, as the hero implosion forced Fawcett to excise its spandex cast permanently in 1953. (To add insult to injury, Fawcett also had to pay National $400,000 to settle their long-standing court case over the character: National had long maintained Marvel was too shameless a rip-off of Superman to go unchallenged.)

Publishers had begun indulging the morbid tastes of comics fans at least in part because of how the rest of the entertainment landscape was evolving. In the age of radio, comics had been a prime source of the spectacular fantasy tableaus the audio-only airwaves were unable to provide. But now comics were no longer the exclusive distributor of other worlds. The formative business of television had begun broadcasting a litany of science fiction scenarios to over eleven million households. Shows like *Captain Video* and *Tom Corbett, Space Cadet* presented papier-mâché planets and plastic spaceships, but to an audience that had never seen such sights beamed directly into their homes, it was galvanizing.

Less than twelve months after ceasing broadcast of the *Superman* radio drama, National commissioned a Superman television unit to be assembled at RKO's studios in Culver City, California. The move was unusual in that the publisher and copyright holder of the character would be forgoing a production company in favor of its own installed crew.

Superman radio producer Bob Maxwell was paired with National editorial director Whitney Ellsworth; Ellsworth had scripted the *Superman* comic strip for some time in the 1940s when Jerry Siegel was drafted into his nation's war efforts. Together, Ellsworth and Maxwell had hashed out scripts for the radio serial years prior.

Ellsworth packed his family into a car and headed for the Grand Canyon. While his family took in the sights, he remained in a hotel room and dashed off the first draft of *Superman and the Mole Men*, a tightly budgeted sixty-minute drama that National intended to use as a calling card for a TV series. The worst result, they reasoned, was that no sponsor would be interested, in which case they could still screen the pilot as a theater attraction and recoup their investment.

Ellsworth returned to California and consulted with Maxwell. (When collaborating, the two would often use the pseudonym "Richard Fielding.")

Satisfied with the template, the producers then initiated an open casting search, in which several hundred gym rats were surveyed and quickly found wanting in charisma.

For reasons budgetary or creative, film serial star Kirk Alyn was not asked to resume his role, a fact that seemed to rile him. "Kirk was very upset when he wasn't asked to be Superman in the TV show," recalled Noel Neill. "I don't think he was worried about being typecast." If not, it's possible Alyn had resigned himself to the role and simply wanted to continue profiting from it.

One day, a young actor named George Reeves dropped by the casting office of director Tommy Carr, who had overseen the film serials and was assisting in the search for Alyn's successor. Reeves had been mired in a ten-day lecture tour on jaywalking, a rather ignoble pursuit for someone who fancied himself a serious actor.

If a casting director were to recognize Reeves at all, it would likely have been from his appearance in *Gone with the Wind* as one of Scarlett O'Hara's myriad suitors. Since then, Reeves had toiled in dozens of forgotten B-movies and assorted roles in *Kraft Television Theatre*. He had an athlete's build, which in that day meant barrel-chested and solid, if not particularly well defined. An amateur boxing career had granted him a nose seven times broken; a strong chin protruded from his face. He was handsome, though his hair follicles lacked the shoe polish–black sheen the role called for.

Carr thought he looked the part. Better, he had a track record as a capable and professional actor. Maxwell and Ellsworth, having found no one even remotely plausible for the role, agreed.

Reeves was offered the job at a time when his decade's work in Hollywood had resulted in little progress. Though film actors faced a certain stigma if they defected to the competing medium of television, and suffered complications when they returned to movie houses, Reeves's underwhelming filmography left him with little to fear. He accepted the role.

Having dismissed the idea of casting Alyn, producers saw little purpose in pursuing his Lois, Noel Neill. Phyllis Coates was hired as the lone member of Superman's regular supporting cast to appear in the pilot film. Her Lane was blustery and demanding, hardly one to shrink away from danger. When push came to shove, though, she could emit a shriek that could shatter glass.

Production on *Superman and the Mole Men* commenced in summer 1951 and lasted a whopping twelve days. Ellsworth had penned a narrative with overt connections to the country's divisive battles over racial tolerance: In it, the town of Silsby is home to the world's deepest oil well. At thirty-two thousand feet, drillers hit what appears to be the center of the Earth, and the titular characters emerge. The slack-jawed townsfolk don't know what to make of the new species, so they do what comes naturally—they form a mob and grab guns.

Reeves's Superman, far slimmer than he would ever appear in the series, wastes little time defeating the prejudiced townspeople. "I'm going to give you one last chance to stop acting like Nazi storm troopers," he warns. Eventually, the Mole Men return to their home at the center of the Earth, and the opening on the surface is blown to bits so each race can continue to exist without fearing the shadow of the other.

With Clark and Lois on assignment in Silsby, the *Daily Planet* and its accompanying staff are nowhere to be found. The Mole Men, while employing the bulk of the film industry's dwarf population, offer little in the way of fantastic science fiction elements. And as in the first Alyn serial, when Superman needs to take flight to catch one of the little people, the film makes the jarring transition to animation.

Released in theaters in November 1951, *Mole Men* was nonetheless a success. More than a money machine for National and distributor Lippert Pictures, it served as an hour-long audition reel for both Reeves and Coates.

"The monkey suit," as Reeves would come to call it, would be his for the rest of his days.

If Reeves entertained bad omens about the series, Jack Larson didn't entertain the prospect of it becoming anything at all. A stage actor, Larson

An undated publicity photo of *Adventures of Superman* stars Jack Larson and George Reeves. Reeves's habitual drinking frequently led to Larson and other cast members having to stay late to finish the day's shooting.

(Everett Collection)

dreamed of emulating the kind of comedy perfected by Laurel and Hardy, whom he had long adored. With his contract-player status under Warner Bros. freshly dissolved, he met with producers for the role of Jimmy Olsen, a character created for the radio serial and later introduced into comics continuity.

"I was told to just take the work and that no one would probably ever see it," he recalled. "I just wanted enough money to get back to New York and do a play. And when the show went on the air and was enormously popular instantly, I realized this was a big danger. Suddenly, in New York, I became Jimmy Olsen. People were following me. I became worried about being typed, and I was very right to be worried because I *was* typed."

With Maxwell and Carr satisfied with Reeves's portrayal of the hero, production on the first season of *Adventures of Superman* commenced in 1951. Joining Reeves, Larson, and Coates was veteran actor John Hamilton as *Daily Planet* editor Perry White; Robert Shayne was Inspector Bill Henderson, Superman's inside man at the police precinct. The entire first season of twenty-six episodes was funded by National and shot at the breakneck speed of two episodes per week. Edited over 1952, it found a home in syndication in 1953. (The pilot movie was split into two parts and repurposed as episodes 27 and 28.)

Then as now, television production schedules were grueling. The pay, however, was not commensurate with the effort: Larson made $250 an episode. "I don't think anybody was very happy with the salaries we got," he remembered. "But in those days, you honored a contract. Nobody ever walked off a series until James Arness walked off *Gunsmoke*. He wanted a lot more money, and jaws dropped all over town. You just didn't know that you could walk out of a contract. It never occurred to me."

Larson nonetheless counted his blessings: Reeves, who was not making substantially more, had to suffer in a wool and rubber costume, padded in the arms and torso for a properly heroic build. With practical flying effects replacing the pilot's animated sequences, he was strung up on wires for takeoffs and landings, which resulted in more than one fall to the floor below him. Reeves spent lunch breaks in the company of Toni Mannix, a married woman, and alcohol. He would often hold up filming until he could sleep off the effects, a gross indulgence that irked Larson.

"They didn't shoot if he drank too much. We had the latest lunches of anyone. Toni would bring him martinis to the studio, a shaker of martinis. George was not an alcoholic, but he drank. The problem was, if he wasn't coming back to work until later, I would have to stay later and pick up the day's work with him once he had rested in his dressing room." Sensing Larson's frustration, Reeves would ply him with steak dinners after shooting.

Both Larson and Reeves got their first bitter taste of Superman's influence in 1953, when Larson attended a screening of *From Here to Eternity*. The military-themed drama, with Burt Lancaster and Frank Sinatra, was seen as a slam dunk at the box office. Reeves had a key role as a uniform who cautions Lancaster against getting involved with the boss's wife. It was a warning that Reeves may have done well to heed in his private life.

By that time, *Adventures of Superman* was thrilling television audiences across the country. Larson waited for his coworker and friend to make an appearance on-screen. When he did, the crowd yelled out "Superman!" with all the grace of burlesque spectators. Producers, scrambling to reassemble the fourth wall of their movie, reduced Reeves's screen time to a scant few minutes.

The respect Reeves had craved in Hollywood was replaced with sheer adoration—that of the half-pint set. No one had ever seen a man in flight on television before, and the novelty of such a sight was enough to elevate the crude method of sticking Reeves on a pole and blowing a fan in his face. On a nineteen-inch TV, it was agreeably awesome. Kids went positively nuts for Superman, sometimes literally.

Around Christmas 1953, National's marketing department hired a square-jawed stand-in for Reeves to don the costume and appear at Marshall Fields department store in Chicago to promote the plethora of Superman product that had begun to roll out, piggybacking on the success of the TV series. "A little kid was there whose parents had bought him a drafting compass," Larson recalled. "He had this thing, and he knew you couldn't hurt Superman. And as hard as he could, he jabbed the pointed end into Superman's rear end. George was very aware of that. He said it just takes one dumb kid with a BB gun to put out your eye."

Reeves loathed personal appearances in costume. He relented when ABC, a popular syndicated destination for the show, coerced him into filming a short vignette that would signal the arrival of coaxial cable on the West Coast. To get up the courage, Reeves imbibed heavily the day of the shoot. He climbed to the top of Mount Wilson outside Los Angeles and symbolically joined two cables together.

Reeves and Larson also agreed to make an appearance in costume at a Memphis movie theater, a PR stunt cooked up by National. When they arrived, they found the theater was segregated.

"George grew up in southern areas. It was all sold out, but he wasn't going to do it if it was going to be segregated. He asked if I was with him, and I said I was." The owner relented, and the stars stayed to sign pictures. The appearance was Larson's only concession to producers: fearing typecasting, he refused to do any more glad-handing on behalf of the series outside of a soundstage.

———

Bob Maxwell's *Superman* took many cues from the seedy comics flying off the stands at that time: the first season was virtually a film noir exercise broken into twenty-six segments. The Man of Steel opposed jewel thieves, kidnappers, and small-time hoods. The show didn't hesitate to torture their hapless victims: a girl afflicted with polio had her braces stolen; animals were gassed to death.

Whitney Ellsworth was assigned the daunting task of making the ambitious show work on a shoestring of a budget. To his benefit, the crew of *Superman* knew how to make anything look good. "Whit was a very good guy," Larson said. "He assembled very good crews. We had two Oscar-winning cameramen, and one of the great editors who edited *High Noon*. He won the Oscar for that. We had a lot of the crew of major filmmakers like Stanley Kramer. Everyone was interested in experimenting on how you shoot a one-camera show under the budgets and time constraints that we had. It was interesting."

Although Superman possessed the powers of a god, budgetary constraints forced the character to avoid any cataclysmic world-saving feats. Reeves wore a permanent look of bemusement as he allowed bullets to ricochet off his chest, humoring whatever stupid local crook dared to even bother. Powers that required viewers to use their imaginations—Superman traveling through phone wire, Superman turning invisible—were welcome script contrivances.

The series also relied on Clark's newspaper sleuthing to make up for the lack of comics-style spectacle, so Reeves's version of the character had to be more capable than previous portrayals. Few men could intimidate the *Planet*'s ace reporter; ditto Coates's resourceful Lois, who got tangled up in the machinations of local gangsters with a decided lack of reservation. (Once, a stuntman decked Coates so hard she fell to the ground, unconscious.)

Kellogg's, which had sponsored the radio drama, signed on to fund the show's second season, with one provision: the gritty stories had to be replaced by lighter fare, the better to pander to its key demographic of adolescents. Moreover, there was substantial hysteria over the near-maniacal rantings of Dr. Frederic Wertham, a psychologist who railed against the violence and (self-perceived) sexual subtext of the comics medium. To him, Superman was a fascist, and Batman and Robin engaged in acts of sodomy in the bowels of the Batcave. Though his ideas were warped, his erudition grabbed the attention of Congress, who held hearings on the matter. Suddenly, Reeves leaving criminals to starve to death on an island didn't seem like such a great idea.

To facilitate the change in tone, National replaced Maxwell with Superman comics scribe Mort Weisinger. The move fractured the camaraderie that had existed for years between Maxwell and a still-employed Ellsworth, and may have prompted Maxwell to try to undermine the show's success by poaching one of its key characters. "It was very clear that the Jimmy character was the most popular, even in comics," Larson said. "They put out *Superman's Pal, Jimmy Olsen.*" Maxwell invited Larson out to New York and offered him the starring role in *Waldo*, a pilot he was preparing about a man and his precocious chimpanzee.

"There were two chimpanzees. They bite, you know. It was a very good pilot script, but I really didn't see leaving the *Superman* show, which was successful, to work with a chimpanzee. I'm an animal person, but I just didn't see it. It made me very nervous." Larson begged off; Maxwell shot the pilot, which went unsold. Despite his noir leanings on *Superman*, he went on to produce the homespun *Lassie*, which ran for umpteen seasons.

During a break in shooting, Coates received an offer to appear in another series, *Here Comes Calvin*. *Superman* producers, not eager to alter their formula, offered to double her salary. She left anyway, though the pilot went nowhere. Ellsworth figured it would be good business to court Noel Neill, who had proved herself a capable Lane in the film serials—though her Lois was not nearly the ornery feminist Coates had developed. She was offered the role sans audition, though on more than one occasion, she would be scolded by Ellsworth to "do it like Phyllis did it."

(Both Neill and Coates wound up becoming the inadvertent objects of a particular brand of affection: when the VCR became a mass commodity in the 1980s, scenes of their inevitable capture and physical restraint at the hands of villains became favored viewing for bondage fetishists. Their shorthand in chronicling these scenes in online databases is clinical: "Overall a good scene of moderate length where Lois struggles mightily against her bonds"; "Would have been a better scene if they used more than one strand of rope to tie her wrists together"; "Lois manages to slip off her gag pretty quickly and remarks upon the fact; fortunately . . . her blindfold stays snug as Clark frees himself and as Superman flies to the rescue.")

Production on the second season commenced in 1953, two years after the first; due to the slavish details of Larson's contract, he was unable to seek work during the long interim. "I had a very odd contract with *Superman*, which Maxwell had done. It was over seven years. The only thing they had to do was to send me a telegram and thirty days later, I had to come to work. It was all very peculiar." Under the threat of being called to return to the *Superman* set at a moment's notice, Larson was unable to commit to any other lengthy production schedules. His uncomfortable tethers to Olsen grew tighter.

Ellsworth's mission to lighten up the show went into effect immediately: gone were such morbid exercises as pushing an old woman in a wheelchair down a flight of stairs. While Reeves likely bemoaned the descent into camp, Larson's comedic leanings helped him embrace it. "That was all very nice for me. Though I liked the first season, Jimmy was just a standard juvenile in peril. We didn't have a standing street scene at RKO, so they used the Hal Roach Studios street scene. I was haunted and excited by the ghosts of Laurel and Hardy. I always wanted to do comedy, and the focus on Jimmy made him more of a comedic character."

If the laughs were increasing on-screen, the inverse was true outside of the camera's view: Larson came to the set one morning to find that Robert Shayne, the series' Inspector Henderson, was being grilled by two stern-looking strangers. After consulting with Reeves, he learned that they were FBI agents. Thanks to the insinuations of Shayne's ex-wife, the actor was suspected of being a Communist.

Kellogg's wanted him ousted. With emotions inflamed by the McCarthy hearings and their blanket paranoia, suspected anti-American activity was as good as proven anti-American activity. Reeves held firm, insisting Shayne remain on the show. He did, though whether that decision was predicated more on economics than goodwill remains in question: actors often wore the same clothes for the entire season so they could film framing sequences from multiple episodes in succession. When the government began bludgeoning Shayne, he likely had a substantial reel built up, necessitating several costly reshoots if the role were to be recast.

Shayne didn't completely escape punishment: he was barred from appearing in any cereal commercials. The cast was expected to shill for the sponsor's assorted boxes of sugar in ads, ancillary income that Larson found to be almost perversely generous. "I made more money doing the commercials for Kellogg's than I ever made on the show," he laughed.

In some spots, Reeves would stroll through a neighborhood in Middle America, using his X-ray vision to confirm that the nation's youth were fueling themselves with Frosted Flakes or Sugar Smacks. (That Superman would have little problem using his powers to peep in on young boys would be a suspect plot device in more jaded times.) In others, he would take a similarly frivolous attitude toward his powers, using them to supply Jimmy and Perry with more cereal on the QT.

The ads were a boys' club. "I couldn't do the Kellogg's commercials," Neill recalled. "The men all did theirs and I said, 'Where's mine?' They said, 'Well, we just don't think it would look so good with you being a single lady with a single gentleman you work with at breakfast.'

"How things have changed."

———

As season two wrapped, Reeves began itching at his wool uniform with greater ferocity. (Literally: wearing it for too long made his skin break out.) As he hit forty, his hopes grew dim that he would ever outgrow the brand. Worse, he was perpetually risking his neck on flimsy flying apparatuses and dubious props; the first season saw him attempt to crash through a balsa wood door, but unfortunately for him, the supports had not been removed. He was knocked unconscious. Reeves demanded additional compensation to continue playing a willing participant to the end of his acting career.

Ellsworth, burdened by the paltry budget Kellogg's had allotted, wouldn't budge. The trades broke stories that Superman would be recast; rumors circulated that Kirk Alyn would be ready and willing to wear the cape again. After some more blustering, Kellogg's relented: Reeves would get $2,500 per show.

More expenses were incurred in season three. Though color televisions were reserved primarily for upper-class viewers with disposable income, Kellogg's and National predicted (correctly) that the format would eventually be the standard; black-and-white programs would prove harder to sell to syndication in the decades to come. Beginning in 1954, they footed the bill for color film, necessitating a change from Reeves's drab gray costume to the conventional red and blue. None of this effort would be seen by viewers until 1965, when the series' reruns began transmitting in color.

To help offset the increased expenditures, producers began editing episodes together and exporting them to an eager feature film market via distributor Twentieth Century Fox. Posters in theaters promised such amalgamated wonders as *Superman in Scotland Yard* and *Superman and the Jungle Devil*. The recycled productions did well enough for producers to commission two scripts for potential feature films, *Superman and the Ghost of Mystery Mountain* and *Superman and the Secret Planet*. Eventually, National likely saw little benefit in risking a box office flop that might tarnish their TV success. Nothing came of either project.

The thirteen episodes that make up the series' third season suffered from the fatigued imaginations of Jackson Gillis and David Chantler, Ellsworth's go-to staff writers, who were left with the majority of scripting chores when Ellsworth fired the other scenarists in an attempt to cut costs. Bumbling scientists and inquisitive kids were often the catalyst for an increasingly tired-looking Reeves to demolish a brick wall or swoop in from a window to give a cursory lecture or a punch to the jaw.

From 1954 to 1957, Reeves and his supporting cast would convene once a year to film a baker's dozen of episodes. With Reeves's mane rapidly turning gray, heaping globs of hair dye became a must-have accessory for makeup artists. The padding on his shoulders and arms masked a body more interested in imbibing than strength training, while a corset hid poor eating habits and a decaying metabolism. His interest was piqued only when Ellsworth allowed him to direct three episodes during the sixth sea-

Actor George Reeves dining with fiancée Leonore Lemmon at the Coconut Grove Playhouse in Miami, Florida, in 1959. Lemmon was present the night Reeves died.

(Everett Collection)

son, though the subject matter—one plot involved the search for a brainy donkey—was hardly substantial.

"We all worked hard for George," recalled Larson. Reeves seemed invigorated by the challenge, enthused by the prospect of having a career in the business that wasn't influenced by his iconic stature in the eyes of children. Larson even encouraged him to approach MGM executive Eddie Mannix, whose wife, Toni, was openly involved with George, a perverse scenario made plausible only by Eddie and Toni's Catholic refusal to get a divorce. "Eddie was known to have a very bad heart," Larson explained. "He was not going to have a long life. This was before heart transplants and heart operations. Toni and George were certainly going to marry when Eddie died."

According to Larson, Reeves "was very friendly with Eddie Mannix. And I said, 'George, why don't you just get Eddie to get you into a film at MGM?' And George looked at me with amazement and said, 'Well, Junior, that would be pushing it a bit, don't you think?'"

By 1958, it was a moot point. Reeves had left Mannix for Leonore Lemmon, a younger woman who, in Larson's words, "made George feel like a boy again." (Lemmon was said to have been a madam of sorts in New York City, a liaison for people wishing to procure sexual favors—including Jimmy Hoffa.) The break-off had sent Toni spiraling into a deep depression: Reeves and Lemmon, newly engaged, would entertain themselves in the house Toni had bought and furnished for her lover. She made harassing phone calls to Reeves. Once, he left his beloved dog in his car while he ran in for groceries, and when he came out, it was gone. Mannix was believed to be the culprit.

Reeves's life was in flux: though he detested being associated with Superman, the series had provided him with a steady income and stable schedule. But now Kellogg's and National had stockpiled more than one hundred episodes to run in perpetuity, and another season of work seemed unlikely.

Reeves's renowned generosity among friends left him with little in the way of retirement funds; he planned to box a series of exhibition bouts, including one against famed former champion Archie Moore. He accelerated a fitness regimen to prepare, including enlisting judo champion Gene LeBell for motivation and instruction. He had even taken to appearing as Superman for performances at state fairs, wrestling LeBell's "Mr. Kryptonite" in faux displays of grappling; in odd juxtaposition, Reeves would also sing with his band.

(During one particularly eventful appearance, Reeves's worst fears about the ill-defined line between his mortal being and Superman's powers were allegedly realized when a kid pointed a gun at him. He was supposedly talked out of firing when Reeves told him bystanders could be hurt by stray bullets. Reeves mentioned the incident to several reporters, though it was never corroborated.)

Reeves had no fortune outside of the series; when he appeared on *I Love Lucy*, one of the most popular programs of the era, it was in the suit. He wasn't credited, which only added to the idea that Superman was real and George Reeves was not.

While Reeves was training for the Moore bout, word came down that National had agreed to fund a seventh season after all. It even intended to extend the reins of the budget to compete with the growing amount of fantasy content on the dial. Reeves would be required to report to work for another twenty-six episodes. The trial was never-ending. At forty-five years of age, Reeves would be asked to bear more twelve-hour days in that wool and rubber suit, more bemused expressions at Jimmy's antics, more empty morality lessons at the expense of his legacy.

It was not encouraging news.

The last time Jack Larson saw George Reeves alive for any length of time was at the funeral of John Hamilton, who had portrayed Perry White. "We were pallbearers at John's funeral, which upset George very much. We loved John. He was just wonderful. He was a great guy. He was Mr. Hamilton to me for many years. He was a single father raising a son."

Larson saw Reeves once more to say good-bye before leaving for a film in Munich. National had yet to announce its plans for a seventh season of *Superman*, and Larson gambled that the series wouldn't be requiring his services. He made the film, immediately dismissed it as pabulum, then trotted off to France, where he used the salary from the movie to buy a Volkswagen. He spent the summer enjoying the company of friends and relaxing.

Like a specter, the role of Olsen haunted him, reaching out to the far ends of the Earth. He received a telegram from the United States, beckoning him home for another round as the *Planet*'s ceaselessly naive photographer. But worse news was to follow. "I was just out of contact and having a great time. When I arrived in Rome, I had tons of mail. There were all these huge envelopes. People had sent me headlines and newspaper accounts of George's death.

"And I thought, 'Well, I guess we won't do any more episodes after all.'"

Noel Neill had last seen Reeves playing cards with one of their directors; Ellsworth had called her to the soundstages to see if Lane's business suit would still fit. "He seemed happy," Neill said. "He was looking forward to starting in September."

Reeves was found dead on June 16, 1959. He was sprawled naked on his bed, a single bullet having penetrated his skull. Leonore Lemmon and other guests had been mingling downstairs. His blood alcohol content was three times the legal limit, which was far from unusual.

The following morning, millions of children who had been captivated by Reeves's portrayal of their favorite comics hero were met at the breakfast table with headlines blaring, "TV's Superman Kills Self." The police had come to that conclusion immediately, though Reeves's body was remarkable for a suicide inasmuch as the shell casing had been found ejected directly underneath him, which some amateur sleuths would later posit as impossible unless George had been holding the gun upside down. Furthermore, investigators never looked for a telltale sign of self-inflicted injury—powder burns on the hand. The body was washed as soon as it got to the coroner's office, making later examination for such particles impossible.

Chief among the peculiarities: no fingerprints of any kind were found on the gun. How a dead man could wipe his firearm free of evidence didn't seem to bother police. Ditto the two additional bullet holes found in the floor, carelessly hidden under a throw rug. Lemmon admitted to "fooling around" with the gun days prior, shooting into the ceiling. Apparently, this kind of reckless hedonism didn't raise any flags, as police seemed satisfied with her answer.

Yet Reeves allegedly had far more to live for than in the years prior. LeBell recalled that Reeves had been offered the lead in *Wagon Train* and had promised his friend a supporting role. Other reports pegged him as the choice of producers for the lead in a television adaptation of *Dick Tracy*, though how enthused Reeves could've gotten about assuming the mantle of another kids' idol is subject to debate.

Then there was the matter of the Mannix duo. Toni Mannix had called Phyllis Coates in the wee hours of the morning in a state of hysteria over the tragedy, seemingly long before anyone outside of those in the house could've known about Reeves's death. Toni had been shattered at losing Reeves to Lemmon, and her husband Eddie was reported to have had long-standing affiliations with the mafia. In a Bizarro motive, some theorized that Eddie had Reeves killed for *not* continuing the affair with his wife.

Of course, with George gone, chances for reconciliation would devolve from slim to none. More adjacent to the crime scene was Leonore, who had been seen arguing with Reeves in a steak house earlier that evening. When the two returned to his house, she insisted on leaving the light on for friends, with whom George had no interest in socializing. Taken collectively, the events of the night were sufficiently tense.

"They had been very unhappy," Larson remembered. "I know that through Elisha Cook Jr., who went to the house. He was a good friend of mine. He had been to George's house shortly before his death and said it was miserable. George's friends didn't like her friends or her. There was a lot of heavy drinking, strangers, arguing. It was a mess."

Leonore returned to the house after the police closed it down, retrieving thousands of dollars in traveler's checks. She skipped town shortly thereafter.

Reeves's mother, Helen Bessolo, was crestfallen, as well as suspicious over the circumstances of the death. She pleaded with lawyer Jerry Giesler to pore over the case, looking for any leads or clues the police seemed apathetic about finding. Months in, despite being funded over $50,000 by Bessolo, Giesler begged off any further investigation. His documents point to a substantial trail leading toward Eddie Mannix and his organized crime ties, a road that seemingly wouldn't end well for someone asking too many questions.

In their 1996 expose of the case, *Hollywood Kryptonite*, Sam Kashner and Nancy Schoenberger theorize that Toni Mannix sent a contract killer to Reeves's house that night—that he crept in and used Reeves's gun against him. Toni may have believed Leonore would be fingered for the alleged murder, but a suicide would be just as neat.

Larson believes the tragedy was self-inflicted, with Reeves too distraught over the downward spiral his life had become, so he had reservations when Ben Affleck came knocking on his door one day in 2005 looking for insight on Reeves, whom he was to play in the biopic *Hollywoodland*. "They wanted to come talk to me before they did the film. I have the best goodwill in the world toward it, but only if they don't accuse Toni. Like in cheap books like *Hollywood Kryptonite*, which I call *Hollywood Craptonite*. They just didn't do it. His death absolutely ruined her life."

There will never be a sufficient progression in cold-case methodology to ever determine what happened to Reeves that night; any conclusion one draws is fed by anecdotal observation and personal feelings. If Reeves's life was taken, it seems plausible that his ten-year relationship with the wife of a mafia-connected mogul took its inevitable course. If Reeves took his own life, it was surely fueled by the unbearable prospect of portraying Superman into middle age.

"I was certainly depressed myself at being typed as Jimmy Olsen," Larson mused. "We never discussed George being depressed about that, though I know he was. But he never complained to me. Never, ever, in all those years.

"Honest George, the People's Friend. That's what he called himself."

One can imagine Reeves as an imperishable being in some kind of afterlife, finally at peace, though still irked by one final ignobility:

The suit his mother Helen procured from his closet for his burial was one belonging to Clark Kent. He had worn it often on the show.

Purgatory

I asked Joe Shuster, "What did you think of the Superman musical?" He said, "Oh, I couldn't afford to go to that show."
—Neal Adams

Reeves's untimely death in 1959 brought with it an abrupt end to what had been a successful franchise for National and Kellogg's. *Adventures of Superman* held strong in reruns, perpetuating its usefulness—and Reeves's eternal bond to the role—long after its star had expired.

If any consideration was given to recasting the role and moving forward with the budget Kellogg's had already allotted for a seventh season, it wasn't voiced to the supporting cast. Ellsworth had had enough trouble finding his Superman once, and the morbidity of replacing Reeves with a lantern-jawed look-alike reeked of crass commercialism.

But for Ellsworth's underling Mort Weisinger, respect for the dead only went so far. Armed with funds from Kellogg's, he coerced Larson into his office one day to propose a spin-off series featuring Jimmy Olsen. "I was stunned and upset," Larson remembered. "I was not going to do it, but there was some question as to whether I was *contractually* obligated to do it."

Weisinger figured he could film thirteen episodes of an Olsen series using fresh Larson material interspersed with stock footage of Reeves. "Mort figured out a way to use all this existing footage that they had cut from other shows. If they needed a new rescue scene, they would send a muscleman through in a Superman outfit to rescue me and carry me out. You wouldn't see him." With John Hamilton also deceased, Weisinger planned to use Pierre Watkin, the Perry White of the film serial, to pinch-hit.

Larson, who dubbed the entire venture little more than "necrophilia," defied the legal threats made by National and simply quit acting, in part to head off any possible injunction coming his way and in part because *Superman* had left him with mixed feelings about the profession as a whole. He had toiled for years on a series that left him unable to walk the streets without people heckling his television persona. Ellsworth—who was as disgusted by Weisinger's plans as anyone—offered the actor a TV pilot in 1960. When the ingenue of the series, Sheree North, insisted she and Larson head to acting class every night after rehearsal, he begged off.

Larson eventually found satisfaction as a playwright, toiling away from the spotlight and thereby circumventing his typecasting affliction. He became the first playbook writer to receive a grant from the Rockefeller Foundation. Years later, an interviewer would ask Weisinger what had become of Larson. Weisinger, who was once described as a "pathological liar" by DC Comics editor Julius Schwartz, told him that he had seen Larson working as a box boy in a Brentwood supermarket. "I called Whit and asked where in the hell Mort came up with that," Larson sighed. "And he said, 'Well, he asked me if I saw you and I said yes, at City Foods.'

"But I liked Mort. Maybe he was disturbed by my response at the *Jimmy Olsen* series. I then did a number of interviews, like with Tom Brokaw [to set the record straight]. I guess people were glad I wasn't in the gutter somewhere."

———

If Ellsworth was unwilling to repurpose the memory of Reeves for the sake of profit, he didn't see much harm in attempting to resuscitate the franchise in other ways.

A week after production ceased on the sixth and presumably final season of *Superman*, and long before Reeves lost his life, Ellsworth shot a pilot
for *The Adventures of Superpup* using the same *Daily Planet* set previously
host to humans. In an effort to make a more overt grab at the adolescent
audience the character appealed to, Ellsworth reimagined the Man of Steel
as a canine; "Bark Bent" was a mild-mannered reporter under the supervision of "Terry Bite." Billy Curtis, who had portrayed a Munchkin in *The
Wizard of Oz* and had some experience with the franchise from his silent
role as a Mole Man, led a cast of little people adorned with oversized animal heads populating the burg of Pupopolis.

The overall effect resembled nothing so much as a David Lynchian
nightmare; the anthromorphism combined with the Superman mythology
made for jarring live-action viewing. Ellsworth sent the pilot over to executives at National, who were simply too stunned to reply. By 1961, their
silence finally convinced Ellsworth that his Saturday morning pursuit was
never going to air.

But National remained adamant that something could be done to reinvigorate their marquee property—and perhaps the answer was Superboy.
The character had debuted in 1944 as an addendum to the character's
history: instead of donning his costume for the first time as an adult, the
alternative continuity had Clark Kent making use of his powers as a teenager. The series was undoubtedly an attempt to marry the coveted abilities
of Kal-El with the profile of comics' target audience: boys who had little
trouble imagining themselves flying around and hurling asteroids in space.
The juvenile character was a vicarious treat.

Under the revised narrative, Lex Luthor is a boyhood chum; the duo
even conspires to find a "cure" for Superboy's aversion to Kryptonite. But
when a lab accident results in Luthor losing all his hair, he blames Superboy
for his follicular troubles. Their hometown of Smallville becomes the origin site for their endless rivalry.

Ellsworth and National figured this was the perfect solution for the chasm
created by Reeves's death: the prequel erased any concerns over recasting,
but the familiar "S" remained. National funded a pilot that was shot in 1961;
John Rockwell was cast as the titular character. Befitting the actor's com-

parative youth, he needed far less assistance from the costuming department than Reeves in filling out his suit. The unfortunately named Bunny Henning assumed the role of Lana Lang, Clark's love before he meets Lois.

Ellsworth, in tandem with other writers, pumped out thirteen *Superboy* scripts in addition to the pilot episode. Perhaps owing to the growing economy of television production, the stories were more ambitious than *Superman*'s: robots, aliens, and time travel were frequent plot points. In an attempt to curtail costs, National dictated the pilot be shot in black and white. The flying sequences were constructed differently from those of the Reeves series: Rockwell's suspension from wires would be married to video, not film, footage, in much the same way local weathermen are superimposed over maps.

Despite the supposed youth of the character, Rockwell was possessed of rather dark, mature looks. His Superboy was stockier than previous incarnations, lending his persona an adult menace rather than the more innocuous disposition of his comics counterpart.

National was nonetheless pleased with the result and began shopping the pilot around for sale to syndication. When General Mills expressed interest in having Wheaties sponsor the show, Kellogg's exerted their remaining influence to have the entire thing scrapped. With *Superman* reruns still churning out a profit, a competing program wasn't in their best interests. *Superboy* arrived DOA, joining *Superpup* as the second (and last) of Ellsworth's ancillary projects never to take flight.

Superman's unplanned sabbatical from live-action entertainment extended from 1957 to 1966, when, curiously, another comic book tent pole suddenly became the darling of the pop art generation.

National's Batman had debuted in 1939 as a sullen sociopath, but when a live-action *Batman* series premiered on ABC in January 1966, the character's television duplicate was a light-footed detective in a world of primary colors. Adam West portrayed Batman as a hero virtually in love with the idea of outsmarting criminals. Unlike the tortured soul found on comics shelves, his Bruce Wayne didn't consider the job a curse.

The show was garish and faithless to the source material; it was also an immediate hit, possessed of a vibrancy and energy few shows on the dial could match. Color television was penetrating the market, and *Batman* designers giddily decorated their sets with all the subtlety of a paint can explosion. The show aired twice weekly, emulating the cliffhanger finales of the movie serials.

Its success was hardly lost on National, which was ecstatic at the prospect that *Batman* was surpassing the heights of the more rigid Reeves series. Eager to transfer the tongue-in-cheek formula to the Man of Steel, they agreed to let Harold Prince orchestrate a Superman musical on Broadway; the idea had been broached by playwright David Newman's wife Leslie, who was inspired by their son's comics collection.

Prince, who had produced the original Broadway versions of *Fiddler on the Roof* and *West Side Story*, and even won a Pulitzer for his work on *Fiorello!* imagined Superman in the same highly stylized world as the *Batman* TV series. He commissioned Newman and Robert Benton to pen the book, and hired composer Charles Strouse and lyricist Lee Adams to create the songs. If the idea of a singing, dancing Superman appeared noxious to purists, it seemed perfectly in step with the contemporary cultural climate, one steeped in irony and camp.

In many ways, Prince had it harder than Maxwell and Ellsworth did on the *Superman* TV series; he needed an actor who, in addition to looking the part, would meet the physical demands of performing stunts onstage—and be able to carry a tune.

Prince held several open auditions until he reconnected with Bob Holiday, with whom he had worked on *Fiorello!* Holiday had toiled as an all-purpose entertainer in nightclubs, sharing bills with the Three Stooges. He was a durable performer; best of all, his six-foot-four frame was kept in shape with regular visits to the gym only a block away from his apartment on West 57th Street.

"When I was a kid, Kirk Alyn was my hero," Holiday recalled. "He was the first Superman. Hal asked me and several other people to audition. They were looking for somebody that could play the part and be credible. It went down to the wire. And fortunately, I got it." Upon his hiring, Holiday supplemented his normal fitness regimen by downing protein shakes and hitting the weights.

Prince hired Joan Hotchkis for Lois and a veteran stage actor named Jack Cassidy to portray a columnist obsessed with unmasking Superman. Newman and Benton devised a plot that had Superman questioning his value as a hero, eventually losing his powers in a plot device that had more learned audience members snickering at the impotence subtext.

Cassidy's stature in the business—he had received a Tony Award for *She Loves Me*—required that he receive top billing over Holiday. "Honestly, I didn't have a problem with that," Holiday insisted. "I was just happy that I had gotten the role." Rehearsals took place in Philadelphia; the playwrights made minor changes to the book, but the most glaring alteration was the replacement of Hotchkis with Patricia Marand.

After a trial run in Philly—which got generally good reviews—*It's a Bird . . . It's a Plane . . . It's Superman* moved to New York in March 1966. Holiday's Superman performed a myriad of live stunts: he'd slip out of his Kent clothes while cloistered in a phone booth onstage; he'd be perpetually strung up on wires and would hover in and out of scenes; in the play's most outrageous sequence, he would hoist an entire bleacher full of extras over his head, aided by an offstage forklift. (Once, Holiday experienced the requisite fall from the suspension cables. Unable to break character in front of the live audience, he landed on his feet and made a quip about his invulnerability, much to the delight of the crowd.)

Holiday recalled that he and Cassidy enjoyed a bit of rivalry onstage. "One time, at the end of the performance, I was coming in for my curtain call. The music is still going, the audience is applauding. I came in, landed, got my applause, and then Jack came on. Then I'd go flying out again, the same way I came in. I'm going up now.

"As I'm just getting off, Jack hands me an envelope and says, 'Would you mail this for me?'"

Producer Prince figured the subject matter was ideal for matinee performances, and scheduled several. Afterward, children would be allowed to mingle with Holiday backstage. Mindful of how enamored he had been with Alyn as a youth, Holiday welcomed the chance to embody their hero. Unfortunately, some of them harbored the same aggressive curiosity as kids from the Reeves years.

"If somebody wanted to take a shot at me, I had no problem with it. I went out after a matinee once and was having something to eat, and there was a little guy with his dad sitting next to me at the counter. They had seen the show. The little guy looked at me, and said, 'Wow, are you Superman?' I said yes. He said, 'Do you really fly?' I said yes. He said, 'Could I hit you in the stomach?'"

Holiday's frame could usually take a little abuse from the pint-sized sadists, especially since he was usually wearing the harness that kept him aloft.

The role led to a string of TV appearances, though as with Reeves, people had little use for him outside of the costume. He swooped onto the set of *I've Got a Secret*, persuading host Steve Allen to fly; Johnny Carson had him for a sit-down session on *The Tonight Show*, where Holiday gifted him with a lock of Superman's trademark spit curl. *Life* magazine's editors were set to feature him on their cover, and photographed him coming in for a landing. At the last moment, they decided to use West's Batman instead.

Holiday was unperturbed, and embraced the role wholeheartedly; he even schemed to fly into Giants Stadium on a helicopter. "I wanted it. They didn't want it. You're young and you do stupid things. I was a Giants fan. I said, 'Why don't we do something like that?' Just go over in a helicopter, and then come down in the same way, on the field, with the harness. Land on the ground and there you are. They didn't want to do it. They felt it was not appropriate for the crowd."

Superman did impressive business for several weeks, at which point ticket sales slowed to an absolute crawl. Four months after its debut on Broadway, Holiday entered the production offices to find a notice posted on the board: the show would be closing down in a matter of days. Neither Holiday nor Prince had much of an idea why things transpired the way they did. In all probability, the matinees infected the show with the stink of juvenilia; adult theatergoers likely dismissed it as little more than a place to take listless kids on rainy afternoons. And with *Batman* permeating the television schedule, audiences may have considered it redundant to go pay for the same kind of camp attitude found on TV for free.

The show was resurrected in 1967, when promoters in Kansas City and St. Louis booked Holiday for a series of engagements. He was hoisted two hundred feet in the air in open stadiums, up and away from the elitist attitudes of the New York theater scene. The hyperbolized Superman was welcomed by crowds of more than ten thousand, most of them children, who still loved their hero even when they could see the strings.

By 1967, National had unofficially become DC Comics, and it was enjoying the kind of circulation it hadn't seen since the wartime boom of the 1940s. *Batman* had morphed into a phenomenon on television, and Superman's stature kept his family of titles aloft. The strength of these two flagship heroes had made DC the largest distributor of comic books in the world.

The resurgence did little to decrease DC's apathy toward Jerry Siegel and Joe Shuster, who had conceived of Superman decades prior and had been directly responsible for the company earning untold millions in the intervening years. Siegel had been employed to write stories for the franchise in an uncredited capacity, a somewhat humiliating form of compensation. More ignoble was the catalyst for his hiring: wife Joanne—the original model for Lois Lane—stormed into the DC offices to shame the company into enlisting him.

Despite the token work, Siegel's attitude was again sufficiently incendiary: he insisted on being recognized, both financially and creatively, for his efforts. DC's response was to fire him outright, leaving Siegel to join Shuster—who was nearly blind and virtually destitute—on the unemployment line.

Siegel's rage over being shunted was palpable, but a DC-mandated gag order forced his silence. It would be another six years before he could

Superman cocreators Jerry Siegel and Joe Shuster in a 1975 portrait. Although Warner Bros. would eventually boast of a billion-dollar profit from their creation, the duo received paltry compensation.

(Everett Collection)

petition the courts for ownership of the icon, and he was advised by his sleepy-eyed legal counsel to keep mum until then. He did; the built-up venom would practically gush out of him by 1975.

Both men clearly had a legitimate claim to the character's conception; a little-known bodybuilder liked to believe he was a third, silent partner. In the 1970s, Mayo Kaan began boasting that he had been the model Siegel and Shuster used to craft the Man of Steel's improbable physique. To prove it, he offered—for a nominal fee—pictures taken of him in a crudely made costume, allegedly from 1936.

The marketable reputation Kaan had attempted to create as the "real" Superman was rejected by Siegel and Shuster, who insisted they had never met him and had no idea what he was talking about. Worse, a building in the background of his "proof" hadn't even been constructed in 1936. Debunked, Kaan went into hibernation until 1997, when he reiterated the story. A more litigious group of copyright handlers were around to mete out legal cautions. Kaan stood by his story until his death in 2002.

In 1967, in one of the earliest examples of media synergy, DC was acquired by Kinney National, a conglomerate that had built up its coffers in the funeral parlor and parking lot businesses. Two years later, Kinney purchased film and music powerhouse Warner Bros.–Seven Arts and renamed itself Warner Communications. DC now had direct access to multimedia platforms through which to build its brands. Unfortunately, few at Warner cared to believe comic books would become a highly touted form of currency in the film and television business, the flash-in-the-pan *Batman* excepted.

By this time, the comic book versions of both Batman and Superman had become far removed from their noir origins. Batman's internal agony over his parents' untimely demise was shuttered to make room for tales featuring time travel, faux Batmen, and inane jaunts into the fantastic. (*Batman* #147 featured the decidedly ungrim hero regressing into literal infantilism in a story dubbed "Batman Becomes Bat-Baby!")

Superman fared no better. Under the dubious direction of Mort Weisinger, his exploits were dwarfed by a litany of supporting roles that turned anyone with even a passing relation to him into a demigod. Beppo the Super-Monkey and Comet the Super-Horse are self-explanatory; mortal friends like Jimmy and Lois would occasionally be gifted with powers. The era is not without its charms—artist Curt Swan's rendition of Superman became the archetype for the character for decades to come—but the tone was generally unsatisfying to anyone over the age of fourteen.

Readers who sought out heroes with more complex emotions needed only to look farther down the newsstand, where rival publisher Marvel Comics was experiencing a renaissance of its own. Under the direction of Stan Lee, it produced a new crop of four-color stars with very human foils. Spider-Man could barely make his rent payments; both the Hulk and the Thing anguished over their hideous visages; Daredevil was blind.

(The charismatic Lee would go on to lecture at college campuses throughout the 1970s, preaching comics as a more respectable medium than what the *Batman* TV series had suggested.)

Marvel had managed to license its most popular character, Spider-Man, as early as 1967. The wall crawler was featured in a primitive Saturday morning cartoon series produced by animation stalwart Ralph Bakshi; the pen-and-ink cast moved with all the grace of cutouts on Popsicle sticks. Despite its parent production company going bankrupt after the first season, it scratched out three years on the air.

In 1966, radio Superman Bud Collyer, who had enjoyed years of prosperity as a game show host in the booming world of television, received a phone call from Filmation Studios. Founded by Lou Scheimer and Norm Prescott in 1963, the animation house was notable primarily for producing decent-looking material on a tight budget and schedule. Unfortunately, none of their original creations (Fraidy Cat, Wacky and Packy) resonated with viewers.

DC had taken notice of what was becoming a lucrative market in children's programming during weekend hours, and had toured the Filmation offices searching for a capable staff to produce a new half-hour Superman animated series. In a bizarre display of premeditated hubris, Scheimer had planted family members toiling away at art tables. When he came through with DC's representatives, he spotted one making an egregious error and promptly "fired" him. DC, presumably impressed with Filmation's no-nonsense attitudes, assigned the studio duties on the Man of Steel project.

The New Adventures of Superman debuted on CBS in fall 1966. The series was a reunion of sorts for the talent involved in the radio drama twenty years prior. Collyer, no doubt soothed by the lightened workload of the new voice-over industry in comparison to his radio schedule, lowered and raised his voice register to depict the Superman/Clark dichotomy; Joan Alexander again suffered the indignity of becoming one of multiple Lois performers, sharing the role with Julie Bennett; Jackson Beck, who had narrated the radio drama, returned for similar duties.

The series took on an anthology feel, with two Superman shorts bookending one tale featuring Superboy. There were no limitations to what animators could depict—an exploding planet was just as cheap to produce as a two-bit hood. Lex Luthor made his small-screen debut; the comic book character's appearance was no doubt influenced by story editor Weisinger assigning scripting chores to several in-house DC scribes.

CBS enjoyed terrific ratings, and mandated a concept change: the series became The Superman/Aquaman Hour of Adventure. Superman's exploits were joined to the oceanic adventures of DC's self-professed King of the Seas; the piggybacking extended the successful show to sixty minutes. By 1968's third season, producers had swapped out Superman's tag team partner once more, retitling the show The Batman/Superman Hour.

With the explosive growth of the television medium came fresh opposition from hyperactive watchdog groups. Frederic Wertham's TV counterpart was Action for Children's Television (ACT), a vocal minority that monitored violent or exploitative content on the dial. Wielding the threat of intervention by the FCC like a weapon, ACT was coercive in its attempts to get networks to rethink programming choices.

Though *Superman* was largely tame in its depiction of action, CBS nonetheless kowtowed to pressure from the family-oriented contingent. The series was canceled in 1969, some months before Collyer died from circulatory problems at the age of sixty-one.

As for live-action programming, networks hoped they could emulate the popularity of *Batman* by continuing to draw inspiration from the comics pages. ABC execs thought they had it made when they spun off their *Green Hornet* series directly from a *Batman* episode. Unfortunately, few viewers cared about yet another millionaire vigilante, especially one who possessed none of his predecessor's light touches; it lasted less than a season. (The Hornet's sidekick, Bruce Lee, would go on to display his martial arts prowess on the big screen.)

Batman producers created a *Dick Tracy* pilot at ABC, with Ray MacDonnell in the title role. They hoped that, like their trademark brand, *Tracy* would rely on camp humor and a rotating rogue's gallery of name actors assuming parts like Mr. Memory and Mumbles. It never made it to air, nor did their brazenly inept four-and-a-half-minute *Wonder Woman* test reel, which they hoped would attract a network order for a full pilot.

At virtually the same time, *Batman* itself had run out of sardonic steam. Twice-weekly airings and an assault of media coverage had conspired to exhaust viewers, who allowed it to plummet in the ratings. Rival network NBC, desperate for even the fumes of an ailing hit, offered to pick it up for a fourth season, but sets had already been torn down.

Adam West found only a few years of respite from the character. In 1973, DC entered into a production deal with Hanna-Barbera to produce a new animated show that would assemble a veritable Who's Who of their roster. The Justice League team of superheroes from the comics pages became the *Super Friends*; the title alteration mirrored the show's homogenized, dumbed-down approach.

The heroes' battles with evil were muted to acceptable levels to appease a still-ravenous ACT council. The series introduced the Wonder Twins, a pair of siblings possessed of rather ineffectual powers: twin Zan could alter his molecular structure to transform into a bucket of water, a seemingly unfortunate genetic gift. The Super Friends rarely exchanged fists with their villains, preferring to do a lot of running, flying, and jumping out of the way. The pacifistic tone was abetted by crude animation that would often insert a third arm or display erroneous color schemes. Kids didn't seem to mind.

In deference to his abilities, Superman was cast as the leader of the group. Batman, Wonder Woman, and Aquaman made up his trifecta of supporting players. The animation studio, in an embarrassing attempt to round out the racial profile of the team, introduced such broadly drawn heroes as Apache Chief and Samurai. West assumed the role of Batman when Olan Soule left after the first few seasons; Danny Dark portrayed Superman for the duration. Casey Kasem, who would find regular work as Shaggy in Hanna-Barbera's *Scooby-Doo* franchise, played Robin.

The series' gee-whiz mentality sated concerned parents but left critics bored. It was still a ratings hit for ABC, who spent the next decade exhausting every possible permutation of the template. The animation business was in a perpetual state of paranoia over appearing stale to attention-disordered youth, and a revolving door of new titles was instituted. Many simply devolved into nonsensical wordplay: *Challenge of the Super Friends, All-New Super Friends Super Hour, World's Greatest Super Friends,* and *Super Friends: The Legendary Super Powers Show.* By the time *Super Powers Team: Galactic Guardians* came around, both producers and audiences were depleted of any enthusiasm. The series gulped its last breath in 1986.

———

For millions of adults and children, no number of four-color heroes could hold a candle to the charisma of Muhammad Ali. In 1978, DC, eager to gorge itself on the boxer's worldwide popularity, made arrangements with Ali's camp to produce the metafiction oddity *Superman vs. Muhammad Ali.* The oversized tome's cover promised that Ali would contest Superman under Queensbury rules. Both men were strapped with boxing gloves, though anyone even casually aware of the hero's mythology would know that one glancing blow from the Kryptonian would decapitate his foe.

Writer Denny O'Neil had an inventive solution to make the match, held on an alien planet for the amusement of a maniacal dictator, more competitive: Superman's powers are zapped by his proximity to a red star, allowing Ali to pummel his opponent mercilessly for round after round. Only Kal-El's recuperative abilities save him from becoming a boxing statistic.

Despite the dopey conceit, purists still found a lot to like in the pencil work of Neal Adams. His cover depicted dozens of celebrities attending the event, including Frank Sinatra and the Jackson Five. In Adams's mind, even Marvel's Stan Lee couldn't resist attending. The novel one-shot sold well, and a Superman/Spider-Man crossover followed three years later. (The notion of DC's and Marvel's premier stars butting heads was contemplated in the Ali special, but legal issues forced Spider-Man's panels to be deleted.)

A more egregious insult to the character came in 1975 courtesy of ABC, which financed a filmed performance of the Man of Steel's 1966 musical for its *Wide World of Entertainment* anthology series. Holiday was not asked to return as Superman; his replacement, David Wilson, would have to settle for the dubious title of being the most miscast metahuman in history. His dumpy, loutish looks lent the title role little dignity. Lesley Ann Warren was cast as Lois; she would later attempt to repeat the role in a more respectable incarnation.

Mercifully, ABC relegated its lone airing to a late-night slot. Any charm the musical possessed as a live performance died on the vine in the prerecorded event. Moreover, the camp nods that had charmed viewers of *Batman* a decade prior were by now hopelessly out of date. The effort remains one of the few ancillary Superman projects that Warner Bros. has yet to exploit on home video.

Warner also had little compunction in allowing Peter Lupus, the "muscle" of the *Mission: Impossible* television cast, to suit up as Superman in a series of Air Force recruitment ads that aired throughout the early 1970s. "It was out of New York," Lupus recalled. "I jumped off a ladder and said, 'Join our Super Team!'" Lupus would appear—in a DC-sanctioned costume—alongside pro athletes like Jerry West. The ads ran through 1974.

By this time, the character had endured more than thirty years of thoughtless handling. Nothing since the Fleischer cartoons had captured the inherent scale and sweeping vistas of the mythology. Thanks in large part to ABC's *Batman*, comics were now reviled as fodder for arrested development; the thought of sinking a studio's vast resources into a strait-laced adaptation of a man in spandex tights was preposterous to everyone with access to a checkbook.

With the crucial exception of a silver-tongued film producer.

Flights of Fancy

I don't think the Salkinds understood Superman, but they knew it was a good idea. And I give them great kudos for thinking so, because Warner Bros. didn't.
—Tom Mankiewicz

Alexander Salkind stared blankly at his son. Over dinner, the excitable twenty-six-year-old had been gushing about a comic book character named Superman. He has powers, Ilya explained. He flies; he's like Jesus.

The elder Salkind was lost. "He looked at me like I was speaking Chinese," Ilya recalled. "My father was born in Poland, raised in France, and he absolutely didn't know anything about the comics."

Born in Mexico City, Ilya had long been fascinated with the escapist allure of motion pictures. His mother ushered him into cinemas projecting the messianic pursuits of Ben-Hur and the stars of *The Ten Commandments*. The "light" of these filmgoing experiences, Ilya remembered, was tempered by the pragmatic attitude of his father, a successful film producer in Cuba. Much later, friend Bob Gale would compare Salkind's conflicted youth to the warring sides of the Force in *Star Wars*. Ilya laid out Gale's analogy: "To simplify it, my mother was the good Force, while my father was more on the darker side of the Force. He was more business-oriented, much more nuts and bolts, tough."

The Salkinds never stayed in one corner of the globe very long. At age seven, Ilya found himself in New York City. Adopting English to supplement his native Spanish tongue, he began following the exploits of comic book heroes and dime-novel adventurers. When an older Ilya moved to Paris to complete his college studies, he would dig up imported copies of *Galaxy* and *Fiction*, in which Ray Bradbury and his contemporaries would spin tales of other worlds.

After finishing school in 1969, Ilya became the third generation of his family to enter the motion picture business, following both father Alexander and grandfather Michael. The family's involvement went as far back as Greta Garbo's first major film, which Michael had produced; celluloid dreams were in the blood.

Recalling his love of Jules Verne's *The Lighthouse at the End of the World*, Ilya persuaded his father to mount a film adaptation. In *The Light at the Edge of the World*, Kirk Douglas opposed pirates who had taken over a lighthouse, their scheme hatched and led by a sneering Yul Brynner. Despite marketing that led audiences to believe it was a family-oriented romp, it was a grisly outing that did only modest business.

Eager to satisfy the morbid tastes of an early 1970s counterculture, the Salkinds mounted *Kill!* in which James Mason prefigures Charles Bronson's vigilante tactics from the subsequent *Death Wish* series. But it wasn't until 1972's *Bluebeard* that the Salkind trio would find success in the States. The film featured Richard Burton as a World War I pilot who murders his lovers, including reigning screen vixen Raquel Welch. Played as a comedy, it became their biggest hit—until 1973's *The Three Musketeers*.

An ardent fan of the Alexandre Dumas classic, Ilya felt his producing clan now had the clout to mount a large-scale production. Again, he would use the swashbuckling narratives of his youth to fuel his adult pursuits. Oliver Reed, Richard Chamberlain, and Frank Finlay signed on as the titular trio. Welch was reenlisted by the Salkinds to feed the audience's more prurient interests; Faye Dunaway was cast as the beautiful but treacherous Milady de Winter.

They also approached director Richard Lester, who had helmed the Beatles films *Help!* and *A Hard Day's Night* but was currently persona non grata in Hollywood. His more recent efforts, like *How I Won the War*, had hemorrhaged money and flopped in cinemas. But Ilya was convinced his reputation for handling actors would aid a complicated independent shoot in Spain. The Salkinds had devised a way to gather enough material for two films by shooting two scripts simultaneously, a cost-cutting measure that would later be used by producers of the *Back to the Future* and *Matrix* franchises.

The Salkinds might have been less enthusiastic about their ingenius plan had they foreseen the legal morass to come. While the actors had shot enough footage for two releases, they were only being paid for one, a situation that resulted in bitter feelings and court proceedings. The confusion prompted the Screen Actors Guild to institute the "Salkind Clause," by which contracts must specify whether talent is being hired for one film or for multiple productions.

(It would not be Alex's only visit to a courtroom. In 1978, he was accused of misappropriating over $20 million from private investors in Switzerland. Claiming diplomatic immunity because he was a consultant for the Costa Rican Embassy, he managed to dodge the charges by fleeing to Mexico. He was petrified of flying and had to be sedated for the journey. The funds were eventually returned in a civil settlement.)

Despite the behind-the-scenes drama, both *The Three Musketeers* and its sequel were critical and commercial successes. Audiences enjoyed the homage to the more broadly drawn protagonists of the 1940s film serials, especially as an alternative to the existential gloom provided in the other movie offerings of the 1970s. But the happiness was mingled with grief: in between releases, Michael Salkind passed away, leaving Alexander and Ilya to continue with the family business.

Faced with financial and creative prosperity, Ilya did what any twenty-something would: he let it go to his head. "I became more like my father: tough, pragmatic, sometimes arrogant. I've not met one guy who hasn't had the same reaction before age thirty. The first one really hits you. Suddenly, everyone invites you, talks to you, wants to make films with you."

By this time, Ilya was the idea maven; Alexander was the one responsible for funding. "A French newspaper called him the 'Poet of Money.'

He was a brilliant wizard at finding funds," Ilya recalled. "The banks were more involved [in financing movies] in those days." With his father's knack for business, Ilya's creative impulse, and the clout afforded by their recent success, the Salkinds spent much of 1973 wondering what to do next. Ilya's thoughts again ran toward the four-color dreams of his youth, particularly toward the allegorical tale of an alien being who comes to be the savior of Earth.

Toward the light.

Despite being firmly rooted in popular culture, Superman had not been seen on the big screen since repackaged episodes of the Reeves series appeared in theaters in the mid-1950s. In the interim, no comics property had managed to sustain the interest of movie audiences. (Jane Fonda had appeared in *Barbarella*, based on a French comic book, but business probably hinged more on her penchant for skimpy fur bikinis than on any sort of brand recognition.) The lone exception—a quickie theatrical release featuring the cast of TV's *Batman*—attracted a flash of interest before the series collapsed under the weight of its own kitsch.

Ilya Salkind detested the tongue-in-cheek antics of Adam West and his ilk; he had once scolded Lester for considering *Musketeers* a children's book. To do Superman justice, he believed, would take a reverential, serious approach. But it still had to be fun.

"What did I see in the character?" Ilya mused. "I think I saw the ultimate good guy. It's something that left a very strong impression on me. He was the ultimate hero. On top of that, he was an alien, which was pretty unbelievable. Everybody says Superman is American. No, he's Kryptonian. It just gelled. Perhaps it was a way for me to express an idea of what I'd like to be."

A dubious Alexander listened to his son's strange pitch about a super-powered man from a distant world, then returned to Europe to gauge the interest of his investors. To his surprise, they responded with enthusiasm.

Superman knew no geographic or language boundaries; everyone could nod in recognition at the sight of a caped man in flight.

With financing imminent, the Salkinds began conspiring with Ilya's childhood friend Pierre Spengler. Like Alex, Spengler was one of the few men in their circle who knew little of the character. But he warned that attempting a production on this scale—with the complex machinations behind trying to make a man "fly"—would cost millions of dollars. The Salkinds took his point, but they didn't care. Done right, they would make tens of millions in profit.

Budget concerns would come later; the biggest hurdle to clear in the immediate future was to somehow convince Warner Bros. to relinquish the rights to the character. Such a proposal would be greeted with incredulity today, in the age of "brands" and Hollywood's obsession with established franchises. To contemplate selling the screen rights to one of the most recognizable icons alongside Mickey Mouse would be dubbed an act of insanity.

But in 1973, Warner—like everyone else—saw no potential for filming silly men in tights. Comic books were children's fare, suited at best for crudely budgeted escapades on television.

Dick Shepherd, then head of production for the studio, received a call in early 1973 that the Salkinds were interested in purchasing the rights to their DC institution. To hear Ilya tell it, Shepherd couldn't have cared less: "They called him from New York and told him the Salkinds wanted to do Superman as a movie. And he said, 'Ah, sell it. It's not worth it. It's not a good property for a film.' He told me that, which is the reason I respect the guy. Admitting a mistake is pretty commendable, especially in this business."

Negotiations were nonetheless protracted; while Warner didn't care if Superman flew to the cinematic scrap heap and back, DC was another story. Its editors had a reverence for the character and his history, and they tortured the Salkinds with minutiae about how they would be able to depict the mythology. "Every breath of the actors would've had to have been monitored by DC," Ilya said. "There were integrity clauses, moral clauses. They wanted approval on everything: costumes, cast list, who was going to play Superman." Protection soon turned to suffocation, and the Salkinds became increasingly exasperated.

After six weeks of talks that went nowhere, Ilya phoned Bill Sarnoff, head of Warner Publishing, to which DC Comics was subordinate. Free of any emotional investment in the character, Sarnoff's division signed off on the deal. The Superman film and television rights now belonged to the Salkinds for the next twenty-five years for the relatively modest sum of $4 million, only $1 million of which was due upon signing. They also wound up with a negative pickup deal, which held them responsible for funding and producing the film. Warner would have first crack at distribution, but there were no guarantees. DC, meanwhile, would supply a production liaison who could voice complaints, though his or her veto power would be limited.

Julius Schwartz, then the editor of DC's Superman titles, met with the Salkinds after the deal had been locked. He suggested screenwriter Leigh Brackett, who had made her name as the scribe on a series of John Wayne films and *The Big Sleep*. Ilya balked when he found out she was on the West Coast, as his base of operations would be in New York. (Brackett didn't suffer too much from the snub; genre fans recognize her embryonic contributions to the second *Stars Wars* film, *The Empire Strikes Back*, prior to her death in 1978.)

Schwartz next suggested Alfred Bester, a noted science fiction author who had dabbled in television and whose wife, Rolly, had briefly played the role of Lois Lane in the radio serial. Schwartz played up his friend's credentials in genre fiction; Ilya Salkind bought the sales pitch and hired Bester for what was to be the largest payday of the author's career. But Ilya's father was not amused. Alex Salkind wanted a big name to author the screenplay—someone who could attract major talent to their project and boost its profile in the industry—and he hadn't heard of Bester. The author got a kill fee and was waved off.

Ilya's next choice was William Goldman, one of the few "celebrity" scribes in Hollywood at that time. Goldman had accepted an Oscar in 1969 for his work on *Butch Cassidy and the Sundance Kid*, and he would later receive a second for 1977's *All the President's Men*. He was well respected in studio circles for delivering literate scenarios that remained palatable to a popcorn-engorged public.

Salkind, Spengler, and Goldman spent three hours hashing out the character and his motivations; finally, Goldman begged off. "He just wasn't feeling it," Ilya recalled. Goldman, who prided himself on gritty reality, couldn't gather enough enthusiasm for the denizens of Krypton. (Ironically, Goldman would later attempt a pass at the screenplay for New Line Cinema's proposed Captain Marvel film.)

Meanwhile, Mario Puzo was becoming a highly valued name. A struggling author of highbrow novels, Puzo figured a story immersed in mafia lore would have commercial potential. He was right: *The Godfather* became a bestseller, and its subsequent film adaptation entered pop culture consciousness with its operatic tone and bullish performances by Al Pacino and Marlon Brando.

Flush with success, Puzo was enlisted for scribing duties on the junk blockbuster *Earthquake* in 1974. But to the Salkinds he offered a high profile and a level of cachet even Goldman couldn't equal.

"We took this enormous corner suite at the Plaza Hotel in New York with a beautiful view of the park," Ilya recalled. "Then I said, 'This suite is not good. It's too flashy.' So we got a very tiny suite with a view of the courtyard, and that's where Puzo came. He was a really wonderful man, but when he walked in, he literally looked like a truck driver. Very simple guy, very earthy guy, not at all sophisticated like Goldman."

Salkind reiterated the story: Kal-El comes to Earth, the last surviving member of an alien planet. He's raised by farm folk. Grows up with Middle American values. Has powers beyond those of mortal men. Decides to use them to protect his adopted race. Wears blue tights.

Puzo liked it, especially the promise of the sort of lavish, sweeping themes he had used to great effect in *The Godfather*. The Salkinds agreed to pay him $350,000 to deliver a screenplay, plus 5 percent of the gross receipts. Over several weeks in Las Vegas, Ilya, Puzo, and DC head Carmine Infantino hashed out the narrative. There was a lot of ground to cover: Superman's origin, his debut in Metropolis, his romance with Lois Lane, and his adversarial relationship with Lex Luthor. A cohesive story had to be intertwined with the kind of spectacular set pieces that fans would expect from a big-budget superhero epic.

(Puzo was cognizant of the challenge. In the 1940s, he had written stories for men's magazines owned by Martin Goodman, the founder of Marvel Comics. When Marvel editor Stan Lee agreed to let him try his hand at a comics fable, he returned a week later empty-handed. "It's too difficult," he told Lee.)

In October 1975, Puzo returned with a work that resembled nothing so much as a phone book. The three-hundred-page opus was lyrical, respectful, entertaining . . . and unfilmable. "If we had made the script, it would've been $500 million," Ilya exclaimed. "He went all the way with the comic books. When you put in the script, 'Superman lifts part of China and puts it in the air,' it's easy to write, but to do it realistically, it's a whole different ball game."

In Puzo's tale, Superman's formative years were chronicled in explicit detail. Arriving in Metropolis, he would oppose a quartet of Kryptonian supervillains that his father had imprisoned. Seeking revenge, they threaten Kal-El's adopted home planet with chaos, usurping the presidency and squatting in the White House. One adversary was dubbed "Kru-El," one of many details indicative of Puzo's bombastic approach to the material.

The swollen script made Ilya frantic. Even something half its length would be unusable. Puzo was disinterested in conforming to Salkind's need for something more practical; in late 1975, he bowed out of the project. Salkind was disappointed but not heartbroken. Puzo's name brand lingered, and they now had a template from which to work. (The author would later receive "Screenplay by" and "Story by" credit for his contributions.)

Ilya's next meeting was with Robert Benton and David Newman, the writing team behind *What's Up, Doc?*, *Bonnie and Clyde*, and, perhaps ominously, the ill-fated 1966 Superman musical revue. More sympathetic to the needs of the film business than the novelist Puzo, the duo began hacking away at the dense narrative.

Not long into rewrites, Benton decided to take up an opportunity to direct his first feature, *The Late Show*. As a replacement, Newman brought in his own wife, Leslie. She provided much-needed female insight into the character of Lois Lane.

Some of Puzo's more egregious alterations to the mythology—like making Clark Kent a television reporter instead of a newspaperman—were excised. Also discarded was Puzo's suggestion that in order to avoid waiting half an hour to introduce the star of the film, the same actor should play both Kal-El and his father, Jor-El. Salkind, fearing audience confusion, scrapped the tactic.

Under advisement from the producers, the Newmans had taken the Puzo blueprint and turned it into two separate scripts. As with *Musketeers*, Ilya envisioned a simultaneous film shoot that would cut costs and anticipate the demands of a receptive audience eager for more. By now, the group of four Kryptonian villains had become three, and their harassment would have to wait until the second film. In the first, Luthor's mayhem would provide sufficient incentive for heroics, especially since a good portion of the film would be devoted to the obligatory backstory of Clark Kent's rocket trip and subsequent adolescence in Smallville.

Impatient to see the polished work, Alex Salkind insisted the Newmans fly to Paris and read him the script aloud. He fell asleep midway through.

―――

Before Puzo signed on in 1975, the Salkinds received a call from the agent of a young director named Steven Spielberg. His client, the agent exclaimed, was a huge Superman fan and would embrace the chance to bring him back into the collective consciousness. All he needed to do was finish *Jaws*, his ode to monster movies featuring a bloodthirsty shark.

Ilya had seen an early screening of *Jaws* and was convinced it was going to be a smash; his father was not. Alex insisted on waiting to see how the "giant fish movie" would do before committing to the unknown director. Ilya sulked, but Alex was the man with the money; the younger Salkind could do little except politely decline the offer. *Jaws* would go on to become one of the most successful movies in history. By that time, Spielberg had the chutzpah to remember the scorn. When Ilya called his agent back, the rep mockingly suggested Spielberg could still do it—as a musical. Salkind took the hint and went on his way.

He proceeded to talk up Superman with directors Peter Yates (*Bullitt*), John Guillermin (the 1970s remake of *King Kong*), and Francis Ford Coppola (*The Godfather*). "Some were really excited about it, some less. They didn't know how to do it. Yates was very excited. We had more than one meeting. But another film came up for him." *Musketeers* director Richard Lester was approached; when he suggested they make it a period piece, he was left alone.

Ilya eventually took a meeting with British director Guy Hamilton, who had helmed arguably the best Sean Connery installment of the James Bond franchise, *Goldfinger*. Hamilton displayed the necessary enthusiasm for the mythology, agreeing with Salkind that they had to avoid the camp mood that permeated other comics adaptations. (At that point, the Newmans' rewrite had still not excised a couple of moments that flirted with self-mockery, such as when Superman runs into Telly Savalas in a gratuitous cameo, or when Luthor begins to eat facial tissues out of frustration.)

Satisfied Hamilton could handle a production of this scale, the Salkinds hired him. Producers now had a workable script, an eager director . . . and absolutely no interest from a studio. "We still didn't have an American distribution deal. A lot of territories were sold, but it was getting very, very bad," Ilya recalled. The Salkinds had wagered that the Superman brand coupled with Puzo's fame would prove to be enticing to someone. Instead, they had come up bust.

Ilya began to eye the financial plug keeping the movie alive. Over a million dollars had already been spent on script development, effects tests, and assorted perks like the Plaza hotel rooms. They had no stars, no shooting date, and no Superman. Days before Ilya was to formally end development and tuck his tail between his legs, he received a call from Kurt Frings, a notorious Hollywood agent and deal broker.

Salkind still remembers Frings's matter-of-fact statement, one that would prove to be his project's salvation: "I can get you Brando."

Though the collective memory is somewhat crowded by the Brando of later years—bulbous and isolated, eccentric and difficult—there was a time when the actor was the biggest movie star in the world. Brooding through films like *The Wild One* and *On the Waterfront*, he ushered in a new era of "Method" acting, in which performers didn't so much emulate their roles as channel them.

With his matinee idol looks fading, Brando used his physical gravitas to lend weight to *Last Tango in Paris* and, most notably, *The Godfather*, as Don Corleone. By the mid-1970s, he was again considered to be the biggest of stars. So big that Ilya had difficulty believing the actor would invest his talents in what was, on the surface, a lark of a movie.

He asked Frings what Brando would expect as compensation; Frings told him $2 million would sound appealing. "I called my father in Paris at four in the morning," Ilya remembered. "He said 'Do it!' So I did it." Frings got a copy of the script and forwarded it to Brando. The response came back: he would do it, but for $3.7 million and a percentage of the gross. Salkind fumed, but realized getting Brando was the only substantial chance he had of moving forward. He agreed to the deal.

News of Brando's massive payday spread across town, and the movie piggybacked on the resulting hype. The day after the signing, Gene Hackman's agent phoned Ilya and informed him that her client wanted to work with Brando; he had appeared in Newman and Benton's *Bonnie and Clyde*, and the duo had forwarded him their latest script. The versatile performer had just come off an Oscar win for *The French Connection* and was considered to be another respected member of the Serious Actor clique. Salkind told his agent that the only feasible part for him would be Luthor, but his character and Brando's would have no scenes together. Hackman didn't mind; such was Brando's cachet at the time that just appearing in the same film was good enough.

(Later, when it was estimated that Brando received $15 million for two weeks' worth of work on *Superman*, Paul Newman was said to have gasped. Ilya Salkind had once offered him his choice of roles, and his deal would've been the same as Brando's—he had declined.)

As with Brando, the price for an actor of Hackman's stature was high. He received $2 million for his concurrent work on the film and its sequel. Vanity crept into the part early on: Hackman refused to don a skullcap to simulate the hairless cranium of the archvillain. Instead, he would play the part as if the character were obsessed with wigs, going bald only at the film's climax. Hackman also rebuffed suggestions that he shave his mustache.

As predicted, Warner salivated at the sight of the newly beefed-up cast list. The Salkinds arranged for the studio to pick up domestic distribution, but it was still an independent production. Father and son had final say over cuts, casting, and catering.

"Without Brando, there would've been no movie," recalled Ilya. "But then it became a huge picture. Throughout all this, there was tons of publicity." Salkind likened the frenzy over his film to the furor over *Gone with the Wind*; he had helped it along by flying elaborate banners over consecutive Cannes Film Festivals that announced, "Brando, Hackman in *Superman: The Movie*."

With several key components in place, it was time to start tangible production. In late 1976, Ilya commissioned workers to begin constructing sets in Rome. Upon arriving in Italy with Brando, the crew were greeted with inauspicious news: Brando's *Last Tango*, a graphic exploration of sexual identity, had recently been dubbed obscene in the country. Its director, Bernardo Bertolucci, had already been detained, and it was guaranteed that his star would share his fate if he remained. Italian police gleefully informed journalists that they had an arrest warrant for Brando idling on their desk.

Any thoughts of replacing Brando were never voiced; he was the reason the film was moving forward, and his absence could mean its collapse. The Salkinds redirected production to Shepperton Studios and Pinewood Studios in London; the latter was where George Lucas had recently finished his space oddity *Star Wars*. Now that his crew had left, the soundstages were virtually desolate. "The pound was very low," Ilya said. "They had fantastic technicians. So we moved to London, and that's when we had the problem."

Left to right: *Superman: The Movie* screenwriter Tom Mankiewicz, actor Marlon Brando, director Richard Donner, and producer Pierre Spengler on the set in 1977. Donner believed Spengler had little business on a film shoot.

(Everett Collection)

As a British citizen, director Hamilton fell into a warped tax bracket that would swallow the majority of his salary for the film. To circumvent the tax laws, he could only remain in the UK for thirty days out of the year. This requirement had driven the Rolling Stones out of the country, and now it seemed poised to further cripple the Superman production. Ilya was faced with a choice: part ways with Brando—who made the film possible—or with Hamilton.

"Obviously, we were not going to lose Brando," Ilya said. He dismissed Hamilton and entered into talks with Mark Robson, who had recently helmed the Puzo-scripted *Earthquake*. DC and Warner staffers agreed with the choice. Then Ilya's wife, Skye Aubrey, mentioned a friend of hers named Richard Donner.

Donner, who was born in New York City, originally had designs on becoming an actor. After some bit parts in off-Broadway productions, he secured a small role in a TV adaptation of *Of Human Bondage*. Director Martin Ritt fumed at Donner's inability to take direction, but figured he might be better suited to giving it. After a brief apprenticeship under Ritt, Donner moved to California and began directing episodes of *Kojak* and various movies of the week. In 1975, Twentieth Century Fox tapped him for a supernatural script that mimicked the biblical overtones of *The Exorcist*, which had proved to be a monster success. *The Omen* was a lurid tale about an adopted boy destined to be the Antichrist, and it remains memorable for a scene in which David Warner is decapitated by a pane of glass.

Salkind was impressed with the visual flair of the film, and Warner Bros. was happy to back the director of a recent hit. But upon receiving the script, Donner was noncommittal. This was a much larger-scale production than he was used to. Fortunately, it came with a larger-scale paycheck:

his $1 million salary was ten times what he had made on *Omen*. The reservations disappeared and Donner flew to London in January 1977.

—————

Pay or no pay, Donner still had concerns about the script. Planned as two movies, it was still a backbreaking tome. And there were those lingering scenes featuring Savalas to discuss. After much debate, Donner convinced Salkind to let him bring in a new writer: his friend Tom Mankiewicz, who had worked on several Bond films with Sean Connery and Roger Moore. (His uncle, Herman J. Mankiewicz, had cowritten *Citizen Kane*.)

"It was a well-written script," Donner told *Cinefantastique* in 1979. "But it was a *ridiculous* script. . . . They had gotten a *wonderful* screenplay from Mario Puzo. And they had . . . a good director—an Englishman named Guy Hamilton. And then they brought in David and Leslie Newman, and Bob Benton to do rewrites. So you had European producers and an English director making an American fable. And . . . I don't think they really knew what the fable was."

Initially, Mankiewicz wanted nothing to do with the project. Donner had phoned at five in the morning, alerting him to a courier who would be delivering the current draft. Mankiewicz mumbled something, then went back to sleep. Donner phoned again an hour later; Mankiewicz blew him off. Eventually, Donner petitioned his friend in person while wearing an ill-fitting Superman costume. Appeased by the director's enthusiasm, Mankiewicz relented.

"Mankiewicz immediately pointed out some of that campy little stuff, which I said was going to go anyway," Ilya Salkind recalled. "He was absolutely helpful and essential in tying up loose ends and making it tighter, getting rid of the tongue-in-cheek tone we didn't want to touch. He came up with some very good thinking." The writer discarded the extraneous presence of a Luthor henchman named Albert and damped down the campier passages; no longer would anyone descend into Luthor's underground lair by way of a collapsing toilet stall.

With the script coming into focus, the issue soon became set design. From Donner's first day in London, designers had eleven weeks before Brando showed up for shooting, a scant window for a film that demanded expansive locales. "We were doing the Krypton of the comic books, the way they drew it," Salkind said. "Donner saw the stuff we had done, and sadly, it was almost all unusable." Donner brought in production designer John Barry (*Star Wars*), who reshaped the design to better conform to the director's tastes. The Krypton they imagined would be less garish, the ice-like structures resembling Superman's future fortress in the snow more than the green color scheme of the comic book locale.

During their stay in England, technicians had experimented with every possible manner of replicating flight. They catapulted dummies through the air; as in the 1940s serials, they tried animation; in blatant disregard for the safety of the stuntman, they even attempted to swing him on a crane three hundred feet in the air. The myriad attempts wound up costing more than $2 million.

None of it was convincing. "Nobody knew how to make the guy fly," Ilya recalled. "It was all experimental. It had never been done before, properly." Desperate to make headway with only weeks before shooting began, Salkind enlisted optical effects expert Zoran Perisic. His "Zoptic" process, which sandwiched a static performer between a lightweight moving camera and a front projection screen, seemed to provide the answer. Both the camera and the screen could zoom out simultaneously, giving the convincing illusion that the subject in the foreground was in motion. Salkind allowed Perisic to produce some audition footage; when it passed muster, he was hired for the film.

Donner enlisted cinematographer Geoffrey Unsworth to photograph the production, a formidable task considering the radically different surroundings Superman finds himself in throughout. With more than seventy films to his credit, Unsworth was considered an innovator in photography, having applied new optical effects methods for *2001: A Space Odyssey*. (Lucas had wanted him for *Star Wars*, but Unsworth was already committed to *A Bridge Too Far*.) Model maker Derek Meddings, effects supervisor Roy Field, and costume designer Yvonne Blake rounded out the cadre of visual professionals.

Because of the time crunch, Donner insisted on a harmonious effects family. "One of my greatest attributes on the picture was that I knew what I wanted," he said. "I didn't know how to get it, but I wouldn't accept anything until I saw it. So these poor bastards had to keep trying and trying and trying. In the beginning, everything was departmentalized, and there were little arguments and things like that. But we'd sit in my office at night and go over things; and gradually props was helping special effects, special effects was helping matte painting, matte painting was helping miniature effects, and so on. And soon it became a totally homogenous group."

In between production meetings, Donner sat down with his cast. Brando, in particular, was renowned for his sardonic attitude toward his work. During one meeting, he suggested to Donner that Jor-El be depicted as a bagel, for which he would provide the voice. (The actor's infamously anemic work ethic would welcome, if not specifically a bagel, any kind of stand-in; his agent had warned Donner that he might suggest playing Jor-El as "a green suitcase.") Quickly learning the ways of the director as diplomat, Donner cautioned that any fan of the mythology would know Jor-El resembles a human, not a starch; Brando relented.

Donner had more fun with Hackman: After learning the actor was adamant about not shaving off his moustache, the director introduced himself while sporting generous upper-lip growth. Appealing to Hackman's good sportsmanship, Donner vowed to shave his off if Hackman would do the same. The next day, a clean-shaven Hackman approached his director in the makeup trailer; Donner had made no alterations to his appearance.

When Hackman grew irate, Donner slowly peeled off his fake mustache.

———

Shortly after arriving in London, Donner hung signs in every production office that read "Verisimilitude." It was a reminder to cast and crew that the subject matter, while decidedly unreal, had to be played straight. "If we can tell this story as if it's actually happening," Donner told Mankiewicz, "as if Superman's date with Lois on the balcony is like two shy teenagers getting to know each other, then we'll have a terrific picture."

"You don't just do a silly comic strip," Mankiewicz said. "You try to make a meal out of it. I tried hard to have Brando symbolize God in that long speech when he sends Clark down to Earth. 'I have sent them you, my only son.' If that's not God sending Christ to Earth, it's as close as you can get without offending the churchgoing public."

Close to the beginning of shooting, Donner also received a warning from *Musketeers* director Richard Lester, who met with Donner and informed him he had yet to be paid for his work. "Lester had been suing the Salkinds for his money on *Three* and *Four Musketeers*, which he had never gotten," Donner recalled. "He told me he's won a lot of his lawsuits, but each time he sued them in one country, they'd move to another—from Costa Rica to Panama to Switzerland. . . . [He] said, 'Don't do it. Don't work for them. I was told not to, but I did it. Now I'm telling you not to, but you'll probably do it and end up telling the next guy.'"

He was right. With a seven-figure payday on the table, Donner would take the gamble. Lester would eventually get his money, as well as an invitation to join *Superman* once creative conflicts came to a boil.

Things began simmering between Donner and producer Pierre Spengler early on. Donner perceived Spengler as clueless to the demands of filmmaking—nothing more than a nuisance. "Spengler was the liaison to Alexander Salkind, and he supposedly had this knowledge of production," Donner recalled, "but my God, I've been in this business long enough to know what a producer is, and it was ridiculous for him to have taken this job. As far as I was concerned, he didn't have any knowledge at all about producing a film like that. If he'd been smart, he'd have just sat back and let us do it; but instead, he tried to impose himself. So, not only did we end up producing it . . . but we also had to counter-produce what he was doing."

Despite the best efforts of the Newmans and Benton, the production still had a mammoth script to deal with. Mankiewicz excised the bloat, paring down the film to a reasonable length and, with Donner, created three distinct beats. The first portion of the film would detail the monotone life of Kryptonians, particularly Brando as Jor-El. With his peers refusing to heed his warnings of an impending natural disaster, he encases his son Kal-El in a rocket and sends him speeding toward Earth just prior to the doomed planet's expiration. The film would then jump from the lavish spectacle of Krypton to the Norman Rockwell–esque scenery of Kansas, where Kal-El lands and is informally adopted by the Kents. Finally, an adult Clark would arrive in Metropolis, ready to begin his career in journalism and his full-time job as savior.

All told, *Superman: The Movie* had everything in place to begin shooting in April 1977.

Except a Superman.

Cape Fears

They were looking for a name actor. They actually had Neil Diamond. He went in to interview with them and I remember when he was coming out. People were laughing like hell.

—Jack O'Halloran

In the late 1970s, morphing diets and exercise regimens conspired to change American attitudes about the male physique. The barrel chest and square shoulders that had typified screen heroes and heavies in the 1950s were now considered quaint; supplements and pseudolegal pharmaceuticals fueled a new ideal, one that had more in common with the muscle-bound body types of comic book protagonists than the fit form of an average exercise enthusiast.

Screen stars who shared traits with circus strongmen were nothing new; Steve Reeves had made an abbreviated career out of portraying Hercules due to the stark amount of muscle packed on his frame. But the emergence of bodybuilding as a valid form of athleticism produced a new crop of men who could essentially deliver themselves as living sculpture, their grossly overburdened muscles straining skin tissue.

The lone star to crack bodybuilding's lurid veneer was Arnold Schwarzenegger, a personable Austrian champion whose effusive ego was put on display in the 1977 documentary *Pumping Iron*. Unlike many of his overdeveloped counterparts, Schwarzenegger had charisma to match his expanded biceps. He nabbed bits parts on episodic television; more infamously, his thick Austrian accent was overdubbed for *Hercules Goes Bananas*, a 1970 spoof that lived down to its title.

The Salkinds could imagine no one who embodied the physical dynamics of a comics hero better than Schwarzenegger. Meetings were held, but in speaking to him, the producers realized that audiences would likely revolt at their treasured slice of Americana being outsourced—even if the accent could be explained away by his Kryptonian heritage.

Talks with the future governor of California punctuated what was, for its time, the most compelling casting search since Fox pined for its Scarlett O'Hara in the late 1930s. *Variety* ran weekly updates on whom the Salkinds had been speaking to. For comic book purists, many of their interviewees would prompt nausea.

Bruce Jenner was a 1976 Olympic champion in the decathlon. Though he lacked the bloated dimensions of Arnold and company, he was clearly fit and capable of filling out the shamelessly revealing costume. "It would've been a perfect choice, physically," explained Ilya Salkind. "He didn't have enough experience as an actor, but he was a lovely guy. We tested him with a camera when Hamilton was directing. We really were going that way."

Jenner's limitations as a performer removed him from contention. At that point Brando and Hackman had yet to come on board, and Alex Salkind was under pressure from investors who wanted some kind of tangible attraction tied to the project. "That's when I started getting a lot of pressure from my father and the bankers: we need a star, we need a star. I reluctantly had to do that. We were partners, but he was the ultimate boss. He said, 'If you don't get a star, this movie's gonna fail.'"

Duly instructed, Salkind began eyeing virtually anyone who had ever proved himself capable of headlining a movie in the past twenty years. Warren Beatty ran around his pool in the suit and felt too ridiculous; Steve McQueen gave a flat no; Clint Eastwood was too busy; Christopher Walken was considered, but ultimately, said Salkind, "he would've made a great Lex Luthor."

The *Superman* casting offices became a revolving door of possibilities: Charles Bronson, James Caan, Ryan O'Neal, Sam Elliott, Perry King, Jeff Bridges, Jan-Michael Vincent, David Soul, Robert Wagner, Lyle Waggoner, and Kris Kristofferson found themselves offered—or, as many of them perceived it, threatened with—the title role.

"I offered the picture to different guys," Salkind remembered, "but the most significant was Robert Redford. I did it knowing it was a mistake, but it was Robert Redford, great actor. He sent me a very nice letter saying, 'Look, I don't think people are going to believe me flying. It's not going to work.'

"It might've worked, but I doubt it. Superman is so ingrained. When Heston played Moses, how many people had seen Moses? There's this systematic bombardment of images of Superman where the guy looks a certain way. If you don't believe it's him, there's no fiction/reality."

Prior to the opening of *Rocky*, Sylvester Stallone openly lobbied for the part. "Stallone wanted to play him. He approached us. *Rocky* hadn't opened, but I had seen the movie. He was fantastic, but it just wouldn't work. He was a wonderful actor, but he's too Italian for the mythology of the comics."

The search for Superman hit bottom on several occasions: once, Salkind invited crooner Neil Diamond for a chat. Diamond had long wanted to break into acting, but he withdrew when he realized how substantial the time commitment would be: the days and nights spent making the film would wind up costing him millions of dollars in performance revenue from touring.

In an echo of DC's still-formulating crossover, Alex Salkind entertained the idea of casting Muhammad Ali. Over dinner at Cannes, Ali's promoter had enticed Alex with the possibility, citing Ali's global popularity. He had just drawn huge worldwide numbers for a mixed-style fight with Japanese pro wrestling legend Antonio Inoki. The prospect of marrying two of pop culture's most recognizable icons tempted the producer, but Ilya intervened, clueing his unwitting father to the fact that Ali happened to be black.

It was only the signing of Brando and Hackman that finally sated the star-lust of the financiers, leaving the younger Salkind free to pursue a lower-profile actor more easily believed in the suit. Donner agreed with the strategy, suspecting that a recognizable face in the role would only serve to alienate viewers. Burt Reynolds in spandex, he believed, would always be Burt Reynolds in spandex.

The aversion to name actors did not completely dissuade Salkind from contemplating other noxious prospects—like when Ilya's wife, Skye, suggested that her dentist be considered. Don Voyne was the epitome of Beverly Hills health care providers: fit, intelligent, and just as camera ready as most of his clients. Voyne was poured into the suit and given a screen test. Physically, he was it. In terms of talent, he made a better dentist than an actor.

When Donner assumed directing duties, he had jotted "Nick Nolte" down on a napkin. Nolte's stocky build and gravel-gargling voice didn't seem to lend itself to anyone's interpretation of the character. Worse, his modest level of fame from the TV miniseries *Rich Man, Poor Man* defied the creative edict to cast an unknown. It was a moot point, as Nolte eventually turned the role down. John Wayne's son Patrick was briefly considered; when his father developed cancer, talks ground to a halt.

Later, as things got increasingly desperate, Jon Voight agreed to be the pinch hitter in the event that no better alternative had been found by the time filming started. No salary agreement was made public, but Voight's respectable stature after his work in *Midnight Cowboy* and *Deliverance* would've necessitated hefty compensation.

Voight was one of the few actors not intimidated by the growing legacy of the costume. By this time, enough incarnations of the character had appeared to call into question the intelligence of embracing such a role. Kirk Alyn's career had flatlined after his serial appearances, while Reeves had met with a tragic end both professionally and personally.

The affliction didn't stop with Superman. Adam West found himself permanently affixed to Batman's cowl after only three years on the air. (In 1979, his Caped Crusader would pop up in an embarrassingly low-rent NBC movie featuring second-string DC heroes "roasting" one another.) Virtually no one who had ever sported tights on-screen went on to collect gold statues or play opposite established stars. Only actors who had kept their faces hidden from public view—like radio's Collyer—had managed to sustain a career.

With weeks to go before shooting began, Salkind and Donner faced twofold pressure: not only was their Superman an absentee but so was his leading lady. In the comics mythology, spunky reporter Lois Lane charges into dangerous peril without a second thought. Make her too forceful, and she might devour the meek Kent; too reserved, and you lose the integrity of the character.

Salkind tested a half-dozen actors for the role, including Stockard Channing, Shirley MacLaine, Anne Archer, and Lesley Ann Warren. (Carrie Fisher was considered, but *Star Wars* had yet to screen.) While Donner and Mankiewicz lobbied for Channing, Ilya Salkind preferred the rougher edges of a young actor named Margot Kidder: "I think Spengler was also for Kidder. We weren't clear, and we saw them again. Finally, everybody agreed Margot was—let's say, less forceful. Channing was so good that she might've overshadowed Clark."

Mankiewicz ultimately reached the same conclusion: "They both played the comedy so wonderfully, but Stockard looked like she could have you for breakfast."

Kidder, born in 1948, didn't possess conventional leading-lady looks. Her skin was stretched thin over her face, her thin lips offset by bulging eyes. But her emotions were broad; she seemed to dominate the room. After graduating from boarding school, Kidder had pursued an acting career, taking bit TV parts. At one point, she shared dinners at a beach house with would-be luminaries Steven Spielberg and Martin Scorsese. "I flew into L.A. from Montana and did a reading," Kidder recalled. "They really liked it and then called and said 'Can you be in London in a day?' and I went 'What?' . . . I didn't have a clue that it was such a big deal because I grew up without comics. I had a very fierce English teacher mother who felt that children should not read comic books."

The casting of another female role, that of Lex Luthor's sultry right-hand woman, provided Mankiewicz with an early glimpse of the Salkinds' infamous business practices, which would soon become a growing cancer in the production. For the part of Miss Teschmacher, Donner pursued Goldie Hawn. Her salary demands were just as exorbitant as Hackman's: she wanted $2 million for her efforts. Unable to raise the funds, the

Salkinds mandated an alternative. Donner and his team rallied behind Ann-Margret, a vivacious Swede who had become known for her charms as Elvis Presley's right-hand woman in *Viva Las Vegas*.

The actor was asked to entertain the producers' offer of $500,000. If she rebuked the opportunity, Donner and Mankiewicz were firmly behind Valerie Perrine, a similarly ravishing beauty who was willing to work for a relative steal.

The production's think tank was gathered at the bar of a Zurich hotel when Salkind friend Pierre Spengler entered the room with good news. "We have just concluded a deal with Ann-Margret," he announced. Donner and his writer thanked Alex Salkind for his vigilance in casting the desired performers.

A half hour later, Spengler reentered the room. With virtually the same cadence, he notified everyone that he had just concluded a deal with Valerie Perrine. She had agreed to do it for $250,000, a 50 percent savings on their ancillary bimbo.

"But you made a deal with Ann-Margret,'" lamented Mankiewicz.

"She can sue," Alex Salkind huffed.

"These are the people we're working with," Mankiewicz thought. "Look out."

———

Late one night in London, Donner and Mankiewicz were sullenly poring over the myriad of head shots that had been submitted to the casting office for the role of Superman. Donner was puffing on a joint; Mankiewicz was nursing a Jack Daniels. The prospects were grim. If an actor looked the part, he couldn't deliver the necessary emotional gravitas. If he could act, he was too short, too blond, too ethnic, or too old.

Eventually, Donner turned to a profile of Christopher Reeve, a six-foot-four Julliard-trained actor. Casting director Lynn Stalmaster had championed Reeve before, but Donner and others had felt that he was too slight for the role. His lanky frame carried little muscle mass, and his

Actor Christopher Reeve at the 1983 Cannes Film Festival in France. Reeve portrayed Superman through four films and earned praise as the most capable of all the character's caretakers.

(Armando Pietrangeli, Rex Features/Everett Collection)

comportment during an informal chat in New York months prior had left Donner unable to imagine him as his Superman. Reeve had classic matinee idol looks but little else in common with the Man of Steel. As a youth, asthma had kept him from sports; alopecia areata had prompted some of his adolescent hair to fall out.

But Reeve's pedigree impressed Salkind: he had worked onstage with Katharine Hepburn and held his own against the aging actor's still-vital presence. Donner and the producers decided to give him a test flight. Reeve had migrated to an off-Broadway play with Jeff Daniels when Donner phoned him with the news. "Next weekend is your lucky weekend!" the director brayed. "On Saturday, you're testing for Superman!" Reeve was noncommittal; he had performances scheduled and no understudy.

In a hyperbolic bit of Hollywood hubris, Donner and Salkind bought out the house for that weekend, though at $5 a ticket, it wasn't a gross indulgence. Released from his duties, Reeve was flown over to London for his screen test and fitted with a cobbled-together Superman ensemble. Dark sweat stains creeped over his armpits.

"Jeez," Donner told his collaborators. "We gotta remember to fix that when we shoot."

For the audition, Donner utilized a six-page sequence that had Lois interviewing Superman on a rooftop. As written, the scene would serve as a gauge not only for the would-be Superman's screen presence but also his chemistry with the actor assuming the role of Lois.

Reeve's suit was ill fitting, his hastily colored sandy brown hair hardly reminiscent of the hero's trademark black locks. None of it seemed to matter. "Good evening, Miss Lane," he rumbled, jumping off the makeshift bal-cony as if he had just descended from the clouds. Donner, Mankiewicz, and cameraman Geoffrey Unsworth exchanged silent glances. *This is the guy.*

"He had an aura," recalled Ilya Salkind. "He was fantastic. He was playing Superman *and* Clark. He hadn't rehearsed it. He immediately developed stuff like, when he would play Clark, he'd bend down so he'd be two inches shorter. He had a lot of that."

Reeve was granted a per diem during his audition weekend and was shuttled around in a limo. The fawning was in sharp contrast to his experi-ences onstage, where he had been making $75 a week. When he climbed into the back of the car after his screen test, the driver turned to him and said, "I'm not supposed to tell you this, but you've got the part."

Reeve returned to the States with little more than assurances from hired help that his life was about to change. Days later, he was in his dressing room talking shop with William Hurt when he got the call. The news was of sufficient gravity in the industry that it was passed along in the media faster than among intimate personnel: Reeve's agent found out about the casting while he was watching *Good Morning America*. Reeve's father was effusive when he heard the news, but only because he thought his son was telling him he had been cast in George Bernard Shaw's *Man and Superman*.

The elder Reeve had always held high aspirations for his son, who had done his best to meet his father's expectations. After graduating from Cornell in only three years, Reeve had gone to Julliard, where he studied alongside Robin Williams and Kevin Kline. During his stint at the presti-gious school, he was cast in a recurring role of lothario Ben Harper on the soap opera *Love of Life*.

Reeve accepted the theatrical role opposite Hepburn while maintain-ing his duties on the soap; the play lasted two months. Though the money was good and the work steady on television, the twenty-four-year-old Reeve was growing bored by the superficial dramatics and subpar produc-tion values of the daytime dramas. With Reeve's career aspirations in flux, *Superman* had come along at a perfect time.

In accordance with the pageantry of the casting search, the Salkinds announced the discovery of Reeve during a press conference in New York

City in February 1977. They agreed to pay Reeve a base salary of $250,000. Unlike Brando or Puzo, he was not entitled to a percentage of the profits.

With Reeve's signature in place, the production went about the business of transforming the reed-thin young man into someone of sufficiently heroic proportions. Earlier, a British bodybuilding champion named David Prowse had lobbied Donner for the role; like Arnold before him, Prowse was a poor fit for a classically American institution, though he found a kind of anonymous success as the physical half of Darth Vader in the *Star Wars* saga. In a consolatory offer, Donner asked Prowse if he would assist in building Reeve's physique.

With roughly six weeks to go before shooting commenced, Prowse engaged Reeve in a rigorous exercise and diet program consisting of heavy weight training, steak dinners, and as much milk as he could down. Reeve was initially overwhelmed by the new physical demands placed on his body and ended his first workout with vomiting. But under the guidance of Prowse, he quickly added twenty pounds of muscle mass. Glowing press accounts during *Superman*'s publicity blitz bleated that Reeve had gone from a 100-pound bench press to 350 pounds, a radical amount of resistance even for a professional athlete. Regardless of his true progress, Reeve was able to rebuff the producers' offer of foam padding.

By some accounts, Reeve's abrupt entrance into celluloid fame brought with it rather abrasive coping mechanisms. When Prowse departed to honor a preexisting commitment to a prince in Saudi Arabia, Reeve was furious. He lashed out at his trainer, complaining that he had lost precious body mass during the ten-day absence. Prowse conferred with Donner, who told him Reeve's impending stardom had already begun to inflate his head. Three days later, Prowse was released from his obligations to the production. Whether it was because of Reeve's indignant attitude or because his work was done—Reeve had put on an appreciable amount of muscle in six weeks—is unclear. But in Prowse's eyes, the newly crowned Superman had already become a diva.

Mankiewicz saw it differently. "Chris was so young. He was a very shy person. He didn't have any money. I remember before *Superman* opened, he came out here a week before. I took him to a poker game, and he lost $400.

While he was losing, one of the other players kept saying, 'Thank God you don't have X-ray vision.' And he couldn't pay the $400. I paid for him.

"He really wanted to be a great actor. And he was very serious about his craft. He was obsessed with the fact that Superman would make him a star and ruin his career, all at the same time."

Reeve's prescient fears prompted him to beg Mankiewicz to call Sean Connery and arrange a meeting; the screenwriter had worked with the archetypical James Bond on *Diamonds Are Forever*. Connery didn't care to occupy himself by coddling a fellow franchise player and begged off. Nevertheless, Reeve got his chance to be advised when the two were mingling at the same party.

"All right, listen," Connery said. "If Mankiewicz here is writing it, it's not very good. Secondly, if it's a big hit, do something completely different for your next picture. And if the second one's a big hit, get yourself the best lawyer and agent in the world and stick it to them. That's my advice." Reeve would heed Connery's wisdom on all counts.

With plans in place to shoot two films simultaneously, casting also had to concern themselves with filling the boots of the three Kryptonian supervillains who would engage Superman in the sequel.

Nothing if not determined, David Prowse made it known that he would make a fine Non, the hulking enforcer of the trio. At six-foot-six, however, he would dwarf Reeve on-screen. Former heavyweight boxer Jack O'Halloran was deemed a better choice. Slightly smaller in stature than Prowse, he was nonetheless a powerful physical presence. He had known, and liked, Hackman from a picture the two were featured in together titled *March or Die*. But like the man he edged out for the role, he took issues with Reeve's behavior.

"Christopher had never done anything," O'Halloran said. "His claim to fame was a soap. Being Superman was a big step into the limelight. He thought he was a superstar. Chris started believing his own press. He wasn't the nicest of people until he got hurt. And when he got hurt, he became a nice person. He helped a lot of people with a lot of courage. Prior to that, he snubbed kids, he was too busy for this, too busy for that."

To audition for the part of Ursa, the cantankerous, man-hating Kryptonian, British actor Sarah Douglas had been called to the production offices on a half-dozen occasions. Each time, she was sent away and told Donner was unavailable to meet with her. Her temper happened to get the better of her during one last attempt at the role, which impressed the finally present director. She was hired.

Leading the pack of Phantom Zone escapees was General Zod, the sworn enemy of Jor-El's bloodline. Christopher Lee and Oliver Reed expressed interest in the role, which promised a healthy diet of scenery chewing. Donner eventually settled on Terence Stamp, further expanding his roster of British performers for the UK-infused production. Stamp's professional accomplishments had been overshadowed in the previous decade by his dalliances with Julie Christie, Brigitte Bardot, and others. After a particularly bitter breakup, he went into self-imposed exile in India. *Superman* would mark his debut as a high-profile actor in the States.

Elsewhere, Stamp's on-screen opposition was busy refining his appearance. Now that Reeve possessed a sturdy frame, his face was dusted with dark makeup to add angles to his still-youthful looks; a more professional dye job gave his locks the required jet-black appearance. Costumers had crafted a series of outfits, each one specifically designed to meet the demands of a given day's shooting. Some looked better while Reeve stood still; others afforded more flexibility in motion. Capes were created in similar permutations, depending on whether Reeve would be "flying," running, or simply standing and looking iconic.

More crucially, Reeve had been perfecting something that Collyer had pioneered so effectively on radio thirty years prior: the dichotomy between the meek Kent and the self-assured hero. For the big-screen Superman, however, the distinction had to be not only vocal but also physical. In the comics lore, only a pair of thick glasses separated the reporter from his alter ego. The conceit was quaint in its day; by 1978, it had the potential to be downright insipid.

"He was better as Clark Kent than he was as Superman," said Mankiewicz. "It sounds like a simple thing, but he said to me one day, 'I'm getting schizophrenic here with Kent and Superman.' I said, 'There's an easy way around that, Chris. You are Superman. You're *playing* Clark Kent.'

"And the minute that really sank in that way, he started doing all these little Cary Grant kind of gestures, getting his coat caught in doors and doing stuff that was really wonderful."

Reeve opted not to rely on gimmicks to differentiate between personas. His Clark was a pile of slouching shoulders and stammering blather; around Lois, the gawkish behavior exaggerated itself. (Reeve took cues from Grant's "charming klutz" persona, particularly his performance in *Bringing Up Baby*.) His Superman corrected Kent's postural problems and stuttering. There was nobility in Reeve's Man of Steel, a kind of grace that had eluded both George Reeves and Kirk Alyn. Reeves had seemed almost bemused by his costumed appearance; Reeve, in contrast, appeared honored by it. For the time being.

"I joked once that if you take the 'S' off his chest, his balls fall off," said Mankiewicz. "What I meant was, I don't think he's a leading man. Which is why he was so good. I was always of the theory—and this is no disservice to Chris—that he was really a supporting actor. If you had a Steve McQueen or Robert Redford kind of hunk as Superman, there's almost overkill in it. But there's a natural shyness in Chris. And it came through even as Superman."

Inversely, Margot Kidder's kinetic persona had won her the role of Lane. By most accounts, her behavior wasn't necessarily indicative of well-being.

Mankiewicz became involved with Kidder during production and lived with her for half of shooting. He bore witness to the erratic tendencies that prompted growing concern from anyone in her proximity. "She always had a bipolar problem that people completely misunderstood. It got worse as she got older. It was misdiagnosed for a long time. But the weird thing in show business is that extravagant behavior is often rewarded. When you're very much in demand and you're a star, people find that charming. But the minute you're no longer a star, you get people saying, 'What is she, nuts?' People turn their backs on you.

"But she was a total pro. I don't think she was ever late one day. She worked her ass off. She would do fine for months at a time, but down the road two or three months, there would be that Black Monday or Tuesday when the world was going to cave in on her. It happened to her all the time. It was terrifying.

"She was a wonderfully talented actress and a truly funny and outgoing and generous human being."

Casting director Stalmaster continued scrambling even after the primary roles were filled. Keenan Wynn was set to play Perry White, but his constitution wasn't prepared for the long flight into Heathrow Airport and a near-immediate slot on the call sheet: the actor suffered a heart attack and was volleyed home. Mankiewicz imagined Jason Robards, whom he was friendly with, would make an excellent replacement, especially since he had just won an Oscar for portraying a real-life editor, Ben Bradlee, in *All the President's Men*. The synergy made Mankiewicz giggle. Robards, not so much.

After Mankiewicz explained the project, Robards was silent.

"You're doing *what?*" the actor finally asked.

"Superman, Jason."

"The comic book?"

"Jason, it's great. Marlon Brando and Gene Hackman are in it."

"That's *their* problem."

Under the gun, Donner phoned Jackie Cooper, a former child star who had evolved into a dependable character actor. Cooper was enthused. "You gotta be here in two days," Donner told him. "If you don't have a passport, forget it." Cooper rummaged through his belongings and found his booklet. "Great," Donner said. "Now get your ass on a plane."

—

Superman: The Movie began principal photography in March 1977. Preproduction costs had exceeded $7 million, the bulk of which comprised the stratospheric salaries of Brando and Hackman. The original director,

Hamilton, had been paid $750,000 in severance; Warner Bros. took $1 million in advance dues for the Superman film rights.

In short, the Salkinds' expenses had gotten out of control before a single frame was even shot. Earlier, they had assured investors that both films could be made for under $20 million; now a third of that had already been spent with nineteen months of shooting pending.

The financial burden was only the beginning. As goodwill evaporated from the production, friendships would be broken and safety would be risked. And in contrast to their indestructible star, more than one crew member wouldn't live to see the premiere.

6

Metropolis Now

If I were arranging a picture like this, instead of hiring people that were more stupid than I was so I'd look bright, I'd have hired the brightest people in the whole goddamned world. . . . And he did just the opposite.
—Richard Donner on Ilya Salkind

Ilya Salkind's mother fondled a steak knife, eyeing Tom Mankiewicz with the dim perceptions of the inebriated.

Then she lunged.

As a close friend of Donner's, Mankiewicz was spared the typical apathy afforded to screenwriters. He sat in on casting sessions, evaluated set designs, and generally acted as Donner's sounding board—a role normally occupied by the producer.

In Donner's mind, Mankiewicz assumed these duties because there *was* no producer. The Salkinds, to his perception, were frantic businessmen who offered little in the way of creative contributions. When they were on set, it was usually to initiate shouting matches over budget concerns.

"I don't mean that they weren't trying to raise money and so on," explained Mankiewicz, "but typically your producer, if you've got a good one, is your Jiminy Cricket, your conscience. You can go to him with script problems, actors, everything. And the reason that I stayed on the picture through locations, casting, editing and scoring, and so on is because Dick didn't have anybody. He was constantly at war with the Salkinds."

Ilya and his father had good reason to be contentious: they had severely overextended themselves with their creditors. The bargain $20 million for two films had morphed into $50 million for just one. Or more. Suddenly, getting it done right was not as important as simply getting it done.

With that pressure inflating by the day, they watched as Donner meandered around set, taking his time with shots and refusing to break a sweat. On one location shoot, in an attempt to improve a take, he waited hours for the sun to shine brightly enough. He was the portrait of a respectable artist. But to the Salkinds, Donner was essentially dangling their money over a toilet and then flushing.

"You're over schedule, you're over budget," Ilya ranted.

"Show me a fucking budget," Donner retorted. But they couldn't; in their constant scramble to appease—then plead with—investors, the amount was in perpetual fluctuation. The producers simply wanted Donner to do less directing and more shooting.

"What is the basic problem with this picture?" Alex asked, exasperated.

"The basic problem with this picture, Alex, is that you're an asshole," Donner replied.

Hemorrhaging money, the Salkinds spent a month regretting the fact that they didn't have a mercenary in play, someone who placed economy over creativity. Donner was too emotionally invested in the material. His conscientious coverage was a liability.

The younger Salkind was struck with an idea: perhaps they could have him fired from the picture. Ilya dashed off a letter to Donner's agent, citing breach of contract issues with his client. He demanded Donner be released from his duties. None of Salkind's propaganda had any substance; legally, there was no way to remove him.

The arguments and intrigue did little for Donner's relationship with Ilya; soon the two stopped speaking altogether. Pierre Spengler became their interpersonal liaison, communicating messages between the two. But Spengler, in Donner's mind, had no business producing a picture. Donner considered him creatively bankrupt, an impression intensified by the Salkinds' insistence that Spengler execute all of their dirty work.

"In a certain way, it wasn't Pierre's fault," Mankiewicz said. "I found Pierre to be a nice guy. He was always sweating. He was caught between what he knew was best for the picture, and the Salkinds, who he worked for."

"Best for the picture" was relative. In an effort to squeeze every last bit of value from their coffers, the producers played fast and loose with crew salaries. Jack O'Halloran arrived on set one day to find a legion of workers standing in line outside Spengler's office. "The crew was lined up to get paid and they wouldn't take a check," the actor recalled. "They wanted cash. And I said to the first assistant director, 'What the hell is going on here?' He said, 'You don't know about the Salkinds, do you? These people have all worked for them before. They don't trust them. They want cash.'"

O'Halloran was speechless. "This is a $50 million picture!"

The Salkinds figured that the longer cast salaries remained in the bank, the more interest they could accrue. To that end, they would write checks from a Swiss account, which would have to clear on both sides of the ocean before being cashed. O'Halloran discovered the game one weekend when he went AWOL from the London set to return home to California.

"I got into Beverly Hills and called my accountant. I said, 'I'm home and I have some things I want to do. How much money do we have in the bank?' She said, 'How much do you think?' I said, 'I've been working eight weeks. There should be a ton of money there.'"

O'Halloran was due a weekly salary and he had already been on set for two months—but there was nothing. Returning to London, he made a beeline for Spengler's office. "I pulled Pierre Spengler right across the desk and I said, 'This is bullshit. I signed a contract to work. I worked. Now pay me.'"

Spengler slumped back into his chair and said, "Are you threatening me?" O'Halloran assured him he was not—he was promising.

"And I was the only person there whose checks cleared in seventy-two hours. Having to do shit like that, though, that's bullshit."

Due to Brando's locked-in start dates, Donner began the production at Shepperton Studios in England with the actor's scenes on Krypton: Jor-El would cradle his only son, played by infant actor Lee Quigley, before sending him rocketing toward Earth. (In 1991, a troubled Quigley would die after inhaling from an aerosol can.) Far from a glad-hander, Brando purposely arrived in London a day late to avoid forced banter with visiting Warner executives. In an effort to play off the gross ratio of income to effort, he told reporters that his record-breaking salary would be used to fund a film about the woes of Indian tribesmen.

Claiming he wished to preserve spontaneity in his performance, Brando didn't memorize his lines. Instead, he tacked them up to every available surface out of the camera's view, including the forehead of Ursa actor Sarah Douglas. Between takes of chastising the Kryptonian supervillains, he would fondle Douglas, who was too starstruck to consider the concept of sexual harassment.

Donner had Brando for only two weeks, a window that prompted panic when his performer began to show signs of a severe head cold. Cost over-runs if Brando had to remain in London would swell into the hundreds of thousands of dollars. Generously, the actor agreed to remain for a few extra days at no charge.

One night, Brando joined Donner and Mankiewicz for a quiet dinner. Somehow, Ilya Salkind had located them; he entered the restaurant, presuming his company would be welcomed. Joining Ilya was his mother, Berta Domínguez, a perpetually aspiring writer. Throughout preproduction, she had submitted several pages of "rewrites" to Mankiewicz, who had dismissed them out of hand.

Not long into the meal, emboldened by drink, she confronted the screenwriter. "Mr. Mankiewicz, I send you rewrites all the time. You never acknowledge them. I don't see them reflected in the script." Mankiewicz made a polite rebuttal, citing time constraints.

Berta rudely announced his salary to the entire table. "You should get on your hands and knees and thank my husband for hiring you," she spat. Mankiewicz, his patience thinning, mentioned Salkind Sr.'s modest height as the reason he was always on his knees during conversations.

"She picked up a steak knife and went for me," Mankiewicz said. "And I'm telling ya, I was so shocked that she would've stabbed me right in the chest. But Brando grabbed her. Brando was sitting on the other side of her, grabbed her, shoved her down into the booth, and said, 'Will you behave, will you behave?'

"And you see her head nodding. And he let her go, and she came up with the knife and came at me again. And Brando took the knife away. Then everybody left."

Shaken, Mankiewicz demanded that Berta be removed from his line of sight for the remainder of the production. Alex, abashed at his wife's behavior, agreed—"kill the writer" made for a cute cocktail party punch line but not necessarily a practical approach to creative differences. Weeks later, Mankiewicz and Donner attended a meeting at Alex's residence; Berta, lurking upstairs, waved over Donner while he was en route to the bathroom. She apologized for the homicide attempt, then declared herself the "Shakespeare of Mexico."

Thank God, Donner thought, I got my salary in escrow.

By June 1977, *Superman* had checked its baggage and moved over to Pinewood Studios. The Salkinds shamelessly informed their existing crew that because Pinewood had an in-house workforce, their services would no longer be needed. Many workers had passed up other projects, believing they would be involved with the film for the duration. Under pressure from creditors, the Salkinds marched them off.

Things had failed to cool between Donner and Ilya Salkind, the latter of whom was increasingly frustrated with Donner's expenditures. Worse,

Superman: The Movie director Richard Donner in 1978. Donner was accused of letting the budget for the film spiral out of control; producer Ilya Salkind prevented him from completing work on the sequel.

(© Warner Bros./Everett Collection)

he couldn't lambaste him personally; firing him had been vetoed, and Warner had seen his rushes and were impressed enough to begin sinking money into the production to keep it humming. For the Salkinds, the funds were like water during a drought.

The assist was, however, conditional on Donner staying.

Ilya had another epiphany: if he couldn't fire Donner, then perhaps he could hire a second director, someone who would emphasize the for-hire attitude he so wished Donner possessed. He immediately thought of Richard Lester. Perhaps the indignity of being shadowed by a peer would force Donner's resignation.

The catch: Lester was still owed money by the Salkinds for his *Three Musketeers* efforts. He had initially won a lawsuit against the duo, but the judgment was rendered against a company in Liechtenstein that was owned by a Bahamian concern. The obtuse paper trail had led nowhere. Now the Salkinds offered to finally honor that years-old agreement in exchange for the director's help on *Superman*. The proposal was sufficiently pleasing to Lester, whose lawyer witnessed Alex Salkind writing a promissory note on a napkin.

Ilya showed up on set one day in June, Lester in tow. For those who recognized Lester, his appearance immediately created a round of gossip about the fate of Richard Donner. Speculation was that he would be replaced or simply storm off.

Neither occurred. Lester made his intentions known immediately, that he was owed money by the Salkinds and simply wanted to get his due. He would not interfere with Donner's duties on set in any way, nor would he ever attempt to undermine his authority in the eyes of cast or crew.

Donner took it well. Much to Salkind's chagrin, the two Richards seemed to operate in tandem nicely, possibly bonding over their mutual difficulties with the producers. Lester took over some second-unit duties, easing Donner's mind over the quality of the ancillary footage. He also suggested the formation of a second model unit. Despite the dire predictions, he was emerging as a valuable new recruit.

Production moved to New York in July 1977 to shoot the *Daily Planet* exteriors. Days into filming, the city experienced its worst blackout in history. The environment became charged and chaotic; Lester alleged he personally witnessed a limo driver beat another to death with a baseball bat over a fare. (The mayhem was duly reported by the *Daily News*, which managed to produce its print run thanks to its neighbors on the film shoot, whose generators provided power.) The blackout conspired to cost the Salkinds five to six times what they had budgeted for the location shoot.

Ilya Salkind threw up his hands. With each new travail came bills on top of bills. During a particularly fierce heat wave, sprinklers were activated in Pinewood, drenching valuable equipment. *Star Wars* had just been released, and the expectations for special effects in major Hollywood productions took on new, costlier dimensions. Even things as innocuous as Gene Hackman's costume fittings and bald cap appliances were somehow costing them $52,000 a day, and $40,000 in petty cash was going out on a weekly basis. T-shirts ordered by the crew were impounded; Ilya had failed to pay the freight company delivering them.

Much later, speculation would arise that Warner Bros. delighted in the overruns, figuring that eventually it could buy out the Salkinds and hoard the return for itself. The studio had found faith in the project, but it came at a price: with each infusion of money came increasing influence over shooting and a growing profit share. Either the Salkinds had a disaster that would break their reputation or a hit that would be devoured by Warner. Either way, the producers seemed hopelessly impotent.

Smallville, the site of Clark Kent's formative youth, was filmed in Canada, where shooting continued in August 1977. Summer storms bled more money out of producers; Salkind announced to the crew—two thousand miles from home—that they would only be getting half of their guaranteed salary. The rest would come later.

In a wheezy display of synergy, DC editors had held a contest that promised the winners cameo roles in the movie. The lucky fans were shoehorned in as jocks during a scene in which a teenage Clark pines for Lana Lang. (Dissatisfied with the vocal inflections of actor Jeff East as a young Kent, Donner had Reeve redub his lines later on.) Ilya's mother-in-law, Phyllis Thaxter, was cast as Ma Kent; Joan Crawford had been Ilya's first choice, but her sudden death left room for some slight nepotism. Glenn Ford, whom Donner raved about as a consummate professional, portrayed Clark's mortal father, felled by a heart attack in order to add pathos to Superman's adolescence.

Throughout shooting, Donner had been juggling sequences for both the inaugural film and its sequel. Because of their schedules, both Brando and Hackman had already finished their scenes for *II*. Trying to assemble footage for one of the installments was formidable enough; finally, all parties were amenable to Lester's suggestion that it would be in their best interests to cease shooting material for the follow-up and focus on the takeoff.

Shooting resumed at Pinewood in late September for eight more weeks of coverage. During a production hiatus in November, Donner was in Los Angeles being interrogated by frantic Warner executives, their imaginations picturing the kind of on-set chaos that had plagued *Apocalypse Now*'s tortured shoot. Donner calmly explained his differences with the Salkinds: how he wished to print a polished take, whereas the producers were begging for more expeditious product.

When Donner returned to greet Reeve in December 1977, he had company: Charlie Greenlaw, an affable Warner rep who was directed to mediate matters and maintain the studio's interests.

Superman was quickly becoming an enormous gamble for the studio. "Warner was established, but not quite with the big guys yet," said Ilya Salkind. "They had done *Exorcist*, which was their biggest film. But they needed another really big one to get there. They had it all riding on

Superman. The merchandising grew to enormous proportions. They sent a very nice guy to watch. He was really helping the tension."

Back at Pinewood, Reeve busied himself with the laborious flying sequences. His profuse sweating (caused by the hours he spent dangling from wires) had costumers lining his suit with additional material and ordering industrial-strength deodorant. Reeve's male "equipment" would shift left to right from take to take; eventually, they fitted him with a cup for continuity purposes.

January 1978 brought with it a rather sobering realization: eight months into shooting, the film was still skeletal. The slavish attention paid to effects, coupled with Donner's self-imposed quality demands—not to mention the weeks spent shooting nearly 40 percent of *Superman II*—had slowed filming to a crawl. Some days, the crew estimated they were getting a meager eight seconds of footage. The summer 1978 release date originally targeted by the Salkinds became a hopeless goal line.

Warner instead settled on a holiday 1978 release. While both *Jaws* and *Star Wars* had ushered in new expectations for the summer box office, the May–August window was not yet the only territory for expensive, expansive eye-candy filmmaking. Warner figured that *Superman* would attract students on Christmas break, especially with parents eager to get them out of the house.

While genre publications like *Starlog* tried to keep abreast of the film's production, and *Variety* was obsessed with the seeming insanity of sinking millions into a comic book adaptation, the mainstream had little knowledge of Salkind's pet project. To incite interest, Warner attached a teaser trailer to the *Star Wars* rerelease of late 1977. Audiences watched from Superman's POV as he moved rapidly through the clouds; great swooping letters trumpeted Brando's and Hackman's participation. Though no actual footage from the film was shown, the teaser was met with a raucous reception from filmgoers newly attuned to the fantastic. *Star Wars* had given them TIE fighters streaking through space—now the Salkinds would show them a man performing the same aerial ballet.

Thanks to George Lucas's breakthrough film, Hollywood was pumping out science fiction by the truckload in an attempt to emulate his success.

Much of it was relegated to television, since the turnaround time for the small screen was more conducive to the fast buck. Comic books became hot properties for producers looking for ready-made storyboards and series bibles.

Marvel Comics, which had yet to enjoy any success in Hollywood beyond a few crude Saturday morning cartoons, was an early beneficiary. After a televised pilot attracted an audience in late 1977, the live-action *Incredible Hulk* premiered in March 1978, starring Bill Bixby as the alter ego of the titular character. Mirroring Salkind's flirtation with Schwarzenegger, producers cast his bodybuilding peer Lou Ferrigno as the green monster. (Circumventing Ferrigno's limited acting experience was simple: the Hulk was mute.) *The Amazing Spider-Man* followed soon after but failed to resonate with audiences; it relied on cheap TV trickery to depict the webslinger's spectacular powers. He was simply too agile for a proper 1970s treatment.

Female heroines seemed to fare better: *Wonder Woman* had premiered in 1976, and it became an oft-visited stop in the development of a teenage boy's interest in the opposite sex. Star Lynda Carter was more the object of adolescent fantasy than *The Bionic Woman*'s Lindsay Wagner, but Wagner's ratings were superior. Equal time for female vigilantes was an idea Ilya Salkind would return to in later years.

For now, Salkind fretted over the influx of superheroics on television. His film obviously had the benefit of top-shelf effects work and a grade-A cast, but would people consider paying for more spandex-clad protagonists when so many of them visited their living rooms for free? He flirted with the idea of screening portions of the film in 3-D, but the gimmick would be costly and likely disappointing. (It would be over twenty years before 3-D effects would become practical, as part of the IMAX sensory-assault revolution.) The idea was abandoned.

Largely oblivious to the hand-wringing, Reeve continued to perfect his flying technique. Much to the delight of Donner, the actor found a particular body language that went beyond a simple extension of the arms and legs. Reeve would grimace during a surge of speed; he would smirk during more leisurely jaunts. He was honoring Donner's edict of verisimilitude.

Reeve's work ethic was so strong that he insisted he perform the flying effects himself, even though stuntman Paul Weston had fallen from the very same wire harness, breaking his collarbone and requiring a visit to traction. O'Halloran had been mortified by the safety measures when he arrived for his stunt work. The harnesses were cheaply produced; Stamp hurt his leg; Douglas was cut.

"There was a guy who had done harnesses for *King Kong* and I said, 'You should hire him. He's an expert,'" recalled O'Halloran. "He had a track record for it. They finally brought him in to do the harnesses for the flying shots. But they had spent a lot of money trying it their own way.

"We were up there doing certain movements, and I remember when we first started, I looked straight down, forty feet down, at a concrete floor. They didn't even have any mats below us. I went crazy. Sarah was scared shitless. And so was Terence. What if the goddamn mold breaks off or an accident happens? You're hitting the floor. This is the kind of thing that these guys did.

"I was up doing flips on the wires and they'd say, 'Oh, the wire will never break.' I'm saying, if they get twisted and they snap, we're screwed."

O'Halloran got his mats, but the production still suffered a fatality. Crew member Terry Hill was killed when a wing of an Air Force One replica snapped off, crushing him.

"They kept that very quiet," O'Halloran said of the tragedy on the closed set.

———

In spring 1978, Donner and his crew traipsed to New Mexico to shoot the climactic earthquake sequence, in which Lois Lane was now slated to (temporarily) expire. As Mankiewicz and the Newmans had envisioned it, the first film would have ended differently: Superman would have flung a rocket meant to destroy the Midwest; careening off into space, it would have shattered the ethereal glass prison that housed Zod and his minions. The second film would have ended with Lois's death, forcing Superman to turn back time by reversing the Earth's gravitational pull. (In a movie that demanded realism, this was the biggest concession to comic book–level theatrics.)

Donner, who held little nostalgia for serials, hated the cliffhanger ending and scrapped it. If the first film were to bomb, the hint of a sequel would inevitably be considered more of a threat than a promise. He accepted Lester's suggestion that the death of Lane be bumped up to the first film, lending it more dramatic weight.

Salkind had originally wanted to shoot the earthquake scenes at Pinewood, which Donner was concerned would result in a substantially cheaper-looking set piece. The director was happy to find that Warner agreed; it sank in the necessary funds for the location shooting. But the weather wasn't as agreeable as the studio: filming was delayed, at considerable cost, when it began to snow.

The Salkinds were now extended beyond their worst expectations. Months earlier, a robber had held up their accounting department at gunpoint. He left empty-handed. There was no money left to steal.

That summer, Donner prepared a three-hour rough cut for Warner executives and for composer John Williams, who had insisted on seeing something closer to completion before he would begin scoring the film. With his *Star Wars* orchestra album having grossed $20 million, he was duly indulged.

By this point, a million feet of film had been shot; Warner's slate for 1978 would have taken a fatal bath if *Superman* failed to deliver on the Salkinds' expectations. But despite the rough cut's grotesque length, the studio was ecstatic. The film was operatic, well acted, and visually stunning. Whether audiences would respond was another matter. But at least all involved had a fighting chance.

The remaining time allotted over the summer was spent wrapping up Reeve's effects work, the most laborious portion of shooting. From the time the actor departed the set in September 1978, Donner had ten weeks to polish a finished print. Editor Stuart Baird led a team of eighteen to assemble footage.

Richard Greenberg had designed the streaking credits used in the teaser trailer; they were such a hit with audiences that he was brought back to mimic the font and style for the actual film. Through no fault of Greenberg's own, one of his entries was the catalyst for legal trouble with the Writers Guild.

Mankiewicz had lobbied Donner for a special credit, one he'd been earning with his advisory role since the beginning of the production. Donner agreed and assigned him a "creative consultant" credit. While the label itself wasn't an issue, its placement was: Mankiewicz's name followed Puzo's, Benton's, and the Newmans', which was an affront to Writers Guild guidelines.

"I was terribly embarrassed that I came after the writers," Mankiewicz remembered. "I'm a very loyal member of the guild. But the arbitration panel said yes, he deserves a separate credit. They corrected it in *Superman II*. I come just before the writers."

Mankiewicz maintains he could've taken a writer's credit as well but declined—partly in response to Puzo's legacy with the production. "Puzo's contribution was practically nil. Mario was a great novelist but not a good screenwriter. He just put down a story from the comic strip. When they said 'Story by Mario Puzo,' I was always pissed because Siegel and Shuster didn't get the story credit."

Siegel and Shuster had remained a source of contention for Warner. In 1975, they challenged the studio's rights to Superman for the umpteenth time, claiming they were in mortal poverty. After failing to secure the copyright in court, Siegel sent out a nine-page press release to one thousand news outlets, placing a "curse" on the film project and railing against what he perceived was the pitiful treatment of the creators of Warner's icon.

The writer spewed bitterness from every syllable. "I hope it super-bombs," he spat. "I hope loyal SUPERMAN fans stay away from it in droves. I hope the whole world, becoming aware of the stench that surrounds SUPERMAN, will avoid the movie like a plague." "Flames were bursting from it," said comics artist Neal Adams, who received a copy of the release.

Adams, who at the time was president of the Academy of Comic Book Arts, grieved at the mistreatment of both men and resolved to do something about it. "Jerry was working as a clerk for $7,500 a year," Adams recalled. "Joe couldn't work anymore because he was legally blind. He lived in an apartment with his brother in Queens, sleeping on a cot next to a window that was cracked and taped up."

Adams ushered Siegel from his California home and Shuster from his Queens apartment and paraded them around news outlets in New York, calling witnesses to hear the testimony of the impoverished creators. Siegel was booked on Tom Snyder's and Howard Cosell's talk shows. These appearances were all that Siegel's limited funds allowed; soon he'd have to return to the West Coast.

His time running out, Adams met with Jerry Robinson of the National Cartoonists Society and asked him to lend a hand. Leaving the society's offices, Adams ran into a man at the coat check desk. "Do you know what this building is?" the stranger asked. Adams shook his head. "This is the headquarters of the Overseas Press Club. You oughta have a press conference." Adams professed no knowledge of how to coordinate a press conference.

"I'm the president," the man said. "You can have one here tomorrow."

The next day, reporters gathered to hear Siegel's tale of being railroaded by the media conglomerate. Dozens of newspapers picked up the story. Eventually, the undesirable attention prompted Warner to sit down with Adams and his legal counsel to try to resolve the dispute. The studio was prepared to offer an annual salary to the duo; Adams was pleased, but that wasn't the end.

"A number of years ago, you took Siegel and Shuster's names off of the *Superman* comic books," Adams told DC.

"Yeah, we did," Jay Emmett replied. Emmett was in charge of DC's licensing agreements and had personally reaped millions from Superman's myriad appearances in store shelves over the years.

"Don't you think they ought to be put back on?" Adams asked him.

"No. Can't do that. That's not going to happen," Emmett replied. "It'll create all kinds of legal hassles and problems." Adams refused to relent. "Is this a deal breaker?" Emmett asked. Adams was noncommittal.

The following day, Adams fielded calls from the media. "We're just about where we ought to be," Adams told a newsman.

"What do you mean, 'just about'?"

"Well," Adams baited, "in order to make this deal, Warner refused to have Jerry and Joe's signature on the *Superman* comics. And I just think that's an outrage. But there's nothing I can do about it." The following day, Adams went to a comics convention in Florida with his family, leaving no notice with anyone except Robinson.

Robinson reached him at his hotel, where Adams had been strolling through the lobby with artist Jack Kirby. Frantic, Robinson demanded to know what was going on. Adams played dumb. "What do you mean, Jerry?" he asked.

Robinson had just finished speaking to Emmett, who had been swarmed by media demanding to know why Siegel and Shuster couldn't get their credits restored. Robinson had told him a signature is all an artist has, and how, as president of the Cartoonists Society, he certainly couldn't argue the point.

"Fine, they got it," Emmett had sighed. "Anything else?"

Robinson mused that it would be a nice gesture, considering it was the holidays and all, for Warner to grant the creators an additional $10,000 each.

There was silence on the other end. "Fine," Emmett said. "They got it. Anything *else*?"

Not long after, executives ordered that Jerry Siegel and Joe Shuster would receive a credit in all future *Superman* titles and adaptations, as well as $20,000 each in annual compensatory salary. While the arrangement met their cost of living needs, it was still a paltry reward considering the billions Warner would eventually realize from their creation.

"I went to the doctor after all this and *my* blood pressure was up," Adams recalled. "The whole thing ate at Jerry. He had a heart problem. He wasn't the type to stay happy. But Joe was cherubic, like Santa Claus."

Despite the slight—and his own ailing vision—Shuster would dash off sketches of Superman on napkins for children, happy to have been part of something that brought them such joy.

As the film shoot wound to a close, Ilya Salkind found the on-set mood improving. "I have a crew picture where they're all together, Lester and Donner. We're all very happy and smiling. That was after the big crisis. This is one thing Dick [Donner] said, and he's right: everybody was in the same boat."

Superman: The Movie was set to premiere in Washington, D.C., on December 10, 1978. No previews would be screened for audiences, meaning that public reception wouldn't be fully measured until the general release. (The studio did share some footage with a contentious fandom crowd at the San Diego Comic-Con, many of whom were afraid of their beloved icon being prostituted; attendees included a young Tim Burton.)

In November, Warner Bros. contacted Alex Salkind and inquired as to the status of the finished print.

Salkind had it ready to go. All that was required, he told executives, was that the studio pay him $15 million. Otherwise, it would remain in London.

The film—in which Warner had, by conservative estimates, invested more than $40 million—was being held for ransom.

Reel Steel

Brando was allegedly paid $3 million for his role, or, judging by his dialogue,
$500,000 a cliché.
—Roger Ebert

As Warner executives reeled from their contentious phone call with
Alexander Salkind, they found grim news in the studio's ledgers. Seven
to ten million dollars was being spent to make sure every potential ticket-
purchaser on the globe was cognizant that Superman was being given the
deluxe treatment on the big screen. Worse, they had already booked 508
theaters in anticipation of receiving the finished print. Theater owners
promised legal action if they didn't have a picture to screen on December
15. The date was three weeks away.

Now Salkind was telling them it would be an additional $15 million,
ostensibly so Warner could obtain the right to profit from more foreign
territories. The studio had not solicited the sale from Salkind—he was
forcing it upon them. Salkind was hardly eager to relinquish more of his
profit margin, but his creditors were sending him into a tailspin.

"They had the negative, and they basically held it hostage unless
Warner would buy three territories from them," recalled Mankiewicz.
"I remember the head of the legal eagles for Warner said to me, 'Those
bastards obviously owed their investors a lot more money and they didn't

Actor Christopher Reeve greets Queen Elizabeth II at the UK premiere of *Superman: The Movie* in London on December 13, 1978. Actors Sarah Douglas and Harry Andrews appear in the background.

(Harry Myers, Rex Features/Everett Collection)

know if the picture was going to be a hit. And they needed cash.'" Warner caved in, remitting $15 million in exchange for the print. (While the studio may have resented the gross coercion, it would turn out to be a bizarrely advantageous transaction.)

The Salkinds, now somewhat eased in their finances, galloped to the premiere, held in D.C. at the Kennedy Center. (Alex's assistant had spent most of his time plotting a travel route by land and sea from Europe to Washington for the flying-phobic patriarch.) The gala was in honor of the Special Olympics; President Jimmy Carter was in attendance. The younger Salkind beamed as he made his way up the steps of the regal building, feeling as though he were literally ascending to a loftier place in the Hollywood hierarchy.

Suddenly, a man sidled up alongside him. Ilya smiled and prepared himself to receive salutations and compliments; instead, the man thrust a manila folder into his hands. Salkind stared at it blankly, uncomprehending.

"You've been served," the man said, and then departed.

Mario Puzo had slapped the Salkinds with a lawsuit, claiming that his profit participation was too meager and that producers were exaggerating cost overruns in order to make the margin thinner. (Though entitled to a share of gross receipts, Puzo could only claim his share after 60 percent of unspecified production costs had been met, a line that became increasingly distant as costs mounted.) "I was crushed," Ilya recalled. "I took it personally. Then you learn not to take it personally. You have a lawsuit, you have a settlement, and then you have lunch. That's how it works."

It would be the first of many litigious surprises for Ilya. But for the time being, he would concentrate on enjoying his moment in the sun. He snapped a photo with the president, betraying little sign of the Puzo disappointment. (Bizarrely, Alex Salkind would later take the photo and crop out Ilya's head, replacing it with his own.) He accepted Schwarzenegger's good-natured ribbing at not being chosen for the part. He even engaged in a little drunken revelry with his crew, including Donner. Liquor had eased their tension, and Salkind walked away feeling like things had finally been resolved. "We were all friendly as hell at the premieres. We were all getting drunk in Washington. Then Dick started saying things."

Army Archerd profiled Donner in his *Variety* column; the director was stone-cold sober in his evaluation of Spengler and Salkind's filmmaking acumen. He lashed out at Spengler, swearing that he would have nothing to do with finishing the second film if Spengler was involved. Moreover, he demanded total creative control over the sequel.

"Then he started publicly calling us assholes, which wasn't very nice," Ilya sighed. Spengler attempted to contact Donner via phone, but his messages went unanswered. Eventually, Donner would bring a suit of his own against Salkind, which accused him of exaggerating cost overruns to diminish his share of the profits.

Spengler scoffed, replying that the director was the one who had caused the overruns, and if he had to blame anyone, it should be himself. A distraught Donner had to pay both British and American taxes on his $1 million salary. His net compensation wound up being less than if he had simply remained in the United States making TV movies.

Donner's abrasive press commentary rankled Ilya Salkind. "Pierre is a childhood friend," he said. "We've known each other a long time. When he said it was on his terms, I said to my father, 'We can't work with a guy like that.' It was a very simple decision. It was based on emotion more than anything else."

The hard feelings surrounding the production continued to flare. Two days after the film's national release on December 15, Marlon Brando sued for $50 million, claiming he, too, had not been delivered the percentage of the gross promised. He filed for a restraining order barring the producers from using his likeness—including the film's footage. (It was denied.) The iconic, laconic thespian eventually took home $15 million for fifteen minutes' worth of screen time, a jaw-dropping ratio in any era.

Margot Kidder followed suit in the literal sense, claiming she had not been properly compensated either. The actor took a less diplomatic approach than her peers, referring to the Salkinds as "scum" in press interviews. She once remarked that crew members were frustrated that their checks were bouncing, prompting Pierre Spengler to threaten legal action for slander. The attitude would not bode well for her participation in future sequels.

Perhaps inevitably, the Salkinds' newly minted star joined in on the chorus of litigation. Christopher Reeve had signed a contract to shoot both *Superman* and *Superman II* simultaneously. In a lawsuit filed in New York, he charged that since filming had been interrupted, the films were not to be considered a single entity any longer. Reeve demanded further compensation to shoot the remainder of *II*. The Salkinds, having filed away an hour of footage for the sequel, had little choice in the matter; recasting the title character in midfilm was a bit much, even for them. They agreed to pay Reeve an additional $500,000 to complete his work on the project.

Despite the personal imbroglios prompted by the labored production, audiences were awed by the end result. *Superman* met expectations in the post–*Star Wars* era of popcorn cinema: the Man of Steel sped through the clouds, caught falling helicopters, burrowed through the Earth. He withstood bullets, juggled warheads, and even saved a cat from a tree, just for good measure.

The 143-minute version of the film that played during the winter of 1978–79 was largely true to Donner's vision, free of any studio or producer strong-arming, though Donner himself excised some scenes due to concerns over an awkwardly elongated running time. (The longer a film, the fewer screenings per day, resulting in fewer tickets sold.)

Donner had enlisted Kirk Alyn and Noel Neill, the screen's original Clark Kent and Lois Lane, to make cameo appearances as a young Lois's parents. Lounging on a train chugging through Smallville, the future journalist insists that a teenager outside is outrunning the speeding transport. Naturally, her parents dismiss the suggestion out of hand. Out of fear that not enough people would recognize the aging actors, the scene was dropped. (Alyn would later go on to portray "Pa Cant" in a no-budget parody, *Superbman*.)

Much later in the film, Superman uncovers Lex Luthor's lair. Before confronting his foe, he's forced to endure a gauntlet that the archvillain has constructed to "test" the Man of Steel's mettle. Fire gaskets blast him with flesh-melting heat; ice surrounds him; a machine gun tears off a cartridge aimed at his chest. By this point, the audience knows of Superman's physical attributes, so the litmus test was removed as redundant. A scene that implied Luthor has a pack of growling, unidentified animals was also snipped; what a snarling beast is going to do to Superman remains in question.

Warner's marketing tagline, "You'll Believe a Man Can Fly," was prophetic. Mainstream audiences had been kept away from the landmark flying sequences, which made them eager to witness whether or not effects experts could match the standards set by Lucas the previous summer. But the studio had difficulty tempering expectations of juvenilia: this was not a kiddie film, and the marketing department had to work overtime to correct early assumptions to the contrary.

By standards both commercial and creative, *Superman: The Movie* was a hit. The film remained at number one for eleven straight weeks, having debuted with $7 million in opening weekend grosses. All told, *Superman* would rake in an estimated $134 million domestically, making it one of Hollywood's biggest success stories of the 1970s. Worldwide, Warner delighted in a take of more than $300 million against a budget of $55 million; in the additional territories in which the Salkinds had forced the studio to invest, it would recoup the $15 million "ransom" many times over. Theater owners, who had grudgingly committed to a marathon thirteen-week engagement, seethed at Warner's majority share of ticket earnings.

Ilya Salkind, though elated, was sore that they had been unable to meet their summer release date. "The repeat business was not as strong as *Star Wars*. The kids liked to see it, but I don't know if they came to see it more than once." Still, so staggering were receipts that Warner granted Siegel and Shuster a $15,000 bonus each.

Critics, possibly slack-jawed over the film's achievements relative to their meager expectations, were universally kind. Roger Ebert took a few shots at the "ponderous" Krypton scenes, but he dubbed the film as a whole a "pure delight" and awarded it four stars. Even notoriously crusty *New Yorker* critic Pauline Kael celebrated Reeve's take on the icon, though she also described his surroundings as "cheesy" and asserted that the film itself seemed to have been "made in panic." The latter allegation was more than a subjective snipe, though perhaps not for the reasons she had in mind.

Screenwriter Mankiewicz took particular delight in *Newsweek*'s glowing review. "The first *Superman* is really three different movies," he said. "On Krypton, it's shot through a fog filter. People talk in almost Shakespearian language. Suddenly, you get to Kansas and growing up in the wheat fields, and it's shot like an Andrew Wyeth or Norman Rockwell painting. And everybody's talking like, 'Gee, Pa. Gee, Ma. Golly.' And then you get to Metropolis and it's all red reds, green greens, and the dialogue starts to crackle. And this was done on purpose.

"That was the thing Jack Kroll in *Newsweek* hit on. Some people haven't picked up on that." (And some did but considered the tonal shifts the product of some Frankenstein production gaffe.)

Genre publication *Cinefantastique* was the lone dissident, sniffing that the film was "poor" and claiming it wouldn't be owed substantial coverage beyond a Donner interview that belabored his criticisms of the Salkinds.

———

Star Wars had ushered in new expectations not only for blockbuster films but for multimedia tie-ins as well. Lucas's space opera was virtually printing money with record sales of albums, books, and toys. Warner Bros. did their best to exploit Superman to similar effect, but legal machinations crippled them early and severely.

Puzo's contract had mandated that his story template was not to be adapted into any other form. That meant lucrative opportunities for comic book adaptations and novelizations based on the film's narrative were immediately out the window. In the novel *Superman: Last Son of Krypton*, comics scribe Elliot S! Maggin (exclamation point his) reflected Donner's vision of the mythology but was mindful not to include any of Puzo's base contributions. Warner also issued a making-of book by David Michael Petrou that was careful not to stoke the fires of any interpersonal drama. Documentaries were dispensed through Warner's TV connections; Atari, a subsidiary of the studio, released a *Superman* pinball game. Counting such trinkets as thermoses and puzzles, more than one thousand items were licensed.

Warner's most promising cash cow, however, arrived stillborn: the studio had failed to secure a toy license prior to the opening. *Star Wars* had yet to begin moving plastic effigies of Harrison Ford and Mark Hamill off shelves with rapidity, and the industry was unaware of the literal billions that were available to them from young boys eager to reenact their favorite movie scenes while in the bathtub.

Mego managed to produce an abbreviated line of twelve-inch collectible figures, though they were a weird amalgamation of comic book wardrobes and vague likenesses of the actors' heads. (Gene Hackman's plastic doppelganger sported green tights.) Standing eight inches taller than their *Star Wars* counterparts, they were also cumbersome to collect. Mego had designs on producing a play set that met the scale of the line, but poor consumer demand scuttled the idea. The company failed to fall in with the trend of offering economical three-and-three-quarter-inch figures; worse, it had turned down the *Star Wars* license. Mego folded a few years later.

DC Comics should have been the arm of Warner to see the greatest benefit from the film: a two-and-a-half-hour commercial for its star creation was playing in rotation across the country. In preparation for what the company expected would be a deluge of new readers, DC publisher Jenette Kahn had expanded its line by a whopping fifty-seven titles in 1976.

But the literal ill winds that had plagued *Superman*'s production wound up being unkindest to DC. The 1978 blizzard that buried the East Coast slowed distribution of its titles to a crawl. By early 1979, DC's presence on newsstand shelves was relegated to a scant few titles. Its business effectively imploded, though its characters were in more demand than ever.

Just as *Star Wars* had promoted a cavalcade of me-too science fiction productions, *Superman* awakened Hollywood to the ready-made wonders of comic book dramatics. Properties that had previously been relegated to cheap pursuits on TV were now being used as currency in the boardrooms of major film studios. *Flash Gordon* was being prepped at Universal; the kitschy take on the comic strip hero made every mistake *Superman*'s caretakers had managed to avoid. Flash was a thick-skulled dolt, and all involved seemed much too aware of their absurd trappings.

"There's a terrible trap when you write something like *Superman* that you fall into as a writer," mused Mankiewicz. "To a certain extent with Bond as well. You want to show your audience that you're somehow smarter than the material, that we're not taking this too seriously and it's all a lot of fun.

"The truth is, the only way these pictures work is if you stay inside the material. You can add all the humor you want, but you need the audience to be laughing with the characters, not at them."

Mankiewicz's genre wisdom had been sought for two follow-ups, one an adaptation of Chester Gould's *Dick Tracy* and the other a more contemporary take on DC's *Batman*. *Tracy* fell through when Gould demanded too much money for the license. In 1979, Mankiewicz began scripting chores on the Dark Knight project, which was intended to be another two-film shoot.

"When I wrote the first draft of *Batman*, everybody at Warner thought that it was going to be like *Superman*," Mankiewicz recalled. Unlike his previous project, however, "it was a very dark first draft. I kept saying, 'You know, he's a guy dressed in a silly suit. This has got to take place at night. It's gotta be dark.'" Ivan Reitman was briefly attached to the project, but he had his own concerns over the foreboding tone. *Batman* sat on the shelf for years until Tim Burton revived it in 1989, turning it into Warner's trademark property of the 1990s.

Despite garnering respect from audiences and critics, *Superman* still didn't hold quite enough cachet to snag any major awards when the Oscars were held in April 1979. Stuart Baird was nominated for Best Film Editing, John Williams for Best Music (Original Score), and the audio crew for Best Sound. It snagged only one statue, a Special Achievement Award for Zoran Perisic's groundbreaking effects work. Giorgio Moroder defeated Williams with his score to *Midnight Express*, though Williams picked up a Grammy for his work one year later.

The snubs prompted Donner to turn his ire toward the Academy. He lambasted them in the press for not recognizing the work of cinematographer Geoffrey Unsworth, who had passed away of infectious meningitis shortly before the film opened. Indeed, Unsworth's task was complicated by the triumvirate of visual approaches the film employed, and his success seemed worthy of at least a nomination.

As for Reeve, if he was disappointed that the sycophantic award circuit had ignored him, he wasn't vocal about it—and he did pick up a Most Promising Newcomer honor from the British Academy of Film and Television Awards. But by his own admission, he adjusted to his newfound celebrity by enjoying a "mandatory" one-year term of being an "idiot," sniping at the media and generally pursuing a freewheeling lifestyle he felt he'd earned. Talking to a *Cosmopolitan* reporter, he felt affronted by insinuations he wasn't being "funny enough" and asked her to leave, reducing her to tears. Possibly in an attempt to resolve his karmic issues, Reeve would don the Superman tights for friends' children and particularly grievous hospital cases.

During his hiatus before filming the rest of *Superman II*, Reeve followed Connery's advice to do something radically different: he accepted the lead role in an earnest picture titled *Somewhere in Time*, based on the Richard Matheson novel *Bid Time Return*. Salkind fumed and threatened a lawsuit, but shooting on *II* had yet to be scheduled. Reeve went off to Mackinac Island to film his pet project, assuring *Superman* producers he would be finished in time for a spring 1979 start for the sequel.

Time was essentially a science fiction fable, with Reeve as a playwright so enamored of the woman in a portrait taken sixty-eight years prior (Jane Seymour) that he "wills" himself into traveling back in time to meet her. While Reeve was not subject to the jeers and catcalls with which audiences greeted George Reeves's post-*Superman* film, the project didn't seem to inspire any kind of reaction at all. Grossing less than $10 million throughout its theatrical run, it was an ominous signal that Reeve's worst fears about his future might become reality.

"He thought he was a box office superstar," razzed O'Halloran. "What did he do other than Superman? He did one nice little picture, *Somewhere in Time.* But he's as stiff as a board in that. He never worked again with Hackman or anybody. That speaks for itself, doesn't it?"

Despite the cool reception in its initial outing, *Time* actually became something of a cult pursuit for fans who appreciated its morbid romanticism. (Reeve literally dies of a broken heart at its climax, after inadvertently rebounding to his own time.) Today, thousands flock to Mackinac Island in pilgrimage to the film's location.

Margot Kidder fared slightly better in the sophomore slump department. She accepted a role opposite James Brolin in *The Amityville Horror*, Warner's attempt to reignite audience interest in the occult. (Their sequel to *The Exorcist* had arrived DOA in 1977.) The film was based on an allegedly nonfictitious tale of supernatural plagues that accosted a family in Amityville, Long Island. Kidder played Kathy Lutz, the family matriarch. The film grossed nearly $8 million in its opening weekend, exceeding *Superman*'s inaugural three-day take, and raked in $86 million in the summer of 1979.

Outside of her *Superman* films, it would be the lone hit of her career.

———

In March 1979, Richard Donner received a telegram from the Salkinds: his services would no longer be needed for *Superman II*. His incendiary statements had continued through much of *Superman*'s media blitz, forcing the producers into either submitting to his chastising or asserting their power over the property. They chose the latter.

Warner, which had supported Donner during the tumultuous shoot, had little to say in the matter. As an investor in the franchise's production, not its orchestrators, the studio lacked the authority to override the Salkinds' decision.

Donner also had the goodwill of the cast on his side, but no one had the influence to insist the producers retain him. They could, however, refuse to work without him—Gene Hackman snubbed offers to come back for reshoots on the sequel, necessitating a stand-in and a voice-over double for some scenes. When Reeve heard the news of Donner's departure, he was livid; he described the Salkinds as "devious" and "untrustworthy" in an interview he gave to Britain's *Time Out* magazine.

"The names we've been called have been really depressing," said Ilya Salkind years later of the perpetually negative reaction to the firing. "This was a very simple decision. The man didn't want to work with us. *We* made the film, *we* took the risk, and *we* worked for three years before he came in. He was absolutely fantastic. He came up with brilliant things. He's a fantastic director. But my father and I controlled the picture."

Donner himself may have subconsciously welcomed the release. After nearly two years on the film, he was spent. He did nothing for the year following *Superman*'s completion except decompress in his California home.

Ironically, some have speculated that if his *Superman* had bombed, he would've been allowed to continue the saga, if only as punishment for his failure. Ilya Salkind rebuffed the suggestion. "I laugh when I see people say, 'Oh, the Salkinds, if it would have flopped they would've kept Donner.' If it had flopped, there would've been no second movie!"

To fill the gap left by Donner, Salkind first approached Guy Hamilton, the original director of the first *Superman*. He was unavailable, which led the studio to put its financial weight behind one of the remaining possibilities. If Hamilton wasn't an option, Warner insisted the Salkinds retain Richard Lester; after all, he'd worked in some capacity on the first installment and had proved himself capable of directing action with the *Musketeers* movies.

Lester was not a comics fan. He considered himself an intellectual filmmaker. And the prospect of finishing someone else's film held even less appeal than the subject matter. But Warner's offer of $500,000 was generous in light of the work already completed. He obliged them.

Because the creative team assembled for the first installment had snipped the sequel's finale, and because Lester's sensibilities ran counter to Donner's, rewrites would be needed. Terry Semel, who was then a Warner vice president, approached Mankiewicz.

"Would you go back to England and work with Richard Lester on the remaining stuff to be shot for *II*?"

"Terry, I can't do that," Mankiewicz replied. "Dick [Donner] is my friend."

"I understand," Semel said. "Could you fly to London and accidentally run into Dick Lester?" Mankiewicz refused.

Despite the plethora of lawsuits that kept the Salkinds' accountants and legal team busy, shooting on *Superman II* would resume in August 1979. The extended hiatus would cost the production some key personnel. Special effects technicians had been recruited for the *Star Wars* sequel, *The Empire Strikes Back*; Hackman had wrapped all the scenes he was going to shoot; Unsworth had passed away. Under the circumstances, it would be challenging to attempt to complete a film and maintain a semblance of continuity.

Done right, though, it would make everyone a lot of money.

Meanwhile, the first *Superman* found new life in the fledging home video market. In order to meet the storage limits of the era's cassettes, the film was squeezed from 143 to 127 minutes using time compression—nonverbal scenes were sped up, and the credits were curtailed. Consumers who were willing to pay a premium for HBO fared better: the cable network's version of the film had only one minute trimmed from its original running time. Video discs, which were briefly a third option, presented the film on both sides of two separate discs; while this edition was complete, it was a hassle to flip discs over during a screening. That annoyance carried over to the relatively more durable Laserdisc format of the late 1980s.

Donner had directorial influence only over the theatrical cut; he was unable to prevent the Salkinds from selling his three-hour-long rough edit to TV stations. Dubbed the "Salkind International Cut" by fans, it runs a full forty-five minutes longer than what had been released to theaters. In addition to the "young Lois" and "Luthor's lair" scenes described earlier, the edit let many scenes run longer.

ABC purchased the cut and broadcast *Superman: The Movie* as a two-night, four-hour event. The sale was initiated without the consent of the studio; the Salkinds, still desperate to recoup their costs and remit payment to their creditors, were being paid by the minute for the film. (Suddenly, Donner's excesses didn't seem cause for complaint.) This version would air many times throughout the 1980s, both on network television and in syndication, plus or minus six minutes of footage.

A hit on screens both big and small, *Superman: The Movie* represented the antithesis of the profane, morbid offerings that had typified the films of the 1970s. That a decade so celebrated for the antiheroes of *Taxi Driver* and *The Godfather* could birth someone as rigidly noble as the Man of Steel seems puzzling. The counterculture movement had dubbed that kind of gross patriotism detrimental, its values archaic; if Woodward and Bernstein of *All the President's Men* had interviewed Superman, their profile would have been far more hard-nosed than Lois Lane's flowery prose. (Revulsion at Superman's messianic stature was uncommon but present: when a reporter accosted Hackman at the premiere, quizzing him on the character's alleged fascism, Hackman called him an "asshole" and stormed off.)

Superman solidified the cinematic change that *Star Wars* and *Jaws* had initiated in the years prior. Studios that had made dozens of films, each of which appealed to a different demographic, could now make a handful of films that featured enough visceral eye candy to satiate the escapist desires of anyone and everyone. Tonally, films would shift from cerebral meditations on culture and life to superficial entertainment.

By the 1980s, Travis Bickle, Michael Corleone, and their conflicted peers would fade away as the movie experience became sensorial rather than emotional. Expensive new sound systems promised further immersion in the worlds of science fiction and fantasy. Releases were bumped from midweek to Friday in order to meet the demand of sluggish workers who saw film as a respite from the mundane, not an intellectual challenge. Studios moved toward the promise of ready-made audiences by using properties that had been well established in the mass consciousness. If it had been a comic book, comic strip, or hit novel, it was likely to get assigned a budget, director, and release date.

In the 1980s, studios would also realize that if something worked once, it would work again. And again. They began to discuss properties like Superman in terms of "branding" and "franchise potential." It was a new perspective that would produce mixed results for the Last Son of Krypton.

But at the moment, the film hundreds of people had labored on for what seemed like an eternity was finally finished.

Years earlier, Donner and Mankiewicz had been returning to their London rentals from a nonproductive casting session. They were only a few nights away from shooting. "We couldn't find a Lois Lane, a Superman," sighed Mankiewicz. "We had this driver, Eddie. We were driving around in silence and Dick looked at me and said, 'Penny for your thoughts.' And I said to him, 'I'm thinking we could be presiding over the biggest financial disaster in the history of motion pictures.'

"And there was this silence. Eddie dropped Dick off first at his house in Chelsea, right next door to Margaret Thatcher, actually. I got to my hotel and I said to Eddie, 'Eddie, would you give the two men who were just in the back of your car $30 million to make a movie?' And he said, 'No, sir, no I wouldn't.'"

For the sake of the franchise, the Salkinds eventually agreed with Eddie. In Lester, they would finally find their mercenary.

8

Dicked

The way "Superman II" was produced is the lowest you can go without actually cheating.
—Christopher Reeve

By his own admission, Richard Lester was acutely apathetic toward comic books in general and Superman in particular. The normal focuses of his attention were intimate character studies, not the globe-trotting exploits of a pseudodeity. If Superman was someone who could do everything, why should he do anything?

It's possible that such emotional distance from the material is what kept Lester in the game, given his frustrating relationship with the Salkinds. On the *Musketeers* films he had viewed Alex and Ilya as ruthlessly economical; they would frequently hire ill-suited crew members because of their attractive price tags. When Lester challenged them on contentious issues, they would abruptly shift the conversation over to French.

There was also the matter of momentum. Lester hadn't been celebrated for any film he'd directed since 1976's *Robin and Marian*, a warm tribute to the aging heroics of Robin Hood. A credit on a near-guaranteed success would go a long way toward restoring his stature in the business.

Whereas Donner felt uneasy conforming to the detached, supervisory style required of a *Superman* director—tooling around Pinewood in a golf cart like Patton—Lester embraced it. He would later tell director Steven Soderbergh that he found the collaborative experience to be refreshing. "The *Superman* films were just a walk in the park," Lester said. "With four units shooting, if you're smart, you could spend most of your time walking between the units. The [crew] would get on without you if they had to."

The kind of emotional investment Donner had made in the project was nowhere to be found in Lester's management style. Creatively, he felt little need to change the alchemy of the mythology. It was a big, loud film with large strokes. Lester was simply seeing to it that the necessary number of setups were resolved each day. One of his few demands was to inject more comedy and human elements into the proceedings; wall-to-wall action, he felt, overburdened the audience, didn't give them a break. If Superman was to spin a tank over his head, reasoned Lester, it should be followed by some kind of quieter scene.

In addition, Lester was underwhelmed by Donner's use of three distinct visual palettes in the first film. He urged new cinematographer Robert Paynter to mimic the garish color scheme of the comics, eliminating any kind of Norman Rockwell–esque influence. The edict would easily be obeyed, considering that *Superman II* would largely bypass the exposition of the first film and concentrate almost exclusively on the Man of Steel's battle with the villains of the Phantom Zone.

Lester caused tension, however, when he opted to retain his standard directorial technique of shooting with three cameras at once; because actors don't know when they're being filmed for a close-up, they're forced to emote at full output 100 percent of the time.

Structurally, the sequel still had several problems to overcome before shooting resumed in the summer of 1979. Lester had inadvertently painted himself into a corner when he convinced Donner to lift the sequel's climax for the first film. Now he was left without an ending. With Mankiewicz begging off, Lester enlisted David and Leslie Newman to help rectify the situation.

"It was a very big challenge without Donner," Salkind admitted. "We were basically starting from scratch. At one point, we had eleven units. I would say Donner shot 50 to 60 percent of *II*. All of Hackman. But mainly, we had to reshape the script, especially after changing the ending to *I*. There was a lot of great stuff that didn't fit into the new continuity."

Scenes shot with Brando's Jor-El and Clark Kent would have to be reworked; the Salkinds had decided that Brando's 12 percent share of the gross was far too generous to allow him to appear on-screen. (Brando's public comments seemed incompatible with his staunch financial demands. Only six months after the first film's release, he complained that he was low on funds. He would later accept $50,000 as compensation for sitting down with a *Playboy* interviewer; ostensibly, the money would be used as bail funds for Sioux activist Russell Means.)

Brando's stature had garnered the project some respectability during more turbulent times, but now Donner's vision of Superman had been properly stamped onto the public psyche. They were no longer in need of a loss leader. "I said, why don't we have the mother talk to Superman?" said Salkind. "The mother talks about love. And it worked, in terms of logic and structure."

Mankiewicz would disagree. "It loses all its impact. The father sent him to Earth. I wrote that long speech with overtones clearly of God sending his son to Earth when he says, 'They can be a great people, Kal-El. They wish to be. They only lack the light to show the way.' The whole full circle, the arc, is him coming back to his father. And Brando, who has very little energy in him left, reaches out to touch him and commits suicide to give his son new life and disappears forever. Well, that is so dramatic and so wonderful, and of course it means nothing if it's the mother instead.

"It drives you nuts when producers, or promoters, really, decide to injure the picture so that they can make a couple extra million dollars."

Unmoved by Mankiewicz's logic, Salkind enlisted Susannah York to reprise her role as Clark's Kryptonian mother, imparting wisdom from beyond the grave at a far more reasonable salary. Even footage of Brando's hand was reshot, in order to make absolutely certain the actor could make no claim of appearing in the film and cause a legal ruckus.

Leonard Maltin's Movie Guide would go on to sum up the sequel's basic philosophy as succinctly as anyone: "Screw the Superman legend, forget logic, and full speed ahead."

———

For reasons known only to Lester, an opening sequence written by Mankiewicz and shot by Donner was deemed unsatisfactory and cut from the print, resurfacing only when a reedit of the film was issued in late 2006.

The intro features Lois examining a copy of the *Daily Planet* emblazoned with Superman's picture. Using a pen to add glasses and a business suit, she realizes she's looking at Clark Kent. Emboldened, Lane sticks herself out a window and urges Clark to save her. He uses his powers covertly to open an awning, which bounces her into the film industry's oft-abused comedic safety net, a fruit cart.

Lester's disinterest was surprising, as the slapstick seemed more in tune with his tastes; inversely, it was also uncharacteristic of Donner's more restrained approach.

The sequence was intended to parallel a later exchange at Niagara Falls, in which Lois, convinced she's discovered Clark's secret, shoots him with a gun. When Clark is unharmed, he reveals his alter ego and reacts with indignation that she would put a mortal's life in danger. "With a blank?" Lois retorts. The scene was used as audition fodder but never filmed properly. Instead, Lester mimicked the spirit of Donner's opener in a later scene by having Lois fling herself into Niagara Falls, only to be rescued by a bumbling Kent.

Lester's alternate introduction was a sequence, shot on location in Paris, in which Lois runs afoul of terrorists at the Eiffel Tower. This non sequitur was an early indication of how sharply contrasted Lester's approach would be to Donner's.

For a scene in Canada, Donner had raised the ire of his colleagues by waiting until the weather was conducive to the shot he wanted. In Paris, Lester appeared oblivious to the heavy precipitation that cast a dark pall over the scene. "They shot in the pissing rain," huffed O'Halloran. "Richard Lester just opened the lens and said, 'Aw, I can fix everything in the laboratory.'

Richard Donner's Lois Lane, actor Margot Kidder, in the late 1970s. In 1996, Kidder would garner headlines for being found disoriented and disheveled, the result of her bipolar condition.

(Everett Collection)

"If you look at the Eiffel Tower shots, the windshield wipers were going back and forth. The cop that's interviewing Margot Kidder, spots are hitting his shirt. He must've changed his shirt six times. Donner would never do that."

That was exactly the point. The Salkinds knew that Lester would perform the minimum orchestration needed to get an acceptable take, and then move on. Kidder would later describe the process as "cheap and fast." (The actor had once come to set distraught over her marital problems; Lester funneled her emotions into a scene in which she's despondent over Superman's responsibilities to the world.)

For scenes in which the Kryptonian villains intimidate the military, Donner had planned on them circling the country destroying familiar landmarks. Instead, Lester shot takes of the trio opposing the army in Houston, pummeling jeeps and sniffing at the arrogance of the military. Donner would later comment that the scenes played jarringly, "an Englishman's point-of-view [of] what America would look like."

The crux of *Superman II* involves Lois and Clark finally consummating their contentious courtship, an idea that had DC caretakers in revolt. Previously, they had harangued Donner over some scattered curse words in the original film's screenplay, backing off only when Donner appealed to Warner for intervention. To DC, having Superman delve into base human desires was a calamity.

The idea had originated with Puzo, who once told *TIME* that Lois and Clark would be seen in bed together and that it wouldn't fall into camp. DC, upon seeing rushes, eventually agreed: there was little on display beyond a bare-chested Kent snuggling with Lois in his Fortress of Solitude digs.

Of greater concern to purists were the seemingly limitless abilities that both Superman and his villainous counterparts exhibit: telekinesis, teleportation. During a climatic battle in his fortress, Superman actually tears off his "S" insignia and uses it as a net to entrap the lumbering Non. Like something out of a fever dream, these powers are never rationalized.

The same holds true for the "super kiss" Clark uses to make Lois forget about his alter ego. Under Lester's guidance, Superman could not only juggle planets but also apparently perform lobotomies. The Salkinds later explained such scenes by saying that Kryptonians have virtually unlimited power; they simply choose not to use everything in their arsenal.

Reeve, who had wavered in weight by as much as thirty pounds during initial shooting, was now of solid construction and well accustomed to the flying sequences. Effects men had devised a more comfortable body mold that would prove to be less chafing than the harnesses utilized during the first shoot, though accidents still occurred. Once, Kidder lost her footing on a set that was collapsing, prompting Reeve to swoop in and catch her. Restless, he spent several nights during location shooting in Norway getting drunk with the locals.

Stamp was less enthused, and spoke to the press often about the strong possibility of breaking his neck. O'Halloran, who had long complained of creaky safety measures, was the recipient of the worst injury to the cast. "At the end, I had a ruptured disc in my back. There was a hyperextension. I wound up getting a back operation."

Though O'Halloran dismissed Lester as a "television director," devoid of any real vision, Reeve sympathized with his plight and remained cordial. At the least, Lester was a professional; he preferred kinetics where Donner preferred myth, and that was fine with Reeve. "I learnt pretty quickly that you can't make a good movie with hostile feelings . . . and I didn't blame [Lester] for what had happened at all," the star told *Time Out* magazine in 1981. "Part of the reason that 'Superman II' is such a good movie is due to Lester's enormous skill as a director."

Reeve and girlfriend Gae Exton had recently had a child, and he had successfully bid for a bigger share of the Superman pie the year prior. Reeve pursued his love of aviation, including hang gliding. (Once, he was nearly arrested for flying in restricted airspace.) After finishing work on the sequel, he went on to perform summer stock as a reporter in a revival of *The Front Page*, ignoring the obvious subtext of such a choice. But his long-held worries over typecasting were dialing into sharper focus. At times, when Reeve the aviator radioed in to control towers, technicians would ask if he was using an airplane.

The comments were inane, but the sentiment behind them bothered Reeve considerably. Just as Clark Kent would grow conflicted about his immaculate alter ego, so would Reeve about his.

Warner Bros. shared Ilya Salkind's concern that the delay of the last film had eaten into their profit margin. The studio announced that the sequel would be ready for a summer 1980 release. However, Lester and company didn't finish additional shooting until March of that year, which rendered this schedule impossible.

When the Salkinds first admitted the film wouldn't be ready in time, the studio had tried to exert some pressure on the production. The effort backfired. "They had a date they were supposed to give up *Superman II* and they weren't nearly finished," remembered O'Halloran. "I was in the screening room when Warner told Alex, 'Well, maybe we won't pick up *II*.' And Alex said, 'Does that mean I can bring in other distributors to look at it?' They thought they were being cocky and said, 'Yeah, yeah. No problem.'

"They brought a whole bunch of people into the screening room. Alex had already shot the fight over New York City, and when we put that up on screen, they couldn't get the bands off their money fast enough. He played them like a fiddle."

Humbled, Warner's Terry Semel devised a strategy with the Salkinds that proved to be a total anomaly in American filmmaking. The studio would hold the film for release in the States until summer 1981. Before that, it would screen the film on a staggered schedule throughout the rest of the world, opening during the season in which each country's film attendance was highest.

The plan put money into the Salkinds' pockets quickly, a boon to their credit-heavy ledgers. Despite the windfall that had accompanied the first release, their staggering $70 million debt to Swiss banks was still accruing. So instrumental was Franz Afman, a Rotterdam banker, in helping to fund the sequel that he garnered a credit on the film. (The investor kept a watchful eye on the production, making a futile effort to keep it on schedule.) Later, money maven Howard Schuster would declare himself so "burnt out" by *Superman II* that he withdrew funding from Francis Ford Coppola's slate of projects.

The release scheme had one pitfall: by opening the picture everywhere but in America, the studio ran the risk that either early word would leak out that the film was not very good or its "money" sequences would be spoiled. Cast and crew were under strict orders not to discuss the film with American journalists. In today's Internet age, foreign fans would have exhaustively detailed every frame months before the film's U.S. release. But in the early 1980s, the ploy largely worked, though some bootleg tapes still made it to New York street corners.

Lester and Ilya Salkind had reenlisted John Williams to score the finished print. After a few minutes in the screening room with the director, Williams marched out and told Salkind that he "could not get along with this man." Composer Ken Thorne was enlisted to pay homage to Williams's title theme.

As Warner prepped for the sequel's release, it began to grow nervous about a TV network's attempt to piggyback on the popularity of the title character. ABC's *Greatest American Hero* debuted in the fall of 1980; William Katt starred as an average Joe who stumbles upon a costume that grants him powers similar to Superman's. The program, which was a mild success for the network, was good-natured in its narrative and not substantially derivative of DC's mainstay. Regardless, Warner sued, claiming copyright infringement. The burst of paranoia didn't meet the judge's criteria for a sufficient case, and ABC was granted a motion for dismissal.

Terence Stamp had once estimated that the sequel would be two-thirds Donner's footage, but because script changes necessitated reshoots, the film would be split nearly evenly between the two directors. Warner Bros. appealed to the Directors Guild to assign the appropriate cocredit, but they weren't receptive. Neither was Donner. When Lester phoned him to ask if he would want his name to appear, he declined, saying, "I don't share credit." Lester had earlier spoken of leaving his own name off the film entirely, figuring that Donner had done most of the important legwork. His name would wind up being the sole director billing on the film.

Superman II was released in the United States in June 1981. In a sign of Hollywood's new summer strategy and audiences' voracious appetite for "event" films, the prints appeared in more than fourteen hundred theaters, nearly triple the net cast by the first installment. The studio had doubled its marketing budget to $17 million, hammering consumers with TV, print, and radio ads, all promising the kind of slam-bang action found in comics panels. Pressured by the media onslaught and enthused by their enjoyment of the first outing, Americans paid out $24 million in first-week ticket sales, shattering existing box office records. By comparison, the prior year's *Star Wars* sequel had netted only $10 million in the same time frame.

In total, the addendum to the myth grossed $108 million in its domestic theatrical run. For the year, it trailed only the Spielberg/Lucas juggernaut *Raiders of the Lost Ark*.

An effusive Ilya Salkind greeted press with news that, like *Star Wars*, *Superman* could continue on for four, six, perhaps eight films. Even the Dickensian misers in Warner's accounting department felt the euphoria: they upped Siegel's and Shuster's annual pension to $30,000.

Superman II did exceptionally well in the home video market. In 1982, only 4 percent of homes owned VCRs, and both Warner and Disney forced retailers to lease their titles; renters would have to pay up to $7.50 a night. The prohibitive fees led a growing number of people to pay for cable channels like HBO, which paid $10 million for the rights to broadcast *II*.

The sequel's success further inflamed studio interest in pillaging the comics industry for material; most attempts—like the woefully morbid *Swamp Thing*—couldn't conjure up even one-tenth of the business. *Batman* was still mired in development hell at Warner, the brass refusing to be sold on Mankiewicz's take. Disney decided to invert the process, developing a film titled *Condorman* and then adapting it into a comic strip. By the time consumers latched onto the comics series, the movie would be ready for release. Unfortunately, readers had little affection for the prepackaged tripe. Both the comic and the film suffocated.

Universal's *Conan the Barbarian* fared far better, taking a grim approach that mirrored Conan creator Robert E. Howard's dank prose and utilized Arnold Schwarzenegger's limited emotive abilities to personify the growling barbarian. Successful monosyllabic heroes were the exception rather than the rule; *Greystoke*, which took a stern approach to the Tarzan mythos, bombed.

———

Despite the patchwork construction, *Superman II* is arguably better entertainment than its predecessor. No longer tethered by the requisite origin story, which took up a hefty portion of the original, the sequel is free to explore the sheer visceral kick of being a nigh-invulnerable hero.

In *Star Wars*, the laconic Han Solo is the audience's avatar, escorting them into a strange world buzzing with the Force and sharing their jaded attitude toward the near-religious mysticism. Superman's first outing has no such point of connection, save for Lois's hyper reactions.

In the redux, it is Kent himself who experiences life outside his physical armor. Stripped of his power because of his need to be with Lois, he's throttled by a redneck in a diner. Reeve stares at his blood with incredulity, painfully aware of how fragile the life of his adopted race can be.

Reclaiming his powers, Superman meets his adversaries on the London-filmed streets of New York, tossing buses and manhole covers with all the ease of a Frisbee. The sequence is the film's crown jewel, a frantic, epic battle that leaves the city in rubble. It's the kind of Grand Guignol display that Luthor's mortality made implausible in the first film. Here, Terence Stamp's Zod is just as swollen with contempt for the Boy Scout as Hackman's original antagonist, but instead of contriving technological threats, he's free to trade punches.

With much of Donner's framework still standing, Lester had little room to maneuver. But several sequences seem infused with his penchant for slapstick humor, most of it in the vein of what had been excised from the earlier Newman/Benton drafts. Bystanders in the New York sequence, despite being threatened with severe bodily harm from General Zod and his crew, still find time to clown: one insists on remaining on a pay phone despite the gust of wind that blows him across the sidewalk; another gets ice cream launched in his face.

The comedy is off-putting, but Reeve refuses to be anything less than the stoic symbol of justice his uniform demands. He's never caught winking at the audience—at least not until he does so literally at the denouement, a smashing of the fourth wall that appears well earned. A scene in which Clark is fraught with anxiety over sharing his secret with Lois shows Reeve at his most capable. His split-second transformation into Superman—his posture suddenly rigid, his voice octaves lower, his expression stern—is a wonder. (Warner, in fact, considered petitioning Reeve for a Best Actor nod. No matter his talent, the Academy was not likely to ever take a genre performance seriously.)

Critics, normally overtly repulsed by the crass commercialism of sequels, found much to like. They declared the franchise to be worthy of consumer dollars and expressed praise for Lester's seamless efforts to reconcile his sensibilities with Donner's.

Mankiewicz took perverse delight in scolding *New York* magazine critic David Denby, who sniffed that Lester was the better director. Under the replacement's guidance, Hackman was given more to do, Denby huffed, his scenes blessed with far more sophistication. The writer dashed off a letter to Denby, politely pointing out that Hackman had shot all of his scenes with Donner and had never once set foot on set with Lester at the helm, so the critique was ignorant. The magazine never printed a correction.

Aside from Denby's inaccurate nod, Lester himself received little credit for the crafting of the sequel. To the genre fans that devoured the incendiary press on the tortured production, he was a villain on the level of Luthor, a hired gun who possessed little trace of Donner's enthusiasm for the material. (Quickly forgotten is Donner's apathy toward the project until the Salkinds dangled a seven-figure check in front of him.) It's an idea that's only grown with the advent of exhaustively detailed Web sites devoted to analyzing the *Superman* films like the Zapruder footage.

Lester was, in all reality, the co-orchestrator for arguably the best *Superman* feature to date. Some of the more inspired ideas from the original film shoot—shuffling big set pieces, economizing crew operations—were Lester's. If Donner created the template for the hero on-screen, Lester is guilty only of abiding by it, much in the same way comic book writers and artists play on the canvas created by Siegel and Shuster. Lester's facility for the material would be rewarded with an offer for another sequel, though the result would be far less appreciated.

Reeve, who said repeatedly that he would only do a *Superman III* if it met the same standards he felt Donner had set on the first two films, engaged himself in a role that would've undoubtedly strained the morality clause of his now-expired contract. As the second lead in *Deathtrap*, he played the double-crossing lover of Michael Caine's playwright; the two share an on-screen kiss. The film died on the vine, but inspired the requisite jokes about Superman's sexual proclivities.

Kidder went on a near frenzy of activity, performing in seven films between *Superman II* and its inevitable sequel. None resonated with audiences.

———

Donner had resigned himself to his exile from *Superman II*. Though he was puzzled by some of the more pointless changes—like the gloomy opening sequence in Paris—at least the character had not been completely prostituted. (That would come later.) Donner was irked, however, that Lester had never phoned him before agreeing to work on the film.

Mankiewicz professed his admiration for Lester but expressed disappointment with the "humorless" nature of some of the new director's contributions. "In *Superman II*, the villains kill a small boy on a truck or something," Mankiewicz recalled. "I thought, 'God this is *so* not what Superman is.'" The Christ metaphor the screenwriter had played with during the first film had been all but erased; whether the sometimes-suffocating allegory was missed depends on the viewer.

After leaving superhero spectacle behind, Donner performed a complete 180, choosing to direct a character study titled *Inside Moves*, starring John Savage. Though a worthwhile effort, it was barely noticed. Better left ignored was his 1982 effort *The Toy*, which starred Richard Pryor as an out-of-work reporter who reluctantly agrees to become the live-in playmate for fat cat Jackie Gleason's spoiled child. The slavery subtext was lost on few people; it nonetheless performed admirably, earning $50 million during its run. Donner would go on to become one of the studio's most profitable directors, chairing the *Lethal Weapon* saga and several other Mel Gibson vehicles; his offices have remained at Warner for over twenty years.

Donner never again went behind the cameras of the Superman franchise, though two projects in the new millennium inspired him to revisit the character. In 2001, fans who had long desired to see the director's original vision of *Superman II* in totality began exchanging Donner-directed footage culled from international TV broadcasts, which the Salkinds had padded to bring in more revenue. Their collective efforts resulted in a bootleg DVD that was circulated online—at no cost—featuring a rough approximation of what Donner's edit may have looked like. The effort took two years and many thousands of dollars, a substantial testament to the esteem in which fans held Donner and his work.

Warner Bros., aghast at the guerrilla tactics, threatened legal action. But the enterprise had its intended effect: in 2006, under pressure from both fandom and director Bryan Singer, Warner released a "Donner cut" of the sequel, which restored scenes he had shot and even made use of audition footage for the "Lois shoots Clark" scene. Most impressive, after Warner settled with Marlon Brando's estate for an undisclosed sum of money, Jor-El's role was restored.

"In the high-tech revolution, I'm driving in the slow lane," said Mankiewicz. "But apparently, there were such bloggers and so on that heard about this scene, that scene. Dick, I must say, always wanted to put his version together, but he wasn't maniacal about it. An editor named Michael Thau called me up one day and said, 'Help. We need you. We're recutting *II*.'" Donner and Mankiewicz sat in on the editing sessions, offering intermittent input. Neither received any compensation for the revised work.

Superman II: The Richard Donner Cut is neither a better nor a worse film than its first incarnation. Lester's labored slapstick has been all but excised, and Brando's presence certainly elevates the melodrama surrounding Clark's conflict over becoming "human." But incorporating the unpolished audition footage is jarring; ultimately, the edit is simply a curiosity.

In late 2006, Donner reunited with his former personal assistant Geoff Johns, now a scribe for the Superman comic books. The director agreed to assist in plotting an arc based on loose story threads that he had informally toyed with for a possible *Superman III*. Free from the machinations of the Salkinds, Donner and Johns produced *Action Comics* #844, the inaugural issue of a four-part arc.

The four-color equivalent of stunt casting worked; the issue sold out quickly and went to additional printings. In it, Superman consoles a small child who is alleged to be another survivor from Krypton. Donner, no longer held to budgetary caps, was free to tell artists exactly what he wanted.

The closing credits of *Superman II* promised that the second sequel would be "coming soon." The tease was presumptuous, as Reeve was now a free agent. Nonetheless, Ilya Salkind began plotting a story that would feature a litany of Superman's supporting characters, including brilliant automaton Brainiac and perhaps even Kal-El's cousin, Supergirl. (The Kryptonian villains of *Superman II* had spoiled their chances for an encore by apparently plunging to their deaths in the Fortress of Solitude. Scenes had been filmed—but not incorporated—of them being arrested instead.)

The film would marry some of the more fantastic science fiction concepts with Reeve's grounded performance. On paper, it was a rousing finale, with audiences finally submerged in the totality of Superman lore.

And had Richard Pryor not been booked on the *Tonight Show* one night in 1982, it may very well have happened.

Pryor Motives

For a piece of shit, it smells great.
—Richard Pryor on *Superman III*

Just as they had done for several consecutive years in the 1970s, the Salkinds buzzed the 1981 Cannes Film Festival with a huge banner, this time announcing *Superman III*. The first sequel had already rung up hefty profits in overseas territories, making the prospect of a trilogy a nearly foregone conclusion.

If Christopher Reeve was happier leaving the series as a two-part saga, a $2 million paycheck went a long way toward persuading him to hit the gym once again. Who he would be training to oppose was another concern, and one that would eventually prove to be the first of several death knells for a seemingly indestructible character.

———

Were DC's top two superheroes to compare attributes, Batman might eventually concede that his sometimes-rival Superman could crush him into a fine paste of bone and flesh. Romantically, Superman's decades-long courtship with the personable Lois Lane would seem to best Bruce Wayne's predilection either for cheap arm candy (to better promote the idea of his being a lazy-brained playboy) or, worse, the kind of woman who might be as likely to kill him as kiss him (e.g., Catwoman).

The lone area where Batman can brag of clear superiority is in his rogue's gallery. The Dark Knight boasts some of the most eclectic and formidable villains in the history of fiction—adversaries who have kept him properly motivated through decades of comics narratives, years of TV series, and five feature films. Joker, Penguin, Two-Face, Riddler . . . all conspire with alarming purpose to challenge Batman's patience and mortal mettle.

Superman, in contrast, has never fared terribly well in the archrival department. The blame lies partially in his sheer indestructibility: a common hood isn't going to offer any substantial problems beyond deciding which police precinct he can be most conveniently dropped into. Lex Luthor presents the greater challenge of a cunning intellect; comics writers often supplemented his smarts with body armor, all the better to confront his metahuman nemesis. Brainiac, a sentient robot that assimilates—then destroys—civilizations, shares Luthor's penchant for trying to outsmart the blue lummox. And Darkseid, the ruler of the planet Apokolips, has tried to skewer the Man of Steel on multiple occasions. But after the potential of these three foes has been exhausted, things begin to look grim in the ranks of the opposition.

Many of Superman's notable adversaries were cultivated under the influence of the acid-trip mentality of the 1950s and 1960s: Mr. Mxyzptlk is an imp who can only be returned to his own dimension by forcing him to say his name backward; Prankster and Toyman occupy much the same space as Batman's Riddler, with little to offer beyond elaborate accessories; Bizarro is an imperfect duplicate of Superman who doesn't possess the intellect to handle his powers responsibly. Such villains didn't provide the sorts of ready-made conflicts that Superman's cinematic caretakers could easily mine.

"Frankly, I was getting to a point where it was just one more *Superman*," Ilya Salkind recalled. "Sequels are great, but I wanted to do something different." To reinvigorate the franchise, Salkind imagined a science fiction opus. Brainiac would seize control of Superman's psyche, splitting his personality into a good half and an evil half. For good measure, Salkind introduced Mxyzptlk and Supergirl, the latter of whom could be conveniently spun off into her own film series.

Salkind turned in his treatment to Warner, who by now had exclusive rights to distribute (or refuse to distribute) the film. With their swollen influence, they dismissed the narrative as "too sci-fi," too deeply embedded in Superman lore. Luthor had been easily depicted in live action, but the studio felt that inserting Brainiac and Mxyzptlk was pandering to comics devotees and would require too much exposition for casual audience members. Salkind's ambitions were scrapped.

Not long after, Richard Pryor appeared alongside Johnny Carson on *The Tonight Show*. The forty-two-year-old performer had starred with Gene Wilder in *Stir Crazy*, a 1980 comedy smash. By most accounts, he was the most popular comedian in the United States. Pryor raved about the *Superman* screen saga, acting out scenes with all the enthusiasm of an ardent fan. Earlier, he had told *Variety* that he would love a role in a *Superman* movie.

Pryor's campaign, whether calculated or not, did not go unnoticed by producers. David and Leslie Newman had caught his Carson appearance, and they consulted with Ilya Salkind. Warner felt that the addition of another major star would lift any sagging interest in the character. Box office rewards would be doubled: some people would come for Superman, others for Pryor. On the surface, it seemed to be good business.

All parties agreed: Pryor would receive $4 million for a costarring role in what was dubbed *Superman vs. Superman*—double Reeve's salary. Reeve had grown accustomed to supporting actors filling their pockets with more rapidity than he filled his own, so he accepted the lopsided compensation with good humor, conceding that Pryor had been around longer and had proved himself a draw.

Pryor's casting was at odds with Salkind's perpetual edict that any and all performers involved with his Superman property be relatively free from controversial circumstances. Marc McClure, who portrayed Jimmy Olsen in all of the Reeve pictures, once referenced a "morality clause" in his contract that prevented him from appearing in lurid motion pictures or engaging in questionable public behavior. (The latter mandate would eventually get one Salkind-endorsed Superman released from his duties.)

Pryor, however, was hardly an avatar for clean living. The comedian had self-destructed in spectacular fashion in 1980 when he set himself

Left to right: executive producer Ilya Salkind, director Richard Lester, and producer Pierre Spengler on the set of 1983's *Superman III*. Some charged Lester with injecting too much slapstick comedy into the mythology.

(Everett Collection)

ablaze while freebasing cocaine; the drug had apparently compelled him to douse himself with rum and then light a match. Though his handlers initially deemed it an accident, Pryor later confirmed he had tried to kill himself. The spectacle was diluted when the comedian made light of the incident in his stand-up routine, eliciting some degree of sympathy from his audience.

Richard Lester was once again offered directorial duties; his participation in the franchise went back to 1977, and he had done a commendable job batting cleanup for Donner on the first sequel. The monetary compensation would be considerable, but Lester was hesitant. His wife admonished him, pushing the idea that it would be easy money. Lester, perhaps recalling the dry spell that had preceded his work on *Musketeers* in the early 1970s, finally succumbed.

"It was his 'fuck you' money," friend James Garrett would go on to label his *Superman* earnings. Many who knew Lester couldn't shake the feeling that he was orchestrating big blockbuster films with something approaching contempt. Earlier, Lester had tried to coerce Warner into backing some of his smaller projects. But films that he had done between the *Supermans*—*Cuba* and a prequel to *Butch Cassidy and the Sundance Kid* sans Newman and Redford—were critically and commercially reviled. He was now a studio's hired gun, and if they were going to pay him handsomely for the opportunity, so be it.

While Brainiac had been excised from Salkind's treatment, Lester was still intrigued by the idea of an artificial intelligence wreaking havoc on the populace. He wanted to include a kind of social commentary on the growing use of computers, giving his project a contemporary anchor. Working with the Newmans, he devised a story that featured Pryor as a meek computer programmer who is enlisted by a billionaire psychopath to help develop a sentient piece of hardware. Pryor's Gus Gorman is a reluctant villain, interested in a fast buck but hardly capable of anything truly sinister.

If Lester had been able to exercise his comedic sensibility only sporadically in the first sequel, he intended to make up for lost time. The tone of *Superman vs. Superman* would be far lighter than its predecessors, a fact that would be obvious from the opening reel. Lester took great delight in choreographing an elaborate opening set piece that had the denizens of Metropolis avoiding calamities as if trapped inside a Rube Goldberg device.

The Salkinds, who finally settled their lawsuits with Brando and Puzo in 1982—the two split a $10 million slice of the profit pie on top of their previous compensation—had all the star power they needed in Pryor. For the role of the scheming billionaire Ross Webster, they approached Alan Alda, who wasn't interested. Eventually, Robert Vaughn would sign on. The character was a clear attempt to fill the void left by Gene Hackman, who refused any further working relationship with the Salkinds after the Donner fiasco. The actor was also in a kind of self-imposed exile, appearing only in a handful of films during the early 1980s.

Placing Superman's inevitable love interest was less cut and dried. Margot Kidder had anticipated a $1.5 million payday for a second sequel, citing prior promises and her tenure as Clark's companion. Unfortunately, the Salkinds weren't quick to forgive her rants to the press. Publicly, they bleated that Lois and Clark's relationship had gone as far as it could go; privately, they were still seething about the verbal attacks. Kidder's role—and paycheck—was reduced to virtually nothing in the script. Lois would appear only in bookend scenes to wave good-bye and hello to Kent.

The actor was unrepentant in interviews, telling *People* in 1981 that "if I think someone is an amoral asshole I say so." She maintained that the Salkinds had the ability to repossess her car. Reeve, caught between the two warring factions, tried to be diplomatic: "If Margot does not play Lois, I hope it's for a damn good creative reason and not some political nonsense."

Eventually, Kidder made peace with the decision—she was fond of saying, "I could play [Lois] till I die, but I'm not going to die if I don't play her"—and went about the business of restructuring her personal life. Now twice divorced, she went on a self-professed "health kick," swearing off all pharmaceuticals. In 1982, she costarred with Pryor in *Some Kind of Hero*, a Vietnam vet drama; audiences, who didn't care to see Pryor emoting, passed. During filming, Kidder ended a six-month affair with Pryor when she caught him cheating. In a bid for closure, she cut his Armani wardrobe to shreds with a pair of scissors.

While scripting *Superman III*, the Newmans struck upon the idea of sending Clark back to Smallville for his high school reunion. The field trip seemed like a perfect opportunity to introduce Lana Lang, Clark's adolescent flame from his days on the farm in Smallville. Lang had only been portrayed on-screen twice before—by Bunny Henning in the failed *Superboy* pilot, then again by Diane Sherry in a brief *Superman: The Movie* sequence—so the character had no prior purchase on the public consciousness. She seemed a perfect substitute for the irksome Kidder.

The Newmans wrote Lang with Annette O'Toole in mind, having seen her onstage in San Diego during a performance of *Yankee Wives*. The thirty-year-old redhead was a professed comics fan, and she remembered the aggressive Lang from her pencil-and-ink incarnation. Despite O'Toole's recent engagement, she agreed to physically separate from her fiancé for the three-month shoot. (She later expressed disappointment that Lang never flew around with Superman.)

The final shooting script retained another aspect of Ilya Salkind's original treatment. In between opposing Vaughn's Ross Webster and putting up with the antics of Pryor's hyper Gorman, the superhero would be forced to face off against his own alter ego. The Newmans had long thought of Superman's "schizoid" nature as the primary component of his appeal, and they developed the metaphor into an actual physical confrontation between a meek Clark Kent and a growling Man of Steel. The battle seems inspired by the Newmans' frustration in identifying a new adversary—when all else fails, have the Boy Scout face off against himself.

Close with the Newmans, Reeve—who by now had script and director approval on the series—harangued them for a copy of the screenplay. When it was finally delivered, Reeve was entranced by the manifestation of Superman's internal struggle. He made a formal commitment to the project, though he was wary that the film seemed to lack some of the warmth of his earlier adventures. Despite the absence of any comics-spun story threads, DC enlisted one of its writers, Cary Bates, to help consult on the film. Bates, who hit it off with Ilya Salkind, also adapted the Newmans' screenplay into a DC comics offering.

Filming for the $35 million *Superman III* began in August 1982 in Calgary, Alberta, Canada. Test groups had declared a preference for titles with numerals, prompting producers to drop the intriguing *Superman vs. Superman* designation, which also spoiled its showcase sequence. The film was slotted for a summer 1983 release, conveniently coinciding with the character's forty-fifth anniversary.

Both the Newmans and Lester had expected the chatty Pryor to veer from his character's dialogue, but the performer largely stuck to the script, riffing only when producers decided to omit a large-scale sequence of Superman saving a coffee crop from a storm. Instead, Pryor described the sequence in pantomime.

Most days, the actor was affable and agreeable to Lester's suggestions. Sometimes, however, he appeared on set moody and disgruntled. Whether the changes in attitude were attributable to drug consumption is unclear, though Pryor was known to have been using crack at the time. Once, in a cruel end run around Pryor's fear of heights, the crew hoisted him up sixty feet in the air without any warning. At another point, perhaps fueled by resentment for their methods, Pryor made rude comments toward the camera operator, who lunged for him and had to be held back.

Reeve, who could practically perform the role in his sleep by now, had re-added thirty pounds to his lanky frame by the time shooting began. He looked forward to incorporating two new wrinkles into his performance. First, fearing audiences would grow impatient with the bumbling reporter of the first films, he would portray Clark Kent as slightly more self-assured this time around. More significantly, Superman's scowling doppelganger would give Reeve a chance to inject a menacing presence into what had been a perpetually bright character.

The variations on a theme were welcome, but Reeve still had reservations about what his career would resemble once he hung up the cape for good. The fears were alleviated briefly when he sat down to the craft services table in full Superman regalia next to Sir John Gielgud, who had business on a neighboring production.

After exchanging greetings, Gielgud looked him over and said, "So, dear boy, what have you been up to these days?"

Back on the set, Lester had been giving Pryor free reign over scenes, letting him dominate the proceedings. In reviewing footage in the editing room, he felt he might have been too generous with the coverage. Lester docked Pryor a minute or so from each of his on-screen appearances.

Warner countermanded his decision. More Pryor meant more money, the studio said. At its urging, the director reinserted his cut moments. (Lester could have taken consolation in the fact that the trims would have inevitably seen the light of day anyway, when the Salkinds made their now-traditional expansion of the running time to increase profits on the film's television broadcasts.) In the end, Pryor's character appeared almost as often as Superman, and twice as often as the humble Kent. The studio was sated; this would be as much Pryor's vehicle as the Man of Steel's, a fact that would go on to rankle fans.

Salkind would eventually agree with the criticism, noting that "there were mistakes that were made that today I can see. When you're shooting a picture, you end up losing perspective, because there are so many things going on. There were moments where Superman was standing still behind Pryor when he does his 'Patton' speech. That shouldn't happen. You can't have a superhero not in movement."

Reeve watched as the film unfolded; with each passing month on set, he began to grow more uneasy at the prospect of sacrificing the character's prominence to Pryor's frantic persona. He missed Donner's allegiance to verisimilitude, the devotion and respect he had for the mythology. Lester's penchant for slapstick humor was no longer tempered by the blueprint Donner had set in place; with Lester in full control, the haphazard physical comedy was coming to the fore. Sandwiched between the loopy comedy was Superman, whose straitlaced presence seemed ungainly and out of place.

Distressed, Reeve took to racing sailplanes during breaks in shooting, a hobby that undoubtedly caused flop sweat to form on the foreheads of insurance representatives.

Free from any of the scheduling fiascoes that had plagued the earlier entries, *Superman III* was released in June 1983. Inhaling $13 million its opening weekend, it ranked second in Warner's all-time best openings, behind *Superman II*. As Reeve had feared, audiences were divided on the jarring presence of Pryor, who seemed to be acting in a different film altogether.

Despite the strong bow, the picture steadily lost business as word began to spread that the tone of the work was as conflicted as Superman himself. It wound up grossing just under $60 million, roughly a 50 percent drop from the previous films. The failure could not simply be attributed to the law of diminishing returns; the third *Star Wars* film, *Return of the Jedi*, did five times the business of the Reeve vehicle.

The timing of the franchise's wheezing could not have been worse: the studio badly needed profits that mirrored the takes of the first two films. In the third quarter of 1983, Warner lost $180 million via its Atari subsidiary. The leading video game developer had taken a massive bath with its tie-in game to *E.T. the Extra-Terrestrial*, paying millions for the rights only to rush out a badly conceived product. As word spread, millions of the cartridges went unsold.

At *Superman III*'s New York premiere, Lester and Reeve approached Warner executives, shaking hands and exchanging pleasantries. (Alex Salkind also showed, having sailed in from London on the *QE2*.) Lester informed them this was his swan song for the franchise; more distressing, Reeve concurred, telling brass that the character's limits had been exhausted. He "guaranteed" *Omni* magazine that he would refrain from reprising the role again, citing satisfaction with the series as a trilogy. At other times, he said he believed that any more installments would test the audience's patience with the character. The Bond movies, the principal actor of which Reeve used as a model for his own career, had become tiresome, he thought. This was the end.

If the parting was bittersweet for Reeve, it was simply a formality for Lester. The director had supervised the character over a film and a half, conforming to company mandates and gritting his teeth through a story that struck him as organized nonsense. As per a verbal agreement, Warner backed his *Finders Keepers*, a frenetic find-the-lost-fortune comedy that the studio dumped on CBS Theatrical Films before finally agreeing to distribute.

Thanks in part to complications from a virulent strain of hepatitis A, it would be five years before Lester directed another picture, *The Return of the Musketeers*, a sequel to his and the Salkinds' earlier successes. Pierre Spengler had pitched his own production tent away from his friend Ilya Salkind, and it was he who enticed Lester into a *Musketeers* encore by describing it as a kind of class reunion for the principal cast. Audiences, however, didn't care about the adventurers' exploits decades after their expiration date.

The film's shooting was marred by numerous accidents and injuries to the cast, primarily where horses were concerned. Actor Roy Kinnear's mare took off, broke abruptly, and threw Kinnear to the ground. He died the following day from internal hemorrhaging.

A devastated Lester would direct only one other film—Paul McCartney's 1991 concert *Get Back*—before effectively retiring from the business. He could no longer find the nerve to be responsible for performers and their well-being.

Undeterred by the absence of even their headlining talent, the Salkinds insisted a *Superman IV* was inevitable. If Reeve could be made to change his mind, so be it. If not, well . . . how many Bonds had there been?

———

Superman III is largely Lester Unchained, a jarring blend of Reeve's iconic presence and Pryor's pratfalls. The film's opening sequence sets the tone, an elaborate slapstick dance that would likely be applauded in another film. In the mythology of a stern comic book hero, though, it's the celluloid equivalent of a sore thumb. Subsequent scenes give little regard to basic human physiology—Pryor skis down a high-rise building, landing on the concrete hundreds of feet below with nary a whimper—and regard

Superman as more a circus performer than a righteous power. (He crushes a diamond from coal, a parlor trick courtesy of the comics.)

The absence of Hackman and Kidder, two seeming institutions of the franchise, isn't as sacrilegious as fans may have dreaded; unfortunately, neither one was discarded for anything better. Vaughn's slick Ross Webster pales in comparison to Luthor, stripped of any real motivations for his deeds; O'Toole's Lana Lang is pleasant enough, but bereft of Kidder's manic energy.

Critics were far less inclined to rave about the third outing, crowing that the film looked "cheap" and its narrative "mean-spirited." "Shallow, silly, filled with stunts . . . without much human interest," summed up Roger Ebert. Most agreed that Pryor's comedic talents were misplaced. The caretakers of the franchise eventually seemed to agree, as the 2006 DVD reissue of the film deletes Pryor's name and visage from the marketing materials.

Reeve, as always, appears not to be in on the joke. The film's key sequence, in which the villains' synthesized Kryptonite splits Clark and Superman into two separate personas, is actually a series highlight. His pseudo-Bizarro Superman is badly in need of a shave; he sneers at admirers and slams shots in a bar. He ignores the frightened pleas of witnesses to a bridge accident, preferring to work his game on an aghast Lana Lang. During a particularly nasty streak, he goes on an international tear, straightening the Leaning Tower of Pisa and blowing out the Olympic torch. This is Superman's id in full, devastating effect: the demigod as petulant man-child.

The routine is largely a guilty pleasure, but succeeds thanks to Reeve's commitment. It's fitting that this was the first film in the *Superman* canon in which Reeve received top billing. (Previously, he had had to defer to Hackman and Brando.) It's the actor's deft touch that keeps the second sequel from being a compete abomination.

For the shoddy finale, the film offers up a menacing supercomputer, seemingly as a way to introduce the base concept of Brainiac without addressing that character's brooding apathy toward the human race. Things barely improved when the Salkinds restored fifteen minutes of footage for network TV broadcasts.

In truth, *Superman III* is no more offensive than the character's glee-fully kitschy comic book adventures of the 1950s, crammed as they were with various types of Kryptonite, an expanded family tree, and revisionist history.

But the comics never had to worry about opticals, and the effects work is clearly inferior to prior entries. With Reeve's support, Lester had abandoned the Zoptic system, preferring to leave the camera stationary while people bob and weave through the air. The results pale in comparison to the quality effects Donner had insisted upon (he once threw out six months' worth of visual trickery when it didn't meet his standards). Upon the film's eventual DVD release, fans razzed producers when the clarity of the medium revealed poorly concealed wires. Other flying sequences contain footage repurposed from the first film.

If this was indeed Reeve's swan song for the character, it was an ill-fitting climax to what had been the actor's honest effort to embody an icon.

Eventually, Ilya Salkind would grow cool toward the idea of recasting the title role, perhaps recognizing the difficulty level inherent in making a flying man in blue spandex believable. It was a task uniquely suited to Reeve's abilities. "After *Superman III*, I said to my father, I don't want to do part four," Salkind recalled. "That's it. For me, I was dried up. I didn't see what else we could do. And the Newmans said they didn't want to do it, but that was irrelevant, because frankly we would've found other people. I just didn't want to do another *Superman*. The third was good enough; that's it."

Except that wasn't it. With Salkind unable to coerce Reeve into an encore, he became increasingly more interested in the library of supporting characters that had appeared in *Superman* comics over the decades.

If another star might be required, thought Salkind, so might another gender.

Girl Power

Jeannot and I fought for Helen Slater; Alex fought for Brooke Shields.
Sometimes it's better to lose.
—Ilya Salkind

Unlike her more renowned cousin, Supergirl did not originate in the imaginations of Jerry Siegel and Joe Shuster. The somewhat dubious honor of creating the female heroine goes to Otto Binder and Al Plastino, two DC (then National) employees who spirited her up in 1959.

Porting over Superman's powers to the opposite sex was nothing new. Lois had sometimes been granted otherworldly abilities, and even Superboy once suffered the indignity of being emasculated when an alien transformed him into "Claire Kent." In *Superman* #123, mischievous Jimmy Olsen fools with black magic to conjure up a Girl of Steel to accompany Superman. (True to character, Olsen doesn't bother to solicit Superman's approval before mucking with the dark arts.)

This proto-Supergirl proved popular enough with audiences that DC rolled out the real thing just a year later, proffering the revisionist idea that an entire city had survived the explosion of Krypton. Kara Zor-El is its last surviving inhabitant, and she, too, is jettisoned to Earth in the hopes she can thrive in another culture.

DC's motivation was simple enough. Aside from Wonder Woman, young women had little in the way of populist icons to cheer for. The new character was intended to stir interest among that demographic, but DC made little headway. Supergirl lingered on the fringes of Superman's adventures; when she received her own title in 1972, it lasted a scant two years. Playing to women in the male-dominated genre of fantasy and science fiction, it seemed, was virtually begging for failure.

The inevitability of that result was apparently lost on Ilya Salkind, who decided—after 1983's anemic *Superman III*—that his profitable franchise was in need of gender reassignment surgery.

"I said to my father, okay, let's do *Supergirl*," he recalled. "It's something different, to an extent. I thought it was a very interesting area to explore."

Salkind had licensed Superman's mythology wholesale; if a character was even peripherally involved with the Man of Steel's narrative, he—or she—was fair game. To his thinking, the adaptation would provide crucial resuscitation to an exhausted saga. Already, Christopher Reeve had sworn off any further flying. His trilogy, capped by the disappointing returns of the Pryor vehicle, was enough. But *Supergirl* represented a chance to begin—as the comics industry so dearly loved to do—with a fresh canvas.

Cognizant of the audience's perpetual apprehension about on-screen musical chairs, Salkind asked Reeve to make a brief appearance in the new film, the better to ease fans into the altered continuity. Reeve made a verbal agreement to do so, but it felt like a hollow promise. He was emotionally disconnected from the character and couldn't believe he was being coerced into returning for a fourth time. That uncertainty would only grow as pre-production dragged on.

As with *Superman III*, Salkind was determined to breathe life into Superman's rogue's gallery. He phoned *Star Wars* producer Gary Kurtz, who had worked with screenwriter David Odell on Disney's *The Dark*

Crystal, to inquire about the writer. Odell joined the production and set to work on a screenplay that, per Ilya's mandate, would include an appearance by ruthless android Brainiac and emphasize cosmic vistas over the grittier, street-based fight scenes of the Reeve films. Multiple planets would be involved, making *Supergirl* one of the more expansive entries in the franchise to date.

While Odell labored, Salkind pondered his choices for the director's chair. Lester had had his fill of the franchise; Robert Wise was approached, but the *Sound of Music* director declined. During a conversation with Reeve, Jeannot Szwarc's name had been mentioned. The French director had worked with Reeve on *Somewhere in Time*, and the actor endorsed Szwarc as a capable orchestrator of fantasy.

Infamously, in 1977 Szwarc had taken over *Jaws 2* from John Hancock a month into shooting. While the end result was seen as cinematic prostitution, Szwarc garnered respect for handling an awkward shoot. It was an ironic contrast to the dismal response to his first major feature assignment, the killer-cockroach thriller *Bug*, which had the misfortune of being released the same day as the original *Jaws*.

When he received a call from *Supergirl* producer Tim Burrill, his first instinct was to assume Burrill had dialed the wrong number. "I said, 'I think you made a mistake with me,'" recalled Szwarc. "They offered to take me to London to have meetings. I thought they wanted someone who was better versed in the mythology, but Superman is an international hero. I figured they wanted someone more like Richard Donner, who is an old friend. But Donner didn't want to do it."

Szwarc took the assignment conditionally: he wanted to substitute the might of Superman with the kind of grace of movement expected from a woman. "I said I would be interested if the tack was, instead of strength, it was elegance. It's a girl, after all. And to do something closer to fantasy." Ilya Salkind agreed on all points.

Szwarc immediately peppered his friend Donner with questions, primarily on how to make his protagonist fly with conviction. "I called him to ask about the technical people involved with the film. Roy Field, Derek Meddings, David Lane, that whole gang. He told me they were great."

Szwarc was particularly interested in working with Reeve again, and story conferences resulted in several scenes pairing the two on-screen heroes. "I had great ideas for Reeve. When she first arrives, there was kind of an aerial ballet with the two of them. I used some of those ideas for when she discovers her powers. But originally, there was a sequence where he welcomes her to Earth and they fly together.

"Then there's a scene later where he's trapped somewhere on top of a mountain and he's an old man. She goes and reverses the process." Superman would essentially be the film's MacGuffin, made submissive by magic in order to be saved by the Salkinds' newest moneymaker.

Unfortunately, Reeve was about to renege on his promise to Ilya. "At the last minute, Chris decided he didn't want to do it," Szwarc said. "For personal reasons, and probably because he didn't want to be tagged as Superman for the rest of his life." The truncated schedule for *Supergirl* had initially appealed to Reeve, but in the end, even two more scenes in costume would've been prohibitive to his career after the cape. He apologized to Salkind and stepped away.

The absence prompted Odell to begin revising his script to excise the Reeve portions. Worse, Warner Bros. hadn't changed its mind about the more insider elements of comics lore like Brainiac and demanded they be omitted. In addition, the landscapes Odell had invented would've cost a prohibitive amount of money. While *Supergirl* would remain more fantasy-laden than its predecessors, its setting would be something more affordable.

As with *Superman: The Movie*, Salkind, his director, and casting maven Lynn Stalmaster embarked on crusade to find a proper fit for the cape. Over the three-month search, hundreds of actors were seen; Stalmaster narrowed the field down to sixty. Mirroring his star-conscious edicts from the first film, Alex Salkind was determined to cast a famous figure in the title role. He demanded Brooke Shields; Ilya finally convinced him to go with an unknown.

"We read every young girl you could imagine," Szwarc recalled. "We read in London, in L.A. We even read Demi Moore. Finally, we were in New York and she walked in. That was it. There was a close-up of her face on video, and she was so captivating. She was still in high school, she had done very little, but she really had something."

"She" was nineteen-year-old Helen Slater, a fresh graduate of New York's School of Performing Arts. Having heard of the audition from the high school's drama department chair, she marched in wearing a home-made costume and her own oversized glasses. With nothing to her credit except a series of TV commercials and a single telefilm, 1982's *Amy & the Angel*, Slater nonetheless impressed her potential employers with a poise and maturity beyond her years.

"At that age, we needed someone who would be serious-minded and capable of that kind of commitment," Szwarc said. "She was very bright. It was apparent immediately. We all got a very good feeling about it, her spirit."

Slater was cast and signed to the inevitable three-picture deal, with the inaugural installment paying her $75,000. Days later, she was engaged in a rigorous fitness regimen designed to get her figure in shape and her muscles prepared for the endless hours of wire and harness work to follow. "We had to hurry, because there was a considerable amount of work to do," the director recalled. "She had to train for at least three to four months, general physical training and then all the special stuff she had to practice in order to do the flying.

"We warned everybody, it's going to be a lot of work every day. Even when she wasn't shooting, she had to be training." Slater's coach, Alf Joint, had her doing ninety minutes of weights daily, along with an hour of swimming, to tone her physique.

With Slater toiling in the gym, Szwarc concerned himself with the supporting cast. Ilya Salkind's template of surrounding an unknown with established performers was xeroxed for the new project. Faye Dunaway was cast as Selena, the diabolical sorceress who opposes Supergirl. The choice was particularly amusing given that Dunaway had clashed with the Salkinds over the *Three Musketeers* payment fiasco of the early 1970s. Still,

Actor Helen Slater and the iconic Peter O'Toole appear in Jeannot Szwarc's *Supergirl*. The 1984 film didn't find an audience, which producer Ilya Salkind attributed to audience apathy for female action heroes.

(Everett Collection)

the actor was interested in pursuing a pseudocomedic role in a big-budget affair and had long envied Hackman's scenery chewing in the original. Like Hackman, she would receive billing over the purported star of the film.

Veteran actor Peter O'Toole was offered a considerable sum to portray Zaltar, Kara's Kryptonian tutor. It was obvious that the respected O'Toole, who had been laboring on George Bernard Shaw's *Man and Superman*, was intended to fill the shoes of Marlon Brando. Mia Farrow was cast as Kara's mother.

No Salkind project would be complete without the requisite consideration of an inappropriate performer for pure shock value. In *Supergirl*'s case, it was Dolly Parton, who was intended to play Bianca, Selena's henchwoman; the role eventually went to Brenda Vaccaro. In lieu of Reeve, Salkind established a tenuous connection with the earlier films by enlisting Marc McClure to reprise his role as Jimmy Olsen and casting Maureen Teefy as Lucy Lane, Lois's heretofore unmentioned sister.

As casting wore on, Odell wrote day and night to make the pending start date. Gone were Brainiac, Superman, and the more epic space battles. He had, however, managed to salvage an exploration of the Phantom Zone, the prison for Kryptonian criminals only glimpsed in the earlier installments.

Ilya Salkind had originally wanted to open the film with the explosion of Krypton. Szwarc rebuffed the suggestion. "I said, 'Look, if we do that, it's gonna be exactly like *Superman*,'" the director argued. "I don't think that's gonna work. It's gonna really look like a rip-off, or repetition. I think we have to do something that has some originality. So then we came up with the beginning with the Phantom Zone."

Supergirl's costume went through several permutations before Szwarc settled on the spandex-and-skirt motif. A headband and curled hair were discarded as too distracting. Initially, her "S" was overlaid on the costume, not sewn into it, but DC reps rejected the idea. The end result was faithful to her comics portrayal; the brunette Slater even bleached her hair blond. Weeks spent in the gym had given her a shapely figure, though some artificial enhancement was applied to her bust, the better to entice male filmgoers who might otherwise remain apathetic toward the venture.

Shortly before filming began, Slater consulted with Reeve on the proper protocol for costumed adventurers. As the two strolled through New York City, Reeve commented on a fire blazing across the street.

Here were two of Earth's mightiest, he told Slater, standing there doing nothing.

———

Production on the $30 million *Supergirl* began in the summer of 1983, just as *Superman III* was capping Reeve's participation in the series. The Salkinds had already sold several foreign territories on the film, offsetting a substantial portion of the privately funded budget.

Nearly all of the main-unit shooting took place at London's Pinewood Studios; between the British crew, French director, multiethnic producer, and American star, it was quickly beginning to resemble the United Nations of filmmaking.

Szwarc experienced none of the contentious interactions with Ilya Salkind and Pierre Spengler that Donner had suffered through on *Superman*. It may have helped that Szwarc was a native of France, where Salkind had spent much of his youth. "I got along with Ilya very well. Pierre, too. Ilya was raised in France, and Pierre is French. Ilya is a bit crazy, and I can identify because I'm a bit crazy myself. We got along very well, like a house on fire.

"I saw very little of Alex. He was like the genie with the finances and deals and distribution. I met him a couple of times, but that was it."

The inexperienced Slater didn't seem phased by sharing screen time with someone of Peter O'Toole's caliber. "He was very generous and very kind," said Szwarc. "We were all very protective of her. We gave her a lot of affection, which she deserved and also attracted. She was game. Peter is a very generous actor. She was working hard. That's what he respected. I think we all had the awe when we started, but after that, once we got into it, there was a very good atmosphere."

Despite her reputation for temperamental behavior, Dunaway was never the source of consternation on set. "I had heard stories about her, but as it turned out, we got along fabulously well," the director said. "She adored Vaccaro. They were inseparable and worked very well together."

In sharp contrast to *Superman*'s sordid shoot, *Supergirl*'s schedule went off without any of the franchise's trademark interpersonal drama. Even the weather was gracious. Producers had constructed a ten-acre outdoor set, intended to be a facsimile of Midvale, Illinois. "I needed twenty-one days of good weather on the back lot. The union crew told me, 'Jeannot, you're crazy. There hasn't been twenty-one days of good weather since England existed. But we got all the sun we wanted.'"

Like the creators of *Superman III*, Szwarc declined the Zoptic system, preferring to rely on the expertise of Derek Meddings to make sure Supergirl flew convincingly. "Meddings was a genius," the director said. "We were very well surrounded. The flying was different from what they had done before. I wanted more in-frame exits. When Sidney Furie did *Superman IV*, he called Dick Donner, and Donner said, 'Talk to Jeannot.' They felt the flying in *Supergirl* really looked terrific."

Szwarc had only minor experience with on-set special effects. He had been responsible for the model beast in *Jaws 2*, which he dubbed the "chamber orchestra": "The shark was controlled by hydraulics, so you needed those five guys to do everything together." For *Supergirl*, the director was responsible for "an unbelievable amount of wirework." He would divide his time between flying, optical, and main units, frustrated that he would be unable to see the end result for months. "That scene where she picks up the tractor? That was done live. It took forever. We had to lift her, the vehicle, everything had to be done at the same time. It was tricky."

The harness work provided other tense moments. During a scene in which Slater was supposed to glide over a lake, riggers accidentally deposited her into it. Later, she would be sailed directly into a tree.

Szwarc was particularly consumed by the sequence in which Kara comes to Earth. "I wanted a very special look for when she's in the capsule on her way to Earth. It never looked right and then someone took me to Oxford or Cambridge and a biochemist there was doing these chemistry films, liquid viscosity films. I said, 'That's the look.' So we got that and made a plate out of it. We blew it up and that worked great. There were a lot of things that I was doing that had never been done before."

For a scene in which Supergirl rises out of the water to make her first on-screen appearance in costume, Szwarc wanted Slater to appear dry, the better to hint at the character's iconic status. Reverse photography was suggested, but the lack of water droplets would've ruined the integrity of the shot. Finally, a crew member suggested they simply use a cutout photograph of Slater and coat it with water repellent. Seen from a distance, the primitive effect was convincing.

Production wrapped in the fall of 1983; Szwarc and his crew threw a big party on the lot, celebrating a technically challenging but otherwise harmonious shoot. The Salkinds appeared close to their first controversy-free franchise entry.

The feeling didn't last long. The producers had intended *Supergirl* for a holiday 1984 release, aware that the revamped brand might become lost in the shuffle of "event" films released that summer. Warner Bros. balked, insisting that the only slot they had open was for a July 1984 bow.

Alex Salkind, who had gotten used to executives kowtowing to his demands, refused to budge. But the studio, having suffered the diminishing returns of *Superman III*, was no longer enamored of its brain trust. By the time the June 1984 deadline passed, he and Warner had stalemated each other. The Salkinds were now free to distribute the film through another vendor, a rather dubious honor. For several months, the industry whispered that *Supergirl* was an abandoned film, a label that seemed to condemn its chances at the ticket counter. Scrambling, Salkind made more deals with foreign territories, slotting it for release overseas during the summer.

The sudden liberation wasn't comforting to Szwarc or his crew. "I found out and I thought it wasn't a good thing. It was something between Alex and Warner. Then we got Tri-Star and everybody started to relax."

Tri-Star was a recently formed venture, the collective creation of Columbia Pictures, HBO, and CBS. Most of their offerings (*Meatballs Part II*, *The Last Dragon*) were unlikely to be making laps on the awards circuit, but the distributor did have a substantial funnel to theaters. *Supergirl's* adoptive fathers slotted the film for Salkind's desired November 1984 release.

What audiences would see would not be what Szwarc intended, however. Shortly before the film's debut, test audiences deemed the original 135-minute cut too rear-numbing. Ilya Salkind excised over twenty minutes of footage, making the director's edit obsolete. Gone were extended forays into Kara's Kryptonian home and early explorations of her powers. Other scenes that ran longer were trimmed.

"There was stuff I really liked, but I didn't have final cut," Szwarc said. "I was very keen on the aerial ballet. We did some extraordinary stuff when she flies for the first time. I wanted to inject lyrical poetry in the film, because it wasn't a guy with big muscles, a little bit more humor. Most of it stayed, but I think the ballet was longer than they showed."

Without the marketing muscle of Warner to boost its profile, *Supergirl* arrived in theaters on November 21, 1984, with little fanfare. The addendum to the Superman legacy grossed just under $6 million in its opening weekend, enough to earn first place but just a fraction of *Superman III's* $13 million take in the same window. By the end of its two-month run, *Supergirl* had earned just $14 million. It didn't help matters that a Japanese Laserdisc was making the underground rounds, offering a cut closer to Szwarc's original intentions. Rabid fans of the series—those who might have purchased multiple tickets—were instead springing for the bootleg version.

Ironically, while the Salkinds had deliberately avoided competing with the inevitable summer behemoth, blockbuster competition arrived later in the year in the form of *The Terminator*, the introduction of Arnold Schwarzenegger's iconic robot assassin. The film trampled on most of its competition that winter, earning $38 million and galvanizing the young demographic that Salkind had banked on flocking to *Supergirl*.

"I never understood why the film didn't do as well as I felt it should've done," Szwarc said. "There's no doubt the fact that Warner not being part of it hurt. Or maybe the audience had another idea of what Supergirl should be like. Maybe if it had been released later, it would've done better. I'm sure there were mistakes made in the release. But *Night of the Hunter* was a disaster when it came out, and now it's one of the great films.

"It was disappointing and hurtful. We had all worked so hard. And we liked the film. I have no idea. I know it did better in some territories."

Ilya Salkind theorized that audiences simply weren't prepared to see a female protagonist. "It's very hard for superhero women to be on the big screen. There is some resistance from the audience, which does not apply to television. Stuff like *Sheena*, it doesn't work. That's a fact. *Supergirl* was beautiful, but it was perhaps not the script I wanted to do." Though it was Warner's influence that had curtailed Salkind's more ambitious plans, the studio then turned and wanted nothing to do with the film.

Critics had little patience for what they perceived as an attempt to move beyond Reeve. With its camp tone, the film "trivializes itself with an almost suicidal glee," ranted Roger Ebert. "Why even go to the trouble of making a movie that feels like it's laughing at itself?" Though the flying effects were regarded as superior to those of the Reeve films, no one from the effects team received any honors. Peter O'Toole was, however, nominated for a Golden Raspberry Award for excellence in bad acting.

Szwarc believed critics didn't look deep enough. "One writer said there was a *Wizard of Oz* feel to the film, which I was aware of. Critics didn't understand; they were very unkind. We were hoping to give a model for young girls. For once, they could have their own icon. But advertising is the key to that. They probably tried to appeal to the hard-core *Superman* audience instead of broadening to a more normal audience, and it backfired."

As with *Superman* in 1978, *Supergirl* received virtually no merchandising push, which would've served to both fill Salkind's coffers and act as pervasive advertising. Aside from occasional appearances in DC's animated universe, the character's exploits have been limited to the comics pages.

Perhaps taking a subconscious cue from the film's failure, DC opted to sacrifice Supergirl in their 1986 opus *Crisis on Infinite Earths*. Because no one in comics ever stays dead, however, she's been resurrected multiple times; in her latest incarnation, it's hinted that she was sent to Earth not to be educated by Superman but to kill him. If we consider his film franchise potential, perhaps she succeeded.

Supergirl failed to ignite audience interest, but it nonetheless served as a springboard for a series of business deals for its participants. Szwarc and Ilya Salkind reteamed for 1985's *Santa Claus: The Movie*, a gaudy portrait of the seminal character. Budgeted at $50 million, it was a relative disappointment for Salkind and Tri-Star when it collected only $24 million in receipts.

Slater did little to contradict the notion that the bright blue costume hindered the future ambitions of capable performers. She starred in only one more film, 1985's *Legend of Billie Jean*, before embarking on a television career. Although several versions of *Supergirl* have appeared on DVD, Slater has repeatedly refused to participate in any of their supplemental material.

Ilya Salkind eventually regretted casting Slater, musing that she was too fragile to portray a mythological creation. In retrospect, he agreed with his father: Brooke Shields would have been the more profitable choice.

———

Taken as a slight confection, *Supergirl* is a harmless film, decorated with the kind of tacky imagery producers believed would appeal to young women weaned on the bright palettes of the early 1980s. She was the de facto prototype for the Powerpuff Girls, though not nearly as infectiously enthused about her adventures as those animated figures.

The plot is pure tripe: in search of the "Omegahedron," the power source that sustains Argo City (originally dubbed Kryptonopolis), Kara comes to Earth to reclaim it from Dunaway's Selena, an amateur witch who has other plans for the object. Superman's absence is attributed to a "peacekeeping mission."

Like Reeve, Helen Slater possesses a dignity on-screen that belies her patently ridiculous attire. Unfortunately, her nobility is diluted considerably by Dunaway's Selena, who doesn't share Hackman's ability to play his hammy grin against Superman's stolid presence. Dunaway's antics—enlisting a "love slave," casting spells—reduce any emotional investment in the film to rubble.

In 2000, Anchor Bay Entertainment released the extended cut of the film for the DVD market, restoring many of the scenes left on the cutting room floor. The version runs 138 minutes in total. Though sequences tend to make more sense, it's ultimately too much of a mediocre thing. But fans, ignoring critical response and spurred by the film's limited availability, embraced *Supergirl* as a welcome relic of 1980s cinema.

Ilya Salkind didn't share the sentiment. Following the second straight disappointment for the Mythology of Steel, the producer was prepared to wash his hands of Superman entirely.

Provided the price was right.

Nuclear Disaster

They're coach tourists who want first-class service. They'll nickel-and-dime you on paper clips.
—Christopher Reeve on the Cannon Group

The Cannes Film Festival is the great unifier of the film industry. Every spring, thousands of artists, studio executives, and carnival-barker producers gather in the south of France to evaluate prospective acquisitions, swap gossip, make deals, and watch in agony as the ruthlessly impatient French crowds pass judgment on their labors.

Seamlessly, the Serious Business of Film is interwoven with the garish attention-seeking of also-ran stars like Jean-Claude Van Damme and Pamela Anderson. B-movie squads swap rights and distribution deals for their execrable tripe. On the same stretch of beach where a high-minded work like *The Piano* receives top honors, adult film starlets can be seen arching their backs for devouring photographers.

The Salkinds had virtual tenure at the event, having flown banners overhead for years leading up to *Superman: The Movie*'s production and again for subsequent installments. They found themselves there once more in 1985, seated in a cafe opposite two men who shared their experiences of being foreign-born powers in the U.S.-dominated film industry.

The subject of conversation, perhaps inevitably, was Superman. After the misfortunes that befell the series with *Superman III* and *Supergirl*, the Salkinds finally declared themselves liberated from the franchise. But their rights to the character and his universe wouldn't revert back to Warner for another fourteen years; it seemed nonsensical to let the property lie dormant for the duration.

Ilya Salkind had approached the Cannon Group with this offer: license their rights for a finite amount of time. The Salkinds would, in effect, sublet their Superman property for a nominal fee. The upstart producers would gain a film with immediate name recognition, and the Salkinds could profit while absolving themselves of any direct participation. (Better yet, if Ilya was correct in his suspicion that the public had grown tired of the series, Cannon would absorb any losses.)

The deal was struck in France: for $5 million, roughly what the Salkinds had paid Warner for a quarter century of benefits, Cannon could produce additional Superman films.

Ilya Salkind had little idea that the two men smiling broadly at their new acquisition would go on to put the final nail in Superman's celluloid coffin.

Nor did he particularly care.

———

In 1979, Israeli-born cousins Menahem Golan and Yoram Globus purchased controlling stock in the anemic production company the Cannon Group for twenty cents a share. The production company's lone hit was *Joe*, a Peter Boyle vehicle from the early 1970s. By most accounts, the duo had overpaid.

Golan and Globus had achieved a measure of success in Israel, producing profitable films exclusively for that country's home video market. But Israel didn't offer the sizable audiences required to turn their modest enterprise into anything substantial. The film industry in the United States was where the real money was being made, most often by budget-minded producers offering pure schlock, cheapie horror flicks and militant revenge dramas.

Under Golan and Globus's leadership, Cannon landed a distribution deal with MGM in the early 1980s. The timing coincided nicely with the advent of the VHS boom. Films deemed too close to the bottom of the barrel for learned critics often found an audience in rental stores. Cannon began churning out unrepentantly violent juvenilia like the *Death Wish* sequels, which starred Charles Bronson as a stone-faced vigilante who goes on killing sprees after his family and friends are repeatedly assaulted by criminals; and the *Missing in Action* series, in which martial arts icon Chuck Norris became a Cannon staple. The Norris films suffered greatly from the actor's complete lack of screen presence but threw mounds of action at viewers to compensate. Both franchises appealed to undemanding consumers who enjoyed the myriad explosions, gunfights, and wry one-liners.

Golan and Globus celebrated their B-movie successes but repeatedly cast an envious eye toward the more bombastic major-studio fare. Golan in particular held higher aspirations for his slate than the Norris/Bronson swill, often backing "art house" attempts like *Runaway Train* and then spending hundreds of thousands in campaigns to get Cannes officials to recognize them. The ploy often failed, though Roger Ebert once declared that "no other production organization in the world today . . . has taken more chances with serious, marginal films than Cannon."

To offset costs, the upstart company would often sell territories on films that were incomplete or had yet to enter production. Distribution in England was guaranteed, as the duo had purchased Screen Entertainment, owner of the country's largest theater chain, for $270 million. Naturally, Cannon films constituted a substantial number of bookings in each location.

By the mid-1980s, the cousins had grown restless with being a niche developer and became determined to make their move into the mainstream commercial market. Their solution: piggyback on the chiseled shoulders of Sylvester Stallone. The genetic wonder had become one of the biggest stars in the world thanks to his *Rocky* and *Rambo* franchises, and he was one of the few performers who could virtually guarantee a strong opening weekend. Even the exhaustingly titled *Rocky IV* had done considerable business, proving that audiences were still enamored with the droopy-eyed icon.

Golan approached Stallone with an offer the actor couldn't refuse. To star in *Over the Top*, a movie about the fringe sport of professional arm wrestling, Stallone would receive $12 million. The salary was an industry record for its time. Stallone, who needed little business acumen to realize the figure would guarantee his lavish lifestyle for years to come, agreed.

The move cemented Cannon's go-for-broke mentality. They had accepted a staggering $200 million from public investors in 1985, and had an additional $100 million in revolving credit from First National Bank of Boston. In contrast, their film slate that year had netted them a meager $15 million in profits. Golan and Globus began to bank their future on sizable catchall hits, not the nickel-and-dime earnings Norris and Bronson were delivering.

So enthused were the partners of their pending arrival as a film force that they couldn't seem to shut up about it. Before actor Dustin Hoffman formally committed to an offered project and accompanying fortune in salary, the Israelis had bragged of his signing to the trade papers. The presumption so offended Hoffman that he retreated. Bizarrely, the cousins also announced they would be teaming up James Bond performers Roger Moore and Sean Connery in the same film. Both men denied any involvement.

Undeterred, Cannon took out a fifty-page pullout ad in *Variety* touting its enormous slate of projects for the coming years, including *Superman IV* and an adaptation of Marvel's *Spider-Man* to be directed by *Missing in Action* helmer Joseph Zito.

Initially, freeing Superman of his tethers to the Salkinds seemed to bode well for his box office prospects. With Alex and Ilya's vengeful mandates nullified, both Margot Kidder and Gene Hackman were agreeable to reprising their roles from the first two films. Hackman, in particular, had further cemented his reputation as an actor's actor with films like *Hoosiers* and *Uncommon Valor*, but he rejected criticisms that the cartoonish antics of Luthor were beneath him. Nearing sixty, he still felt infused with vitality and saw the rambunctious criminal as a way of working off that energy.

For Kidder, it had been a full ten years since her debut as Lois Lane, and the ingenue of the first film had been replaced with a more life-worn individual. From the outset, Cannon figured Superman's love life would need to be supplemented by a younger attraction. They eventually cast Mariel Hemingway, granddaughter of Ernest, as the less weathered damsel.

Retaining the franchise's star would prove slightly more problematic. Reeve had written off the role of Superman years prior, but his follow-up projects had failed to find an audience. *The Aviator* was a particularly distressing failure, as Reeve's love of (mechanically facilitated) flight had made him an ardent supporter of the project.

The absence of the Salkinds, whom Reeve had found to be a general nuisance and insufficiently concerned with the proper care and handling of the character, was one point in Cannon's favor. (Reeve called the Salkinds "scummy" in an *L.A. Times* piece, the latest invective hurled at the family.) But Golan had another lure: if Reeve would consider reprising the role, Cannon would promise to fund a more intimate project of his choosing.

Before filming *Deathtrap* in 1981, Reeve had been handed a script titled *Street Smart*. It was a gritty tale about a TV journalist who fabricates experiences with a pimp; the deception eventually leads to real danger for the fame-hungry reporter. Reeve had become enamored of the story, perhaps subconsciously enjoying the character's moral complexity in comparison to the bumbling Clark Kent. Cannon eagerly promised to produce the feature if he would don the tights once more.

Reeve agreed to reprise his starring role, but only in exchange for a $4 million salary, double Reeve's compensation for *Superman III*. He was back in blue despite sworn statements to the contrary—following in the footsteps of his idol Connery, who had returned to Bond in *Never Say Never Again*, twelve years after his farewell performance. And unlike Sean, Reeve reasoned, he wasn't graying just yet.

Satisfied that the most crucial component of their marquee release of 1987 was secured, Cannon opened its checkbook and left Reeve to go shoot *Street Smart* while it located a director. Richard Lester had been approached, but his ailing health only reinforced his commitment to stay away from the series. Wes Craven, who had found a measure of fame with his *A Nightmare on Elm Street*, was also courted, but he declined.

With the help of Warner Bros., which had agreed to provide *Superman IV* with a hefty $40 million in financing, Cannon turned to a no-longer-exiled Richard Donner. Warner chieftains Terry Semel and Bob Daly knocked on the door of Tom Mankiewicz, who had a standing office on the lot. "Will you guys do *IV*? We gotta get this thing back to where it was. Price is no object," Semel pleaded.

Mankiewicz conferred with Donner. Ideas were batted around, but eventually both men realized they had depleted their creative reserves regarding the character. "Dick and I sat down and talked and said, 'Jesus, we already did everything in the first two,'" Mankiewicz recalled. "Dick was into *Lethal Weapon*. I was convinced I was going to be a great director, so I was off developing my own movies.

"We brought him here from Krypton, he grew up in Kansas, came to Metropolis. In *II* he loses his powers, he regains his powers, Kryptonite had been introduced, missiles, saving the world. He turns the world backward. What's left to do, you know? It's futile. We've done it. Let's move on." Mankiewicz returned to Warner with word from both filmmakers: let someone else pilot it.

For a time, that someone else was to be Reeve himself. Like George Reeves before him, the actor began to figure that the best way to escape the Superman persona was to make a gradual move behind the scenes. He and Cannon toyed with the idea of having the star take over the directing chores, but eventually they mutually decided that the scope of the picture might be beyond the ability of a novice. As a compromise, Reeve would do some second-unit direction.

Sidney Furie had come into the Golan-Globus offices to pitch another project. The Canadian director had impressed Cannon with his minimalist approach to *Iron Eagle*, a rah-rah aerial drama that had done significant business. Furie, enamored with the prospect of directing a big-budget attraction, accepted Golan's offer to helm *Superman IV*. Despite the seeming enormity of the task, Furie had little to lose: *Superman III* had underwhelmed, and Warner made it clear that they would be satisfied with even half of that sequel's take. The director began soliciting both Donner and Jeannot Szwarc for advice on the best way to orchestrate the flying sequences.

While Furie busied himself with technical lessons, Reeve was petitioning producers to settle on a story with a social conscience. The prior *Superman* films had been largely heartfelt, but the dramatics were limited to immediate physical danger. The stories didn't deal with "issues," something that Mankiewicz had purposely avoided. The writer tried to hammer the point home when Reeve approached him for advice.

"Here are the rules," he told Reeve. "Don't ever get involved with something Superman could fix. He could disarm the world in fifteen minutes. He doesn't have to go to the UN. If he feels that strongly about it, he could get rid of all the missiles. Superman could feed the world if he wanted to. He could establish agricultural fields in outer space. Don't bring up things like that."

It was the same concern that had afflicted the comics writers for decades: Superman could have ended World War II in seconds. As the most powerful being on Earth, his will is absolute. Better to keep him busy with the assaulting aliens and natural disasters.

Reeve wasn't convinced. Having seen a documentary titled *A Message to Our Parents*, he was compelled by the debate over the nuclear arms race. During a story meeting with screenwriters Mark Rosenthal and Lawrence Konner, the trio escaped a rainstorm by taking refuge in an IMAX theater that happened to be screening *The Dream Is Alive*, a visceral tribute to the beauty—and frailty—of Kal-El's adoptive planet. Inspired by the subject matter, Reeve convinced the scribes to make nuclear disarmament the main story thread for *Superman IV*.

Golan and Globus didn't raise any objections. An earlier, shakier concept had imagined Superman suffering from an accelerated aging process and dying, visiting a kind of Valhalla for superheroes. The patriotism promised by Reeve's suggestion seemed better suited to the property. Konner and Rosenthal, in concert with Reeve, began hammering out the story beats, with Reeve of the mind that Superman could act as the candy around his "pill," the warning of nuclear danger. This serious business, Reeve believed, would be a proper antidote to the misguided folly of *Superman III*.

The grim issue had actually been explored through superhero theatrics at least twice before. In Marvel Comics' mid-1980s miniseries *Squadron Supreme*, a cadre of heroes take it upon themselves to disarm the world's superpowers. Their control soon becomes dictatorial when they institute further revisions to society, enforcing mind control in prisons and even influencing medicine to come up with a solution to death. The dangers of absolute authority are revealed when the team eventually suffers casualties and civilians revolt.

More distressingly, the idea was also present in a treatment written by Barry E. Taff and Kenneth P. Stoller and submitted to Reeve in 1985. In the story dubbed *Superman: The Confrontation*, the titular character immerses himself in nuclear disarmament and even perishes—curiously similar to what was later pitched for the film.

The two novice screenwriters sued Reeve for $45 million, claiming intellectual property theft and submitting that Reeve had even phoned them to discuss the screenplay. Reeve acknowledged that the document had been sent to his office and insisted that the writers had then harassed his secretary on the phone. To placate them, Reeve had phoned and offered compliments on the story, which he later claimed he had not actually read.

The suit dragged on for three years. After an L.A. court found Reeve had done nothing wrong, the writers took the matter to the California Supreme Court, where it was summarily tossed out. Though Reeve was not required to pay any form of compensation, the legal costs would burn up a good bit of his *Superman IV* salary.

He would not be the only one suffering the indignity of vanishing funds. In 1986, Cannon bore the brunt of a $60 million loss, its enormous slate of forty-three pictures a lesson in gross excess. Its E ticket to mainstream respect, *Over the Top*, had been greeted with incredulity by audiences. Though they revered Stallone in action roles, the endless close-ups of his grimacing maw, struggling through a sport as viscerally dull as arm wrestling, was box office Kryptonite. Golan, who had actually directed the picture, was devastated.

Bankruptcy was imminent, and in an effort to curtail runaway costs, Cannon slashed *Superman IV*'s budget, redirecting all but $17 million of Warner's $40 million grant to their thirty other films in production in an attempt to spread the risk around.

The repercussions were obvious. At a third of the original film's budget, with ten years' worth of inflation to contend with, this would be the most economically strapped *Superman* production in decades. Crew members who had been hired for their prowess in effects work were dismissed for cheaper, substandard talent from Israel who had little experience with a film of this scale. That was never more evident than in a scene in which Superman was to march down the streets of New York and into the United Nations building. Cannon had purchased Elstree Studios in England and insisted the footage be shot there instead of on location; the result was a shoddy mess.

The haphazard production suffered a further setback when stuntman John Lees fell and broke both his arms while dangling from a harness. He successfully litigated against what he dubbed "poor working conditions" and was awarded $422,000.

Reeve was livid. His aim had been to deliver a literate, substantial film, but the producers wanted something akin to their endless *Death Wish* franchise—a quick and dirty cheapie. His contract, unfortunately, wasn't contingent upon how much money was spent on filming. He reported to work on schedule, diverting his energy into second-unit duties. If the film were to be crippled from the outset, at least he'd be able to log time behind the camera. At one point, Reeve took costar Jon Cryer aside and told him to steel himself. "This movie," Reeve cautioned, "is going to be terrible."

The disillusionment was evident in Reeve's physique: he had not been as diligent in the gym as he had for prior entries. (An emergency appendectomy on the *Street Smart* shoot had also cut into valuable training time.) Now thirty-five, Reeve considered Superman an eternal thirty, and while age had largely been gracious to him—and he wore a hairpiece to better simulate Kal-El's youthful hairline—there was no denying the disappointment in seeing a dumpier-looking Man of Steel.

Luthor's "muscle" of the film, Nuclear Man, shamed Reeve in the physical development department. Director Furie's son worked at a talent agency, and introduced one of the office's clients, Mark Pillow, to his father. The son of a military man, Pillow had tried (unsuccessfully) to market his sunburned good looks in the film business. But since the part of Nuclear Man required little more than some snarling and flexing, Furie enlisted him. (Reeve had toyed with the idea of playing him as a kind of Superman doppelganger, but *III*'s junkyard fight between Superman's personas made the suggestion seem redundant.) In Rosenthal and Konner's script, the villain—a synthetic creation of Luthor's experiments with nuclear power—was more of a tragic figure. On-screen, he was a grunting palooka.

Despite Cannon's attempt to infuse its business with cash—it accepted $25 million from Warner in exchange for some of its catalog—the *Superman IV* production was essentially bankrupt months before completion. Reeve was in a kind of purgatory: not only was he reprising a character that may have crippled his career but he was doing it on a pauper's production budget.

———

By 1986, comics had become largely a fringe market, no longer the coffee-table institution they once were. Home video and Nintendo systems began taking up the majority of adolescents' free time; reading was laborious, static. Why read about Superman when you could control his actions via a game cartridge?

Those who did peruse comics were usually suit-and-tie professionals with nostalgic spending habits, or college-age literati who preferred the troubled souls of Marvel's *X-Men* to the cosmic adventures of the Man of Steel. The mutant opposition sold five hundred thousand copies per month; *Superman*, under one hundred thousand.

DC's hopes hinged on two factors. First, celebrated comics writer/artist John Byrne, who had helped catapult *X-Men* to the top of the sales charts, was signed to an exclusive deal. He was directed to reboot the Superman mythology with whatever alterations he deemed necessary to make the character more accessible. Second, Cannon's big-screen outing was poised to lure general audiences into sampling the updated comics series.

Byrne held up to his end of the deal; Cannon did not.

The Man of Steel, the six-issue miniseries that added a contemporary spin to the Superman lore, was a smash hit, selling two hundred thousand copies in 1986. Readers were directed to dismiss anything that had gone before as alternate-Earth fiction. Clark's powers did not develop until his late teens, erasing Superboy from existence; the sole survivor of Krypton, he had no cousins; his mortal father, Jonathan Kent, remained alive; and most important, his powers were lessened to Max Fleischer–era levels. He could no longer juggle planets, and extreme effort—like moving an oil tanker—would cause him to break a sweat.

With sales reinvigorated, DC anticipated that the summer 1987 release of *Superman IV: The Quest for Peace* would prove to be a further boon to their market share. What they were forced to rally behind was an abomination. A test screening had gone so disastrously that Furie was directed to excise thirty minutes from the film's two-hour running time, including a major subplot about a failed Nuclear Man prototype. Even after the hackwork, the optical effects shots—which, inverse to the competency level of the staffers, were more numerous than in previous installments—were mediocre at best, laughable at worst.

Released in July 1987, *Superman IV* was a bomb by any standards, grossing under $6 million in its opening weekend and crawling to a meager overall take of less than $16 million. By way of comparison, the first film had done roughly $7 million in its first seventy-two hours, despite playing in only one-third as many theaters. Cannon, completely devoid of any finances, spent next to nothing on marketing.

Reeve put on a brave face for the media, emphasizing the more mature message of the film. It contained the action fans had come to expect, he promised, but also aspired to get people thinking about the enormous responsibility the world's superpowers have to their people. Kidder was equally diligent, though even propaganda-spouting television hosts could barely hide their amusement at the proceedings. David Letterman chuckled through the obligatory clip on his late-night show and then heckled Kidder about its quality.

Even the stoic Pillow did his part, showing up to the premiere at the Royal Hall in London in full Nuclear Man costume, a bizarre personal choice that wasn't solicited by the studio. Prince Charles gamely shook his hand, ignoring the gold spandex.

Fans dry-heaved at the end result, a clunky morality play that seemed oblivious to its egregious errors in basic logic. At one point, Nuclear Man carries Mariel Hemingway's character off into space. Not only is she still able to breathe, but Superman carries on a conversation with her. Critics found it insipid, even in relation to the modest expectations propelled by the third installment.

Cannon found itself on life support, and suffered further when its other brand-name property bombed with equally destructive force in August. *Masters of the Universe*, an attempt to capitalize on the wildly popular He-Man toy line and cartoon, was dead on arrival, grossing only $17 million. The alpha male barbarian made for poor live-action fodder; so severe was the disillusionment that the toy line's gross profits, which had reached an obscene $400 million in 1986, tumbled to only $7 million the following year.

The twin disasters crippled Cannon's plans for *Spider-Man*, which had been scheduled to coincide with the shoot for a *Masters* sequel. Oddly, since Joseph Zito had left the long-gestating Marvel project, both movies were now to be helmed by Albert Pyun. He even cast surfing legend Laird Hamilton as He-Man—replacing Dolph Lundgren—before Marvel raised hell, complaining that Cannon's check, intended to re-up the rights to the wall-crawler, had bounced. With its finances drained, Cannon shut down Pyun's second film as well. Sets for both features had already been built; Golan directed Pyun to utilize them for the trashy Van Damme movie *Cyborg*.

Cannon had gambled everything on the big hit that never came. By 1989, the company was forced into Chapter 11 and under investigation over accusations that they had misrepresented their earnings. Golan parted ways with Globus, who remained to try to salvage their enterprise. The separation was far from amiable. Globus, who had landed at MGM along with the Cannon film library, announced that he would be producing a film based on the lambada dance craze. Not to be outdone, Golan's independent banner announced its own lambada project. Globus trademarked the "lambada" buzzword, forcing Golan to retitle his work *The Forbidden Dance*.

Incredibly, both films about the niche fad were released the same day, March 16, 1990. Predictably, the hastily shot and edited offerings bombed in equal measure. Golan and Globus reconciled in 1992, over dinner at— where else?—Cannes.

——————

Initially, Cannon was unwavering in its support of the Superman legacy. It announced a *Superman V* in 1988, braying that Arnold Schwarzenegger had expressed interest in portraying an ally of Superman's. In truth, Schwarzenegger—one of the world's biggest stars at the time—had no incentive whatsoever to align himself with a decaying franchise. Privately, Cannon's interests in a sequel extended only to the idea that they could make use of the thirty to forty-five minutes of unused footage from *Superman IV*. To their thinking, half a movie was bought and paid for. They approached Albert Pyun to direct, suggesting that the Nuclear Man prototype that had been left on the cutting room floor might make a good adversary for the sequel. Eventually, their financial burdens erased any notion of such a decrepit pursuit.

Reeve certainly wouldn't have been party to it. The crash-landing of *IV* had soured him permanently on the franchise. Ever since Donner left, the character had been passed through a series of handlers who had little or no respect for the integrity that Reeve had tried to bring to the character. His attempt to become more involved with the production had been crippled by Cannon's financial collapse. And by the time someone was foolhardy enough to sink more money into the character's big-screen exploits, he would be middle-aged, his metabolism no longer conducive to the physical perfection the role required.

Mankiewicz had warned him of the "rules," that Superman wasn't meant to solve the big problems. "But he went ahead and did it anyway," Mankiewicz said. "And while it had a very noble theme to it, it was the least effective of the *Superman* movies. Even though people may not consciously think about, it's in the back of their heads: 'Jesus, Superman could just *do* this.'"

Reeve was still smarting from the cool reception his pet project had received earlier in the year. *Street Smart* had grossed less than $2 million, though at least critics hadn't used it as batting practice. Absent of his trademark success in costume, his career now appeared rudderless.

***

If Reeve's misfiring denouement was disappointing, 1988 would top it in the sheer quantity of misguided attempts to resuscitate the Last Son of Krypton, a feat made all the more discouraging by the timing. It was the year of Superman's fiftieth birthday.

Joe Shuster's cousin-once-removed Rosie was working as a staff writer on NBC's *Saturday Night Live* when CBS enlisted her and *SNL* patriarch Lorne Michaels to produce a prime-time special celebrating the character's golden anniversary. Former *Superman* radio announcer Jackson Beck provided the opening narration, which introduced a series of sketches and tributes that were largely unsuccessful. Superman wasn't fodder for *SNL's* often-scathing wit; he was only lightly roasted by his "dry cleaner" and the "deputy mayor of Metropolis."

Clips from the various Superman productions were interspersed throughout, and an earnest Dana Carvey hosted. Noel Neill made an appearance; Peter Boyle, who had once been considered for the role of Luthor's henchman Otis in the Donner films, put in time, as did Ralph Nader and Hal Holbrook, the latter of whom sported a Superman costume for no apparent reason. Superman himself appeared at the climax, albeit in animated form.

More respectful was *TIME*'s cover story commemorating the superhero's anniversary. It acknowledged Superman's cultural influence as something other than a springboard for lazy sketch comedy.

Also set to debut in time for the 1988 media frenzy was a new cartoon series, which CBS had come to an agreement with Warner to produce prior to *Superman IV*'s debasement. Ruby-Spears, an animation house headed by the titular duo of Joe Ruby and Ken Spears, was on board to produce. The cofounders had created *Scooby-Doo* for Hanna-Barbera in the late 1960s.

Superman hadn't been seen in animation since the 1986 demise of the near-immortal *Super Friends* franchise. Here, he would pursue solo adventures that held the character's earliest comics template in high regard. Ruby-Spears enlisted comics scribe Marv Wolfman to be the story editor, though not for the obvious reasons.

"I had done an episode of the *Garbage Pail Kids* featuring a Superman parody," Wolfman recalled. "I'd been given it because the people who story-edited *Kids* knew I had done the *Superman* comic. CBS had no idea [I'd written the comic] but really liked what I had done on *Kids* and asked me to work on the actual *Superman* show."

Because of his working relationship with DC, Wolfman had little problem adhering to the publisher's expectations for the character; the network was another matter. Scripts would often come back with odd notes from executives. "Network notes were often weird and impossible to understand. We pitched Superman vs. a team of robot baseball players. The note came back that Superman and the robots would be on one side and ordinary humans would be on the other. That's not exactly fair."

The show's epilogues would feature "Superman's Family Album," vignettes that explored the stress of having a superpowered youngster at home. One short explored a little-seen detail of early Superman lore—namely, the fact that the Kents had briefly gone to an adoption agency to drop off their baby before changing their minds. It's not explained how the adoption agent, who witnesses Superbaby's property-destroying escapades, would not be able to connect a young Clark with his adult alter ego.

CBS fought Warner's licensing fees, deeming them to be too exorbitant in light of the network's cool attitude toward costumed heroes. "CBS wanted a Superman show, but the person in charge of children's programming actively disliked superhero shows and put it on much too early in the morning," Wolfman said. "This was a show for 9-to-13-year-olds and they put it on at 7 A.M., which was usually designed for 5-to-9-year-olds. It wasn't surprising that we didn't get great ratings." *Superman* ran only thirteen episodes, its full first season, before getting pulled.

At the same time the animated series was gearing up production, a restless Ilya Salkind found himself exploring territory initially scouted by Whitney Ellsworth back in 1960. As a feature film enterprise, Superman was dilapidated.

As a small-screen pursuit, well, that was another matter entirely.

Escape the Cape

Some people were turned off by a show called *Superboy* because they thought it was something that would appeal directly to kids. It didn't have a lot of crossover.
—Gerard Christopher

Since 1984, the Salkind film empire had suffered substantially from the absence of its staple hero. Devoid of any mass-market templates to work from, Ilya and his father had managed to assemble only one complete project, 1985's *Santa Claus: The Movie*. The production revealed an increasing gulf of opinion between the two filmmakers, stemming from what Ilya perceived as a generational gap.

"He got tougher with age," Ilya recalled. We didn't see eye to eye. We disagreed on things. After *Santa Claus*, we really separated."

The younger Salkind entered his third marriage, to Jane Chaplin (Charlie Chaplin's daughter), and added to his brood with two sons. While residing in Madrid, Spain, in 1987, he got a phone call from his father.

"My father or someone came up with making a Superboy series. The rights were still there. They still belonged to us. He got excited. But I didn't want to work with him."

Salkind had sold Cannon the option to create Superman films, but the contract was not all-inclusive: his family retained the authority to produce live-action television if they so desired.

By the late 1980s, the television industry was experiencing seismic shifts. Cable TV was becoming more pervasive, offering videophiles and rural customers the option of accepting stations via grounded coaxial connections instead of the spastic and uneven over-the-air signals. By 1980, fifteen million households had signed up for the service; by the latter part of the decade, fifty-three million living rooms were wired for the upgrade.

By accepting cable fees directly from their audience, programmers could afford to market more niche content and rely less on advertising income. And with the expanded dial came an increasing need for something to fill airtime. Syndication dealers could offer the fledgling stations preproduced wares, usually expired series, game shows, or movie packages. In exchange for a nominal fee, a station wouldn't have to bother itself with producing its own original programming.

Star Trek: The Next Generation was an early syndication success story, building upon the established sci-fi brand to help shatter the notion that syndicated content was low-budget tripe. *Friday the 13th: The Series* also resonated (though its occult trappings had virtually nothing to do with the hockey-masked sociopath of the film franchise). Such specialized genre content was frowned upon by the Big Three networks, who looked to reach the widest audience possible in prime time, but in the world of syndication, fantasy programming would soon become a staple.

Alex Salkind estimated that, like *Trek*, Superman possessed an ingrained awareness level among viewers. Although they may have finally tired of spending time, money, and effort to view the series' lessening returns in theaters, surely the visceral appeal of seeing a man in flight would prove to be an enticement for bored boob-tube frequenters.

He was, however, essentially at an impasse with his son. Their agreement with Warner Bros. dictated that any Superman-affiliated projects would have to be coproduced by both Alex and Ilya. Without the younger Salkind's name on the credits, the series would be stalled indefinitely.

By this time, however, Ilya had been five years removed from the DC mythology, and the idea of experimenting in television intrigued him. Despite his reservations, he agreed to come onto the show—but as an employee. They would no longer be partners.

Salkind Sr. reached an agreement to distribute the show with Viacom, a syndication company that had made millions by repurposing *I Love Lucy* and *The Andy Griffith Show* for a generation that had missed their first-run broadcasts decades prior. Principal photography would take place at Walt Disney World in Florida, a dubious choice, though set designers didn't need to concern themselves with hiding palm trees in Metropolis— the series was set during Clark Kent's college years at the homage-heavy Shuster University of Siegelville, Florida.

Ilya recalled *Superman: The Movie* casting director Lynn Stalmaster's discernment in championing Reeve for the title role, and he again enlisted Stalmaster to help him weed through the hundreds of rope-muscled applicants. During the search, Stalmaster was prepping the woefully morbid comedy *Weekend at Bernie's* for Twentieth Century Fox. A young actor named John Haymes Newton auditioned for one of the lead roles. Stalmaster, struck by his boyish demeanor and advanced fitness level, asked him to come to Florida the following weekend to audition for *Superboy*.

By all accounts, Newton was not an accomplished performer, nor did he exhibit any natural inclination toward the camera. Busing tables at the time of the meeting, he had no televised credits on his resume. Nonetheless, he appeared sincere in the Superman costume and properly mawkish with the oversized Clark Kent glasses on. Ilya Salkind hired him.

Initially, producers figured that Clark's roommate at Shuster U would be Jimmy Olsen, but someone wisely pointed out that Olsen was—in both years and personality—a bit of a man-child, and certainly not Kent's social peer. Instead, T. J. White was introduced as the progeny of *Daily Planet* editor Perry White. James Calvert, a regular in gosh-gee adolescent roles in episodic TV, was slotted for the role. Stacy Haiduk, a redheaded ingenue, would be the third actor to play Lana Lang, Clark's earliest infatuation. Cary Bates, who had been a consultant on *Superman III* for DC, was hired as an executive producer.

———

"The beginning," Ilya Salkind admitted, "was a little rough."

Salkind's memories are perhaps too generous. The first season of *Superboy* ranks as the most inept, poorly performed, and nauseating treatise on the franchise since its inception.

Production on the first episode had commenced on August 14, 1988, to make an October air date. (A Writers Guild strike had ceased production of several shows, but Salkind hammered out an interim agreement to keep working.) With two months allotted for filming and postproduction, the half-hour premiere is a marvel of shoddy staging. Despite the fact that Salkind enlisted many of the same optical effects workers who had kept Reeve aloft in the film series, the budget constraints of syndicated TV conspired to set a new low for Superman's airborne stunts. Newton appeared superimposed over video backgrounds, an unconvincing, cringe-worthy illusion. (Worse, the muggy Florida weather wreaked havoc on the Superman costume; the Man of Steel, after all, is not supposed to sweat.)

No attempt was made to provide exposition regarding the revised Kent lore. He was simply a college student who performed de rigueur feats of heroics when summoned. Lex Luthor was reimagined as spoiled preppie classmate, complete with feathered hair; Scott Wells, who had the considerable task of living up to the echoes of Gene Hackman, was a model of histrionics. His performance appeared to be a parody of bad acting. To cap the painful experience, Luthor's sports car actually crashes into a fruit stand during the episode's climax. It's a testament to the series' general awkwardness that it's impossible to tell whether the wheezing cliche was intentional or not.

Letters from affiliates began pouring into Viacom offices. "This," they wrote, "is abysmal." Viewers were disgusted; critics wept. "Worst comic adaptation to date," declared the *L.A. Times*.

"I wasn't totally focused," Ilya Salkind later admitted. The producer, who was rarely on set, was smacked with the threat of cancellation. "After three or four episodes and some letters from the stations saying it was terrible, we changed many things and the show became better and better." After an initial order of thirteen episodes, ratings were encouraging enough to produce a full season of twenty-six.

The dismal debut didn't leave room for things to get any worse. Salkind enlisted low-watt guest stars like Abe Vigoda and Leif Garrett to try to beef up the cast of unknowns. (Garrett's oily villain collects comic books, a trait that fawning girls in the episode laughably dub "totally cool.") He briefly toyed with the idea of casting Kirk Alyn as Superman's still-breathing father, Pa Kent, but Alyn's declining health interfered. Stuart Whitman, the eventual Jonathan Kent, bore more than a passing resemblance to Glenn Ford, Donner's choice for the films.

As the local Florida crew began to adjust to the economical trickery the budget required, things did begin to improve, though there was still much to dislike about the show. In one episode an explosion resulted in a limp-limbed dummy being projected through the air; minimal takes meant that actors often flubbed or stepped on lines; guest stars like Michael J. Pollard, who was once nominated for an Oscar for *Bonnie and Clyde*, made no attempt to hide their boredom. (Pollard portrayed Mr. Mxyzptlk, finally sating Salkind's long-standing interest in the character.)

In the first season's twenty-six episodes, only one sequence approaches anything commendable. For a charity baseball game, Superman plays all positions on the field, zipping around the bases and catching his own hits. The scene captures the spirit of the Superboy mythos, with Kent using his powers in more mundane, albeit clever, scenarios. The infusion of mirth was likely the result of numerous DC staff writers who were brought on during the latter half of the season. Their efforts were appreciated but tardy; few narratives could withstand the sheer viewer bile induced by lines like "Turn it off, Lex! You're killing the ninja!"

As the anchor of the show, Newton seemed to actually get worse as the season wore on. His Kent was shy as opposed to bumbling, his Superman stilted as opposed to stoic. Audiences surveyed clamored for a return to the clumsiness of Reeve's portrayal, but Newton wouldn't relent, refus-

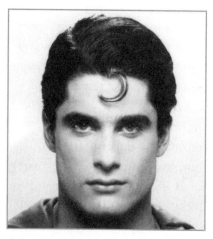

Freshman Superboy John Haymes Newton poses for a publicity photo for the 1988 syndicated series. After a DUI arrest, Newton was released from any further obligations to the character.

(© Viacom/Everett Collection)

ing to devolve the character into his nerdy facade. (In an interesting bit of hubris, he warned reporters that he had signed a four-year contract, and he'd be "done" after that.) The former bodyguard possessed none of Reeve's quiet charm or dignity in spandex. Worse, he was beginning to have serious concerns for his safety. Twice, handlers had "flown" him dangerously close to telephone and power lines.

Newton believed the risks he was assuming were deserving of a 20 percent raise; the actor was either oblivious to or unconcerned with the Salkinds' infamous talent relations. Whatever the case, he was the victim of poor timing. At the close of the first season, Newton was arrested on a DUI charge in Orlando. "Superboy Busted," the papers screamed. An on-screen bore who demanded more money while simultaneously violating the producers' moral clause hit the trifecta of motivations for dismissal. Ilya gave him his walking papers.

The recasting of the eponymous character was the catalyst for a series-wide overhaul. Emboldened, Ilya also released Scott Wells and James Calvert. (Haiduk was spared, though her screen presence was as questionable as anyone's.) The moves were made in preparation for a second season of *Superboy*; incredibly, the brand recognition had been significant enough to stave off further affiliate complaints, and the ratings had sufficient pulse to warrant the promise of another season.

Or threat, depending on one's perspective.

Newton expunged *Superboy* from his resume, fearing the connection would be detrimental to his career. He garnered regular employment on television, with recurring roles on *The Untouchables*—another syndicated synergy attempt—and *Models Inc.* Post-*Superboy* malaise was far more unkind to Wells; after a lone appearance, in 1991's putrid *The Taking of Beverly Hills*, he disappeared from the business, entering drug rehab in 1998.

Salkind had precious little time to reconfigure the central cast of his modest success. For the role of Superboy, Stalmaster immediately suggested an actor who was slightly closer to Reeve, at least in regard to lineage. Like his predecessor, Gerard Christopher was a Julliard grad. He had once foiled a mugging attempt in New York, prompting the city to issue him a citation for bravery. He even knew John Rockwell, Whitney Ellsworth's Superboy from the failed 1961 pilot, though he had no idea Rockwell had assumed the role. Endearingly, Christopher was also a genuine fan of the character.

"I was pretty much raised on the old series with George Reeves," Christopher recalled. "That was my experience with Superman. As a kid, I used to run around with a towel around my neck and all that stuff."

Nearing thirty, Christopher was thinking of quitting acting to focus on more stable pursuits. Getting called for Superman was, to his mind, serendipitous. "I was thinking if most actors don't make it by the time they're thirty, chances are they're not going to make it. Since the Reeve movies came out, I had heard on a daily basis from strangers that I looked like Superman. I thought, 'This could work.'"

Christopher auditioned and agreed to a meager salary in advance of Ilya Salkind's final decision, cutting off any negotiating power the actor would have had if Salkind had tipped his hand. Before the first day of shooting, he was ushered into Salkind's palatial Florida office, its walls covered with sound-deadening corkboard.

"I was in there alone with him, and I remember standing up like a recruit would in front of his colonel in the military or something. He said, 'Gerard, the show is ranked number thirty-eight in the ratings right now. They were going to kill it, but I fought to save it and said we would make changes. If the show's ratings don't go up immediately, we're going to be canceled and you're out of work and so is everybody else. If you consider that to be pressure, consider yourself pressured.'

"Those," Christopher laughed, "were his encouraging words."

Salkind and executive producer Bates also decided to revert Luthor's persona to the middle-aged archetype of the comic books, casting Sherman Howard in the role. (While they didn't bother to rationalize Superboy's change in appearance, the second season premiere explains that the villain had plastic surgery.) T. J. White was removed from continuity completely; Clark's new roommate had no tethers to existing characters. Generally, Salkind and his writers weren't beholden to the comics structure. If they had been, there wouldn't have been any show at all—John Byrne had deleted Superboy from the Man of Steel's history two years prior.

Superboy's second season premiered in the fall of 1989. Spurred on by the infusion of talent in front of the camera, comics writers like J. M DeMatteis and Mike Carlin began porting over some of the more compelling portions of the illustrated mythology to the small screen. Heretofore unexplored villains like Nick Knack and Metallo were introduced. DC released a *Superboy* title based on the TV narrative, with photo covers of Christopher and Haiduk. Shooting had been moved from the Disney studios to the more financially hospitable Universal.

The second crop of episodes revealed two distinct traits of the evolved series. First, it was surprisingly violent. Characters would get stabbed, shot through the hand with arrows, and bleed. Second, it captured the utterly ridiculous spirit of the earliest *Superboy* comics adventures. Superboy would find himself in situations that rendered his appearance absurd. Crippled at the hands of Luthor, Superboy must learn to walk again; true to his noble spirit, he maneuvers his wheelchair over to Luthor's apartment to confront him. A later episode, "Young Dracula," is self-explanatory.

To balance its comics karma, the series introduced the first live-action rendition of Bizarro, Superman's tragicomic nemesis. A faux Frankenstein's monster, the awkward duplicate of the Man of Steel proved so popular with audiences that he logged a total of seven appearances on the series. "How am you?" the monster genially asks a young boy, who shrieks in terror at his block-faced visage. "Me no understand women," he sighs after Lana rebuffs his creepy advances.

As Luthor, Howard embraced the machinations of the villain with barely contained glee: he'd cackle, snort, and contort his face into impossibly wide grins. Though broad, the performance was Oscar-worthy in comparison to Wells's stiff presence.

Christopher's appearance ran counter to the "Superboy" moniker: though his character was a college student, the actor was thirty—six years older than Reeve was when he assumed the role—and looked a decade removed from teenage awkwardness. Whether the audience was prepared to embrace a more authoritative Superman or not, ratings improved dramatically. By the end of its second season, *Superboy* was a top-ten hit in syndication.

Regardless of its popularity, *Superboy* was plagued by much of the same obtuse neglect that had haunted earlier Salkind productions. Christopher was particularly annoyed by a rambunctious stunt coordinator who preferred to entertain females on his lap than supervise the actor's stunt work.

"He would tease the actors, both me in my first year and John Newton," Christopher said. "Stuff like, 'I make more money than you.' He was a real pain in the ass.

"Once, I was on wires. The crane was on a bridge, and the bridge was probably fifty feet in the air. And then I was up another fifty feet because of this crane. And the stunt coordinator, as he was oft inclined to be doing, was down below me sitting on his chair with a girl on his lap, goofing around."

Christopher's handlers brought him within feet of high-tension wires, which threatened to scorch him if he kept moving. "I had to start screaming at them to stop, because my 'safety officer' down below was not paying attention to me. That was strike one."

Strikes two and three came when Christopher was shooting an episode in which part of his body chemistry was to be used to make Bizarro more human. "They put me into a telephone booth–type thing. It had a double layer of Plexiglas because they were going to put CO_2 in the outside to make the fog, and I was supposed to be on the inside and away from the CO_2."

Again, the stunt coordinator was a slave to his hormones; again, Christopher paid the price. "The thing started leaching the CO_2 into my chamber. I was overcome by it. I collapsed and destroyed the set." After regaining consciousness, Christopher demanded the inattentive crewman be replaced or he simply wouldn't show up. Producers caved; the offending coordinator was cut loose, freed to pursue women full-time.

The unlikely success of the show made minor repairs to the Salkinds' embittered relationship. Flush with their triumph, Ilya Salkind relinquished active duties on *Superboy*, and he and Alex began planning to produce a big-budget biopic of Christopher Columbus. With the film scheduled for the 1992 quincentennial of the explorer's voyage, Ilya stormed Cannes and promised full-scale replicas of the *Nina*, *Pinta*, and *Santa Maria*.

Ilya hired director Ridley Scott, who had made his name with *Alien* and *Blade Runner*. Most impressively, Salkind enticed dormant screen icon Marlon Brando to appear. (Brando, unsurprisingly, insisted on getting his money up front.)

Not long into production, Scott was dropped from the helm; Salkind cited creative differences. Fueled in some part by vindictiveness, Scott struck his own deal for a competing Columbus picture. The trades soon began having fun as Scott's rival movie raced to release against the Salkinds'. Ilya and Alex sued the director, claiming that he had taken privileged production information with him.

The fiasco severed whatever was left of Ilya and Alex's familial bond; the relationship reached its breaking point when Ilya brought legal action against his own father. Ilya's wife Jane had handed over a check for $6.75 million to Alex in order for him to pursue the Columbus picture. When the elder Salkind refused to pay her back, Ilya went ballistic and charged Alex with breach of contract, fraud, and racketeering. The suit was eventually brought to the Supreme Court, which ruled in Ilya's favor.

Alex had gotten deeply into debt with a number of vendors for the film—drivers, security people, barge operators. His seeming disinterest in settling his bills prompted Ilya to sever all contact with his father in 1992. "My father and I totally separated," Ilya said.

Alex passed away in 1997. The two never reconciled.

———

For no obvious reason, *Superboy* was retitled *The Adventures of Superboy* at the beginning of its third season. (Perhaps, like his animated counterpart in the Super Friends, Superboy feared impending audience boredom and felt a brand alteration would stave off channel changing.) Since Ilya Salkind had been diverted to the Columbus project, Julia Pistor replaced him as executive producer.

With a gelled creative team in place, producers felt free to explore more compelling corners of Superboy's mythology. In the alternate universe of "Roads Not Taken," Clark is found by someone other than the Kents and grows up to be a ruthless dictator; "Mindscape" uses the silly conceit of an alien parasite to reveal Clark's psyche, exploring his fears of abandonment and the crushing pressure from society to be their savior. The bold experiments in narrative resulted in *Superboy*'s most substantial and creatively satisfying season of its run.

Clark and Lana had migrated from Shuster to begin internships at the Bureau for Extra-Normal Matters, which allowed Clark a base of operations to investigate less mundane threats. The new setting was partially responsible for the series' change in visual tone from sunny daytime adventures to nocturnal fisticuffs. The more substantial influence, however, was Warner's *Batman*, which had been released in the summer of 1989.

Batman absolutely obliterated the negative connotations that been attached to comic book adaptations in recent years, packing theaters week after week with casual fans who devoured Tim Burton's portrait of a gloomy Gotham City and an even gloomier Dark Knight. Batman himself was no longer the self-amused sprite Adam West had portrayed in the 1960s; Michael Keaton played him as a stern vigilante in a molded rubber muscle suit. The diminutive Keaton, who had fought fan backlash over his casting, ushered in a new era in comic-book-to-screen heroics—that of the grim and gritty antihero. Though he was long separated from the project,

Tom Mankiewicz had been correct in his approach. Contemporary audiences wanted something more from their screen protagonists.

Batman also prompted Ilya Salkind to reevaluate his dormant *Superman* film franchise. By this point, Cannon had self-destructed and had no means of picking up their option for a fifth film, and Tim Burton had proved that comics characters were once again in vogue in Hollywood. Though *Superman IV* was a scant three years removed from the public consciousness, perhaps *Batman* had cleansed audiences' palates. Moreover, in *Superboy*, Salkind figured he essentially had a half-hour infomercial for the mythology on television every week.

Salkind began hammering out ideas with Cary Bates and screenwriter Mark Jones for a resurrection of Superman's screen incarnation, both figuratively and literally. The trio hashed out a narrative that had Superman coming back from the dead, a story that echoed Cannon's earliest passes on *IV*. Again, Salkind mandated a potpourri of elements from the character's comics origins, including the Bottle City of Kandor, a shrunken remnant of Krypton populated with tiny citizens.

"Superman died and somehow was resuscitated in the City of Kandor," he recalled. "Brainiac collected cities or planets and had shrunk them in this gigantic ship. It was a fantastic script. Then it became very difficult because Terry Semel, I don't think he liked sci-fi, although Metropolis was also encapsulated inside the ship. It was a very exciting script. It was completely the Superman universe."

Warner's Semel was less than enthused with the fantastic yarn; Salkind received little support from the studio, his key distribution channel.

Of equal concern was just who exactly would portray the rebirthed character. Earlier, Salkind had toyed with the idea of a *Young Superman* film with Newton, but the actor's legal hassles and frail charisma had eighty-sixed it. Christopher was eager to carry the role into full heroic adulthood in theaters, but schedule concerns meant that Salkind might have to pull *Superboy* from the air. That left only their perpetual go-to guy.

"I went to meet with Chris Reeve in New York, and of course he was in great shape," Salkind recalled. "That was in the early 1990s. He read

Replacement Superboy Gerard Christopher heads the 1989–1992 cast of *Superboy*; Stacy Haiduk portrayed Lana Lang. Christopher's hiring in the second season coincided with a boost to the ailing series that placed it among the top ten offerings in syndication.

(Everett Collection)

the script, and he would've done it. We did talk a little bit about Gerard Christopher, but we really wanted Chris." Bates and Jones—who had been told to ignore the three sequels—had written Superman with an older Reeve in mind.

Reeve had done little to alter the base composition of his career since the stillbirth of the fourth installment. He had gotten positive notices for his work—in yet another newsroom setting—in 1988's *Switching Channels*, but few offers had come in. Not only was Reeve blanketed in the cape, but the mediocre sequels had also dulled that lone claim to fame. By 1990, he was accepting roles in made-for-TV films such as *Bump in the Night* with Meredith Baxter Birney.

If Reeve was tempted by the financial promise of *Superman: The New Movie*, he kept it to himself. Speaking with Jay Leno after the comedian took over for Johnny Carson on *The Tonight Show*, Reeve acknowledged his pending fortieth birthday and felt that a younger caretaker should assume the role for a new generation. In the end, the actor lamented that his responsibility to the character had waned with the latter sequels. He was not eager to put himself in a position to disappoint fans yet again.

Superboy's fourth season, which aired from fall 1991 to spring 1992, would continue the production's new tradition of offering plot threads torn from the comics pages. Salkind's fetish for more sensational science fiction elements, rebuffed by Warner for features, found airplay in his absence: episodes featured body switching, alternate time lines, and alien adversaries.

"Obituary for a Super Hero" is the series at its most clever, offering a faux newscast that reports the grim news of Superboy's expiration. "Know Thine Enemy" explores the oppressive childhood of Lex Luthor, part of a disturbing trip through the villain's mind. In "A Change of Heart," when Superboy is framed for Lana's "death," he submits to the legal process and allows himself to be booked and jailed.

Adventures of Superman costars Noel Neill and Jack Larson, who had developed a close offscreen friendship, appeared in "Paranoia." Neill deemed Christopher a worthy successor to George Reeves. (That same year, cable network Nick at Nite began screening the 1950s series to an eager prime-time audience; baby boomers who had been glued to the show as children turned their nostalgia into strong ratings for the channel.)

After Pistor departed to oversee other Viacom properties, Christopher approached executives with the idea that he assume executive producer duties. The actor argued he was on set every day; he had even written several episodes. Viacom agreed, and Christopher enjoyed roles both on and off camera.

Warner, which had been virtually oblivious to comics properties in the 1970s, was keenly aware of the current demand for their valued icons. The studio was prepping *Batman Returns* for a summer 1992 release and had just debuted a live-action *Flash* series for CBS. That the Salkinds retained control of their star character began to strike executives as unacceptable.

Warner's comics arm suddenly became less receptive to the faithful adaptation the Salkinds had been producing. "Let's say DC Comics became very difficult with the approval process," Salkind sighed. Desired guest characters from DC continuity didn't receive the necessary clearance; the former allies became indolent about cooperating.

"The way to make our show go away was to not approve our scripts anymore," Gerard Christopher explained. "So they basically stopped us."

Salkind, who had himself pioneered a myriad of backdoor business techniques, recognized the tactic. Warner was hoping that by snipping the series' umbilical cord to DC, it could convince the Salkinds to voluntarily remove themselves from the Superman business.

Salkind eyed the horizon: he and his father were virtually estranged; Warner refused to approve any of his treatments for a new film; DC refused to grant use of their expansive mythology for the TV series. The tactics were repugnant, but Salkind had to respect a checkmate.

The Adventures of Superboy aired its final episode in spring 1992. Realizing there would be no opportunity to tie up loose story threads, producers aired "Rites of Passage," which allowed Clark to learn more about his alien heritage. "It really set me up as Superman," Christopher recalled. "If we'd done another season after that, we would've had to have been more about Superman than Superboy. We kind of grew up."

Viacom assured disappointed viewers that they would distribute a series of TV movies that would provide closure, but they were vaporware. Sets that had been struck were put in storage in the unlikely event that DC would relent; it never happened. The disenfranchised Salkind duo finally sold the rights back to Warner Bros., nearly twenty years after their acquisition.

Worse, *Superboy*'s potentially lucrative afterlife in second-run syndication—it had filmed the requisite one hundred episodes needed for a proper sale—was crippled. Viacom, Warner, and the Salkinds each claimed a stake in the production and refused to cooperate with one another. The series was blacked out until 2006, when an agreement was finally reached to market the abysmal first season on DVD. In the interim, Christopher peddled bootlegged copies from his personal Web site, inviting the ire of Warner, who politely asked him to stop.

The actor felt particular resentment over a missed opportunity behind the camera. Pistor had promised him a directing gig on the series, but her word went unfulfilled, both during and after her tenure. Christopher was instead paid a salary to direct a future Viacom show that never came to pass.

"To me, that was probably the biggest disappointment of being involved with the show. I really wanted to direct. That's a cliche, but I really wanted to. I had studied directing. And if I had a TV show like that in the can, my show or another show, it would've started me on the road. I would probably still be directing now."

———

Despite DC's plugged creative funnel, the company had little problem being inspired by the series they helped slay. Editor Mike Carlin, who had acted as a liaison to the Salkind venture, was intrigued by their fourth-season plans to "murder" the Man of Steel.

Despite the media frenzy over the *Batman* film franchise, comics sales had flatlined among casual readers. At the same time, the speculative market had exploded: "investors" would purchase new comics in the hopes they would become valuable collector's items. Publishers initiated a series of stunts to catch the attention of speculators. Comics series were frequently rebooted to issue #1, the better to imply a clean slate; multiple covers compelled buyers to snap up several copies of the same issue; holographic images and better-quality paper also contributed to the new emphasis on gloss over content.

Marvel had gobbled up an appreciable market share thanks to their relaunches of popular titles like *X-Men* and *Spider-Man*, many of them helmed by name-brand illustrators like Todd McFarlane and Jim Lee. DC had no affiliation with pencil wielders with that kind of recognition, but they did have one advantage over Marvel: the mass penetration Batman and Superman enjoyed in mainstream culture.

Word began to leak among news outlets that Superman would be perishing in an upcoming issue. The gimmick was nothing new to the medium—the character had "died" umpteen times in his fifty years on the racks—but never before had the hype been so effective. Fans not accustomed to the conventions of the comics medium actually believed he would be buried forever; local newscasts filmed the emotionally gullible sobbing as they stood in line for *Superman* #75, ostensibly his final appearance. Others morbidly wore a black armband with the "S" insignia.

The ruse worked. *Superman* and its ancillary titles enjoyed circulation into the millions, with speculators snatching up multiple copies with the expectation that they would increase in value. Their hopes were pathetically ill informed. Comics that commanded high prices on the secondary market were ancient titles that had been discarded by rueful mothers decades prior. With so few copies remaining, high prices met demand. But with so many buyers now hoarding issues and practicing immaculate storage policies, pristine copies of Superman's death issue—like so many comics stunts of the era—were plentiful.

Much to the embarrassment of weepy fans, Superman returned less than a year later, both in the comics continuity and, perhaps more surprisingly, on television. Warner felt its *Batman* saga was filling its coffers nicely in the film market; Superman, it believed, was better suited for a workout in prime time.

Krypton by Moonlight

It's pretty stunning for a show to go from being very popular and having a buzz,
to all of a sudden being in the toilet.
—Susan Nathan, McCann-Erickson ad agency, on *Lois & Clark*

In November 1993, Warner Bros. purchased a full-page ad in *Variety* touting its most ironic acquisition to date: the total and complete film rights to its own comics headliner Superman and all of his myriad supporting crew. The Salkinds were no longer responsible for adapting the character into other media, a fact that ardent enemies of the later Reeve sequels would likely find comforting.

In a preemptive welcome-home party, producers of the *Tiny Toon Adventures* direct-to-video movie *How I Spent My Vacation* had animated a Superman cameo alongside the teenage protégés of Bugs and Daffy. Meanwhile the studio, eager to flex its litigious power, brought legal action against the comics fanzine *Hero Illustrated*, which had used Superman images for a series of trading cards without permission. The messages, both genial and harsh, were clear: Superman was home.

Like many tentacle-armed studios of the day, Warner had been structuring their business around the concept of synergy. A property would be dispersed throughout their various outlets for maximum profit potential. *Batman Returns* had performed to expectations at the box office; fans clamoring for more Bat-mythos could then turn on their television for appointments with *Batman: The Animated Series*. Perhaps a bowl of Batman Cereal would sate appetites afterward. And if one wasn't completely overwhelmed by then, there were always the half-dozen Batman comics titles on specialty store shelves. (The printed media that had birthed so many iconic film heroes was, as ever, largely ignored by the machine it helped create.)

Batman was a pillar of Warner, a perpetual cash cow that could be milked indefinitely; there was no reason Superman shouldn't be able to emulate his morbid ally's success. Salkind had done little to attempt a licensing push for his *Superboy* series, virtual blasphemy to a studio that had shilled everything Batman, from toothbrushes to beach towels. Hundreds of millions could be made in ancillary product: George Lucas had built his Skywalker Ranch, emancipating himself from Hollywood, with such a strategy.

Superman would be renewed on film, the studio plotted. And live-action television. And cartoons. Video games.

The only question was which incarnation would be the first to welcome audiences back to Metropolis.

DC's president and editor in chief Jenette Kahn had long held the belief that a Superman TV series should build to the long-teased consummation of Lois and Clark's eternal whatevership. In the ultimate display of corporate unity, the marriage ceremony would take place simultaneously on television and in the comics pages.

Kahn was partial to one particular twist of her own creation, a concept for a television series called *Lois Lane's Daily Planet*. The program would place the emphasis on the female reporter's dalliances with gutsy journalism and her meek oddball of a peer, Clark Kent. The title alone would hint to audiences that this wasn't a smash-'em-up action series but a courtship with a twist. The future groom would just happen to be the most powerful being on Earth.

Kahn's template had been discovered when Warner Bros. bought Lorimar Telepictures and the production company's staffers began combing through the Warner archives for salable series ideas. Kahn's idea was essentially *Superman* meets *Moonlighting*, exactly the kind of pithy high concept embraced by the industry's impatient decision makers.

The format was agreeable, but *Lois Lane's Daily Planet* was deemed too limiting a title; execs contemplated *Metropolis* before settling on the slightly unwieldy *Lois & Clark: The New Adventures of Superman.* Deborah Joy LeVine, a writer/producer who had overseen several telefilms and written for the short-lived legal drama *Equal Justice*, was asked to script the pilot. The studio was adamant about the series putting emphasis on the relationship between the titular duo, but the pilot could be as expansive as LeVine wished. Superman would see plenty of action, as long as his contentious interaction with Lois was paramount.

LeVine consulted with her brother, a ravenous comics fan, for details on the character's tumultuous history with Lane and other minutiae. She drew from the snappy, staccato dialogue of films like *The Thin Man* to give the series' leads the appropriate interpersonal style. Properly armed with key points of the mythology on one hand and cinematic inspiration on the other, LeVine wrote a feature-length pilot, which was scheduled to be shot on 35-mm film and given an $8 million budget, generous by the medium's standards of the day.

LeVine would then be charged with one of the more intimidating tasks of genre filmmaking: finding an actor who looked believable in red underwear. Hundreds of male mannequins flooded open casting calls; most possessed the requisite looks, but few seemed to have any degree of charm or performance ability.

Gerard Christopher, who had found himself unemployed as a result of the Salkind-Warner wrangling, figured he might as well go for broke. "I felt like I deserved to get the role," he said. "I had done one hundred episodes of this thing and had the character down by now."

Producers agreed: he walked into the audition and impressed evaluators with his poise and comic book looks. The meeting was successful, right up to the point when one of them looked at his filmography and stared agape at his three-year stint as Superboy. Screaming, the producer threw down the photo resume and charged the actor with deceptive audition practices. Christopher was ushered out.

Finally, producers settled on two choices: Kevin Sorbo, a hulking actor who had found a modicum of success playing beefy guest stars in episodic television, and Dean Cain, a writer/actor who had been a free agent for the Buffalo Bills before getting sidelined with a knee injury. (He would later find some measure of tabloid infamy when it was rumored he had taken Brooke Shields's virginity when both attended Princeton University.)

To LeVine's mind, Cain was more Superboy than Superman. The twenty-seven-year-old had a juvenile energy about him, which was hardly welcome on a series debuting only a year after Salkind's *Superboy* had exited the airwaves. Born Dean George Tanaka, the quarter-Japanese Cain was also ethnic-looking, a departure from the WASPy Men of Steel from years past. Still, his audition was impressive. Cain's Clark was self-assured, a trait demanded by the show's focus on Superman's mortal alter ego.

LeVine brought both candidates to ABC and Warner executives, who settled on the affable Cain over the stiffer Sorbo. While Cain had unconventional good looks, Superman was, after all, an alien from another planet. It was logical that he wouldn't look like a fugitive from Middle America. The actor, who had figured on a career in screenwriting thanks to his Princeton pedigree, ignored both a friend's warning that he would be "forever known as Superman" and the offer of a writing contract with Hollywood Pictures. A fan of *Super Friends* from his cereal-gobbling days, he thought the part would be too much fun to pass up.

"I remember the first day I worked there was the same day Dean Cain got hired," recalled Bryce Zabel, one of LeVine's coworkers on *Equal Justice* who had been invited to step on as supervising producer for the series. "I just remember how thrilled he was. I remember saying to him, 'Hey, man, your life is never going to be the same. You're Superman. Very elite club.'"

LeVine used Cain as a sounding board for auditioning Lois candidates. Teri Hatcher, an actor who had been a recurring damsel on *MacGyver*, was the twelfth and final prospect for the costarring role. Her energy impressed LeVine, who hired her with the provision that she cut her long hair into a style more practical for a city-hopping reporter.

———

LeVine's *Moonlighting* homage instantly began a homogenization process when ABC slotted the series for Sunday nights at 8 P.M. Relegated to "family hour" viewing instead of a midweek 10 P.M. slot, the series could flirt with sexual subtext but never become overt with it. The warring reporters would have dalliances, but the focus on Superman's spandexed exploits increased. The sophisticated romantic comedy was morphing into an all-ages adventure hour.

The devolution was irritating to LeVine, who really had little interest in spearheading a superhero series. She found little to embrace about Superman's truth and justice spiel and constructed the show to play up the schizophrenic love triangle between two people. Had she known she would be orchestrating endless takes of Superman crashing through walls, it's likely she would've passed on the project. "She felt very strongly about this being Lois's story," Zabel said.

The pilot episode of *Lois & Clark*, however, was already in the midst of production, and it carried with it LeVine's preferred approach to the material. Superman himself wouldn't appear in costume until the climax; the majority of the show would be devoted to the title characters' inaugural meeting and subsequent three-way flirtation. To LeVine's mind, Clark wasn't a necessary deception but who Superman truly was. The blue tights were to shield his private life from intrusion, not the other way around. Cain's dual roles even inverted the character's traditional hairstyles: it was Superman who had a business-slick look, while Clark's locks were softened. Lois, meanwhile, was poles apart from the Noel Neill interpretation of the character; she knew karate and wasn't afraid to use it.

Clark's heroics, which included salvaging a botched space shuttle mission, pushed the budget past ABC's comfort zone. Economically stubborn, at one point they threatened to come in and shut down production if work continued past 5 P.M. In case they weren't bluffing, LeVine locked the doors from the inside. She later cut out twenty-plus pages of action sequences to trim costs.

The fretting didn't stop the network from ordering six more episodes before the pilot was finished; the order was later extended to thirteen, and eventually a full season. The stuttered backing was indicative of the network's slow build to confidence in LeVine's take on the material.

In an effort to balance LeVine's point of view, ABC installed David Jacobs as a producer; the writer had an impressive television resume, which included creating *Dallas* in the late 1970s. "I don't think David Jacobs had a feel for the characters at all," offered a source involved with the production. "I don't think he and Deborah particularly got along. It strikes me that David was used to being treated as the king, and Deborah doesn't treat anybody like the king."

After assembling a substantial amount of footage, LeVine and executives made a pilgrimage to the San Diego Comic-Con in the summer of 1993. Attendees were fanatical about their comics adaptations, and they would provide producers with crucial feedback about how the series would resonate with fans of Superman's four-color universe. The promo reel, which highlighted ABC's expensive effects work, was met with applause. At least fandom wasn't about to raise any ire.

Debuting in September 1993, two months before Warner made their "official" declaration of Superman ownership, *Lois & Clark* was ABC's counterprogramming answer to one of CBS's perennial Sunday-night institutions, the Angela Lansbury crime drama *Murder, She Wrote*. Immediately, the press trumpeted *Lois & Clark* and rival NBC program *seaQuest DSV* as locked in a battle for second-place supremacy. *SeaQuest* sported a brand association as strong as Superman himself: Steven Spielberg, one of the few directors who could command attention on name alone. And like *Lois & Clark*, *seaQuest* was an action-adventure hour designed to appeal to audiences bored with Lansbury's geriatric detective.

LeVine's pilot was well regarded by critics, who were shocked that the series could balance spirited fantasy with a grounded romance, seemingly appealing to multiple demographics with panache. It was, however, less

Actors Dean Cain and Teri Hatcher in a 1997 publicity photo for the last season of the ABC series *Lois & Clark: The New Adventures of Superman*. The program's ceaseless teases about impending nuptials angered devotees and led to anemic ratings.

(© Warner Bros./Everett Collection)

a hit with viewers, who had ignored ABC's flashy promo ads over the summer featuring a sleeveless Cain cradling Hatcher, a Superman logo tattooed on his arm. Predictably, *Murder, She Wrote* throttled both actioners in head-to-head competition, providing journalists with ready-made analogies about an elderly woman besting both the Man of Steel and Hollywood's premier power player.

With the show's warring conceptual ideals, the first season swayed uncomfortably between romantic entanglement and the standard, mod-estly budgeted superheroics of Supermen past. In most instances, Lois's investigative moxie would launch her into dangerous situations, which Clark/Superman would then have to salvage. John Shea's Lex Luthor popped up as a recurring menace, using his billionaire profile to stir up trouble. In other episodes, woebegone scientists would watch as their mis-guided experiments put the people of Metropolis in mortal danger.

Staff writers had several interesting ideas for drumming up conflict in the *Daily Planet* offices. At one point, they suggested that one of the *Planet*'s employees reveal he or she has AIDS in order for the show to explore topical issues. When that was vetoed, they offered that Clark could encounter more mundane evils like wife beating or child abuse. Violating Mankiewicz's rules, they also proposed Superman become aware of a hole in the ozone layer that even he can't fix. ABC and DC weren't receptive.

Zabel once advised the staff that the series could infuse itself with a suf-ficient amount of gravitas by killing Jonathan Kent via heart attack; when that didn't fly, it was discussed that, in step with the current generation's marital woes, Jonathan and Martha could separate, with Pa ending up the occupant of Clark's couch. Again, those with final say refused to be that daring with the narrative.

Superman's physical prowess was the subject of much debate. Like Reeves before him, Cain was limited in his powers not by imagination but by the economic realities of television. DC suggested more emphasis on sound effects work to better depict his various abilities. They made specific reference to Max Fleischer's Superman and the corresponding signs of his physical effort: veins popping, sweat beads forming.

Because the show was slotted in the family hour, LeVine was insistent that Superman never beat anyone with his fists, requiring the more frequent display of his other extranormal abilities. She railed against X-ray vision on the grounds that the red eyes reminded her of a rabid animal.

Cain's costume was a constant work in progress, with the cape alternately deemed too invasive or too flowing, and the "S" crest either too large or too small. Early on, Zabel and staffers petitioned DC to allow them to change Superman's costume color scheme.

"We wanted to change his outfit to accent black over blue," Zabel said. "And that just got gonged. Our attitude was, he was just a little bright for today's sensibilities. One of our proposed changes was that the red trunks became black. We just thought they looked a little crazy in today's world. Then we came to love the regular costume."

When not at the mercy of costume designers, Cain lobbied producers for an opportunity to write an episode; his "Season's Greedings" would become a second-season entry. Perhaps because the series allowed Cain to flex some of his other creative muscles, he seemed enthused about the role. "Some people are thrilled to be working and some people don't realize their good fortune at the time. But Dean was thrilled," said Zabel. "His range as an actor, there's that Dean Cain range, which I find comforting."

Zabel also had praise for Hatcher, describing her as "an actress that can just blow you away in a scene." But both stars could be petulant: they would often complain to LeVine about each other's behavior. One day, a man appeared on set bearing a measuring wheel, normally used to measure the proximity of motor vehicles after traffic accidents. When asked what he was doing, the man responded, "Teri thinks Dean's trailer is closer to the set than hers."

It was, by a foot. Producers had it moved up.

Near the end of the season, his hostility toward LeVine growing, ABC-installed producer Jacobs went off on his own writing trek, scripting a story that was scheduled to go into production the following week. When he returned with a draft, he was met with staffers who couldn't believe he had finished a teleplay without first introducing the idea to them or allowing for story conferences.

"He didn't run it past anybody; he just went and wrote this thing at home, brought it in, and said, 'Here it is,'" said a source. "We all read it and kind of went, 'Wow, this isn't very good.' The Emperor suddenly had no clothes." Jacobs was shown the door not long after.

Ratings continued to flatline throughout the season. Fortunately, ABC, which had spent a literal fortune on the pilot, was not in a position to get out of the Superman business prematurely. Nothing was in the wings that would provide substantial competition to CBS's mature murder mystery. Television, which normally prided itself on excising dead weight with all the speed of the Flash (itself a first-season casualty on CBS three years prior), would offer respite to the beleaguered hero.

With a few concessions.

By the second-season premiere, LeVine was out. The producer understood ABC's strategy to counter both *seaQuest* and Lansbury with visceral action but had no interest in deviating from the romantic focus of her initial pilot. Robert Singer, a producer on *Reasonable Doubts* and the cult hit *Midnight Caller*, was assigned LeVine's chair. The writer's room, formally home to scribes who leaned toward romance and flirtatious dialogue, was repopulated with action-adventure scenarists.

Tracy Scoggins, who portrayed lecherous gossip columnist Cat Grant, had been conceived as a foil for Lois and a potential suitor for Clark.

Unfortunately, few believed the earnest Kent would ever seriously consider doting on the amorous Grant. Moreover, Grant's sexual innuendo, welcome in LeVine's conception of the series, was a poor fit for ABC's family hour mandates. Scoggins was given her walking papers.

Michael Landes, who portrayed Jimmy Olsen as a somewhat naive but smooth cub photographer, was also shown the door. Some viewers had complained his dark looks were too similar to Cain's, his persona too mature for the normally bumbling Olsen. The dimpled Justin Whalin was hired as his replacement, presumably to help counter the young-girl demographic appeal of *seaQuest*'s Jonathan Brandis. Lane Smith, who made a formidable Perry White (and whose audition had convinced producers not to cast White as an African American), escaped the ax.

John Shea was not so fortunate. The actor had portrayed a particularly devious Luthor in a recurring role throughout the first season, succeeding as a menace even with a full head of hair. Singer felt that after innumerable appearances in Superman's adventures over the years, the undefeatable villain would inspire apathy in viewers. Of all the changes instituted for the second season, the displacement of Luthor, a crucial component of Superman's story, was the most egregious. Jim Crocker, a writer and walking library of DC lore, came on to consult with Singer over such sweeping decisions but left over personal differences with the producer.

If *Lois & Clark* could take solace in anything, it was that *seaQuest* was faring equally poorly in the battle for Lansbury's leftovers. Series star Roy Scheider, who had been featured in Spielberg's *Jaws*, was a public relations nightmare, dubbing his own show "childish trash" in interviews. Spielberg's *Jurassic Park* had been a breakthrough in optical work, but the trickle-down effect was in evidence in his tightly budgeted show's underwater escapades. Alien life-forms were often nothing more than glorified cartoon characters, a demerit when the show's producers were given the same edict as *Lois & Clark*'s: action was prioritized over all.

SeaQuest floundered, making it to a third season primarily due to Spielberg's influence. Scheider insisted he be released from his contract and appeared in only a few final-season episodes.

At ABC's insistence, *Lois & Clark*'s second season was more heavily invested in the villain-of-the-week template. Sitcom star Bronson Pinchot had a recurring role as the smirking Prankster; the Sound Man (Michael Des Barres) was a self-explanatory ham; also-ran guest stars provided little in the way of energy. The show was skirting the line drawn (and crossed) by Adam West's *Batman* three decades prior.

Producers even attempted to woo Marlon Brando for a guest spot, with predictably negative results. Even known Superman fan Jerry Seinfeld begged off, not willing to incur the wrath of his own personal ATM, the NBC network.

Despite the alterations, ratings plummeted. The sole ray of hope was Hatcher's appeal to young males and her timely emergence as an early Internet superstar. One of Hatcher's publicity photos, which featured her draped in Superman's cape, became a trivia answer: the shot was downloaded twenty thousand times over a six-month period, crowning her the most-viewed (and, truth be told, most-masturbated-to) cyberwoman in the world.

The eager response from the technologically inclined swayed ABC into rethinking their current strategy. Perhaps viewers would embrace a return to the courtship aspect of the series, particularly if it meant more of Hatcher swooning and batting her considerable eyelashes at Clark, himself an avatar for the romantically bereft among the audience. The network finally recognized the dynamic that had kept the entanglement alive for decades in the comic books: the genial frustration viewers felt whenever Clark was tempted to reveal his secret to Lois.

Ratings picked up considerably toward the latter half of the second season, when more adult themes were reintroduced. (By this time, ABC had plotted to migrate the series from its Sunday-night home to a mid-week slot, though the network never went through with it.) Increasingly, the series would tease the revelation, only to have conceits like time travel restore the status quo.

For the season finale, Clark proposed to Lois, finally expediting their romance, though ABC had no intention of capping their relationship so quickly.

———

Lois & Clark's upcoming third season would end with the series among the year's top twenty-five programs, one of the more accomplished about-faces for any network show. As the season began, viewers were properly invested in Clark's struggle to maintain his facade with Lois, though it was clearly a conflict with an expiration date and no agreeable resolution. Either Clark would reveal his secret, ending the tension, or he wouldn't, bloating viewer frustration.

The series had been embraced by a surging contingent of online fans who, inevitably, used Internet message boards as a forum for debating the finer points of genre offerings like *Star Trek*. Producer Singer would frequent threads, gauging viewer interest in particular areas. Most amateur op-eds demanded that Clark be honest with Lois.

ABC finally agreed. The third-season premiere saw Clark offer full disclosure to Lois about his secret habits. (True to her investigative leanings, Lane had her suspicions all along.) Fans were excited over the revelation— though, inevitably, many questioned the viability of the series in the long term minus the undercurrent of suspicion and dual identities.

Shows that relied on the sexual and emotional tension between its leads, only to consummate it, often suffered from what critics would come to call *Moonlighting* Syndrome, after the Bruce Willis/Cybill Shepherd series from the mid-1980s. Once Willis's David and Shepherd's Maddie admitted their feelings, the show lost its reason to exist. To avoid this problem with *Lois & Clark*, LeVine had once mandated that the supercouple not embrace each other until the fifth season, allowing just enough time to explore their post-vow lifestyle before the show came to its natural conclusion.

Instead, Singer and his staff turned to a new conceit, allowing the duo to become romantically involved but teasing viewers over when they would finally be married. The thread dangled over much of the third season, culminating in a story arc that had them making definitive wedding plans; ABC even circulated publicity photos of the couple in full nuptial regalia. While the climax to the narrative would seem to seriously impede story potential, ABC, fueled by the strong ratings of their junior year, had renewed the show for two more seasons.

Whether the network had second thoughts about allowing producers to paint themselves into a corner or whether the showrunners had that revelation on their own is unclear. Regardless, Lois and Clark's union was nothing more than a big tease. As it turns out, Clark was inadvertently preparing to marry a *clone* of Lois, not the real thing.

Such swerves had long been a hallmark of *Superman's* comic book lore, so the writers may have considered the story in keeping with the spirit of the franchise. For series fans not weaned on the machinations of comic books, however, it did not amuse. The faux wedding incited a substantial backlash from viewers, hardly salved when producers had Clark reengage the real Lois—who promptly got amnesia.

Lois & Clark lost over six million viewers during the non-wedding fiasco, a figure that made ABC very nervous over its two-year commitment to a series that suddenly appeared to be treading water. The generous pickup was met with clenched teeth from ABC's new superiors at the Walt Disney Company, which had just purchased the network in its ongoing attempt to branch into every media platform available.

Disney's pervasive influence, which had long frustrated Max Fleischer, was set to ground another one of Superman's caretakers.

———

Hemorrhaging viewers had one benefit: it allowed producers to trump ABC's concerns over Lois and Clark's partnership and finally satisfy impatient fans by setting a wedding date. The decision was hastily passed on to DC editors, who had long been promised that the event would provide an opportunity for some synergistic interplay between the two arms of Warner. Having virtually no time to prepare, the company issued *Superman: The Wedding Album*, which proposed to detail Lois and Clark's "real" ceremony. Cramped by deadline constraints, the book didn't hold much in the way of emotive magic for readers.

Cognizant of their errors the previous season, the crew planted tongue in cheek and titled the fourth-season marriage episode "Swear to God, This Time We're Not Kidding." Fans swore to God that they found it all to be too little, too late. Worse, the threats from wheezing *Murder, She Wrote* were replaced by the upstart FOX network's *Simpsons* phenomenon. Lois and Clark's expedited marriage seemed to only hasten their departure from the air.

Though ABC had assured producers the series would get a fifth-season pickup, no formal agreement was in place. Sensing the network was losing faith, Warner offered a talent exchange: if ABC would guarantee another season—putting the show up and over the one hundred episodes needed for syndication—Warner would agree to offer the studio's highly coveted *Rosie O'Donnell* daytime talk show to a huge slice of ABC markets. The deal was agreeable to both parties, and fans anticipated another year.

ABC, however, had failed to consult with its new supervisors at Disney, particularly Michael Eisner. The CEO's pet project was resurrecting the *Wonderful World of Disney* anthology series for Sunday-night family viewing. Suddenly, the network's promise to renew the show seemed to run counter to Eisner's demands.

Quietly, ABC shuffled the remaining fourth-season episodes to Saturday nights, the graveyard of network television. Fans, predictably livid, began populating the Internet with petitions for clemency. They even collected funds to take an ad out in *Variety* to plea for the show's resuscitation. ABC, in a demoniac stunt, offered to match their charity dollar for dollar, then held off placing the ad until it was virtually too late for it to have any impact. The faux placating went over like a lead balloon.

Lois & Clark's fourth-season finale held the promise of what was to come in the show after its planned renewal. A baby shows up on the newly-weds' doorstep, inviting questions as to who it is, where it came from, and if Clark will be willing to replicate the Kents' sacrifice of time and emotion to raise the foundling. But no opportunity was afforded the series to tie things up conclusively.

ABC paid dearly for hewing to Eisner's orders. Because it had committed to another season—and had taken advantage of Warner's offer to syndicate

Rosie to its affiliates—it was forced to settle with the studio for reneging to the tune of a rumored $40 million. (*The Wonderful World of Disney* ran eight seasons to generally strong ratings, repurposing select films from the Disney oeuvre and offering the occasional original telefilm.)

Fans who presumed themselves blameless were in for a shock when newly unemployed producer Robert Singer began making the eulogy rounds for the series. Singer insisted that the show met an untimely end thanks to its ardent viewers, who had demanded the couple be married off.

The accusations did little to endear Singer to an already irate group of supporters, who, determined to rise above network dictatorship, began writing their own version of a fifth season. Eventually, their homegrown tales grew and multiplied to fill online story depots that numbered in the thousands. Some writers explored what happened to the mystery infant, while others concerned themselves with the more intimate details of Lois and Clark's love affair. Particularly lurid corners of the Web housed explicit fantasies about Clark's hidden obsession with Jimmy Olsen. The erotic escapades were clearly noncanonical.

For his part, Cain seemed indifferent to the controversy, telling the *Boston Herald* that he had grown tired of the role and wished to move on. The actor's restlessness may have been fueled by his fear of heights, the latest in irony for any performer donning Superman's cape.

Both Cain and Hatcher experienced a degree of resistance when trolling for other roles. After unremarkable appearances in several TV movies, Cain—like many Supermen before him—gravitated to business behind the camera. He produced (and hosted) TBS's *Ripley's Believe It or Not!* an often morbid enterprise that spotlighted the bizarre undercurrents of society: weird piercings, medical mysteries, and useless talents. The show was a financial success story for Cain, who lamented its cancellation after four seasons in 2003. Commenting on TBS's replacement programming, Cain wished that "they die a miserable burning death." Hatcher's career had a longer hibernation period, broken in 2004 when she costarred in ABC's hit *Desperate Housewives.*

Superman had, for the time being, outlived his usefulness on television. The emphasis placed on his relationship with Lois was a clever maneuver, but one born out of necessity. To appropriately document Superman's superhuman activities, budgetary requirements would far outsize the limitations of network product.

Warner, which had seen *Lois & Clark* teeter on the edge of the abyss for years, had put plans in motion to resume the character's big-screen adventures almost immediately after retaining the rights to do so in 1993. And the first man they phoned was Jon Peters, a former hairdresser turned maverick film producer, with all the accompanying baggage such a background promised to entail.

Down, Down, and Astray

The studio spent upward of $50 million without shooting a single frame of film.
It went beyond disaster, into fiasco.
—Kevin Smith

Jon Peters is, by the accounts of many disgruntled former employees, an egomaniacal and violent man with a propensity for shouting down his subservients and taking only cursory interest in the fine details of a project. Many claim he suffers from a severe lack of reading comprehension; some have pegged him as functionally illiterate. Others have complained that his preferred method of resolving disputes usually involves physical threats.

In spite of those qualities—or as a result of them—Peters was also, for a time, one of the highest-paid producers in the film industry. He had supervised Tim Burton's record-shattering *Batman*, which granted him a degree of cachet that few production chairs enjoyed and landed him and producing partner Peter Guber leading roles at Sony Pictures. They were paid multi-millions to essentially run that fledgling studio into the ground.

Undeterred by the spectacular implosion at Sony, Warner offered Peters a job in the spring of 1994, after Guber—who considered Peters an emotional terrorist—schemed to oust him from the rival studio. While Peters had not thrived across the avenue, his track record was undeniable: Peters had championed *Batman* as well as *Rain Man* and *Flashdance*. His commercial instincts could often swing a studio's bottom line into the black.

In late 1993, soon after *Lois & Clark* premiered to meager ratings, Peters found himself in the company of producer Joel Silver and new Warner executive Lorenzo di Bonaventura at Silver's plantation in South Carolina. While jogging, di Bonaventura casually mentioned to Peters that the studio had recently reacquired the screen rights to Superman and considered his resuscitation in cinemas to be a high priority. Peters was ecstatic: after the Sony debacle, a high-profile franchise project that mirrored his success on *Batman* would be a welcome return to form.

Before the run was over, Peters and di Bonaventura had agreed: Peters would orchestrate a new Superman film.

Minus, Peters thought, that stupid goddamn costume.

Jon Peters was born in 1945, got his fill of formal education by the seventh grade, enrolled in beauty school as a teenager, and had opened up his own salon by his early twenties. When Peters wasn't busy provoking street fights, he was making himself romantically available to his star clientele, including Donner's Lois Lane auditionee Lesley Ann Warren and, most notably, Barbra Streisand. In a stirring metaphor for their odd coupling, Peters once tried to convince Streisand to have Evel Knievel perform a stunt during a concert scene in *A Star Is Born*, a film the hairdresser was inexplicably put in charge of producing.

Peters's peculiar brand of machismo entranced Streisand, who was sufficiently enamored with her new beau to allow him such responsibility despite the fact that he had no experience on a film set. Peters promoted his creative choices by getting into shoving matches with other producers and insisting he costar in the film when first choice Kris Kristofferson turned down the the project. (Kristofferson would later agree to star.) When director Jerry Schatzberg left the production, Peters demanded to take his place. He was not granted his wish.

Maverick producer Jon Peters in a 1995 publicity portrait. After being tasked with resurrecting Superman for the big screen, Peters drew criticism for his hollow knowledge of the character.

(Everett Collection)

Incredibly, the volatile production resulted in a financial success for Streisand, cementing Peters as a credible player in the industry. Other hits followed, including the cult comedy *Caddyshack* and *The Color Purple*, a Steven Spielberg composition that saw the director ban Peters from the set. Newly estranged from Streisand and partnered with the more grounded Guber, the combustible Peters went on to other profitable projects during the 1980s, culminating with Warner's *Batman* phenomenon.

It was Peters who demanded the studio release the minimalist teaser poster for the film, which consisted of the Batman logo and a release date. The lack of exposition intrigued audiences, who figured such an arcane marketing campaign must herald a worthwhile film. Peters also sank an additional $100,000 into the movie's church-tower finale, insisting that it needed a more spectacular climax. *Batman* sold out screenings across the country, eventually ringing up nearly a half-billion dollars in worldwide business.

Peters's subsequent work at Sony was less impressive. The production of *Radio Flyer* was disjointed: Peters scrapped two weeks of shooting and hired Richard Donner to take over; the film left audiences agape at the odd pairing of fantasy and child abuse. *Hudson Hawk*, a vanity project for Bruce Willis, became a punch line. Most uncomfortably, Peters signed Michael Jackson to a high-profile film deal shortly before he was accused of molesting juvenile guests at his Neverland estate.

Returning to Warner in early 1994, Peters was rewarded for his rash of failures with a five-year production deal, to be christened with his manning of a new Superman film. To the studio, the pairing seemed perfectly logical. Peters apparently knew his comics lore. He had shepherded *Batman* through nearly a decade of development hell, and he could be counted on to rescue the Superman franchise from its own recent difficulties. More important, Peters was fully cognizant of how Superman could be used as a multimedia commodity. He had merchandised *A Star Is Born* with albums and assorted ephemera to huge returns.

Peters, who had genuinely adored Batman, had mixed emotions about the Man of Steel. The producer fancied himself a streetwise rebel and related to the scowling determination and dour attitude of the Dark Knight. Superman, in contrast, was a model of nobility in both appearance and demeanor.

Batman, in short, was a badass. Superman, not so much.

Fortuitously, DC had recently injected an aura of melancholy into Superman's life when he was "killed" at the hands of alien brute Doomsday. It was part of a latter-day movement in comics that spotlighted the emotionally wounded over the bright parade of more gleeful heroes. Readers dismissed Spider-Man's joy at swinging through the Manhattan skyline; they preferred to see him buried alive at the hands of nemesis Kraven the Hunter, who committed suicide at the end of the tale. The Punisher was essentially Batman without a moral compass, a vigilante who shot criminals dead rather than leave them to a depressed justice system. (In a true sign of the times, the gun-toting sociopath even crossed paths with perpetually flummoxed teenager Archie in one of the most bizarre intercompany amalgamations ever, *The Punisher Meets Archie*.)

Peters found the "Death of Superman" story arc to be sufficiently angst filled. He contacted Warner-controlled screenwriter Jonathan Lemkin, who had done some episodic television work and had several unproduced screenplays circulating at the studio, including a well-received draft for a fourth entry in Donner's seemingly endless *Lethal Weapon* series. With his experience in multiple genres from sci-fi to action to horror, Lemkin was believed to have the proper mentality for the hero's fantastic journey beyond death.

Lemkin was met with two constrictive mandates from the studio and Peters. Warner asked to see his ideas before the 1995 Toy Fair, which would help the studio connect with potential toy licensees and reestablish Superman as a viable marketing brand. Peters himself took Lemkin aside and insisted that Superman never be seen flying on-screen. He hated the conceit of Superman zipping around in the air. It struck him as ridiculous and juvenile.

Bound by the superficial restrictions of both his producer and his employer, Lemkin sequestered himself to hammer out an outline for *Superman Reborn*, a loose adaptation of DC's media event. Lemkin, who held no particular allegiance to the character's history, structured a story that held its hero in much the same regard as Warner's *Batman Forever*. That sequel, developed without the input of Tim Burton, was essentially a return to the Adam West mentality of mocking the mythology. Val Kilmer's Batman sported protruding nipples on his sculpted rubber outfit; the morose vigilante loosened up enough to spout "Chicks love the car" when pondering the origins of his sex appeal. Warner had more or less coerced director Joel Schumacher into delivering a two-hour toy commercial. The result was an incoherent mess.

In Lemkin's *Superman Reborn*, as in the comics, Superman is felled at the hands of Doomsday. As he lies dying in Lois's arms, the hero infuses his "spirit" into his Earth lover, impregnating her like the Virgin Mary before expiring. Their progeny grows up in record time to save the world from the villain's threat. Superman's rebirth, literal in the comics, would be the result of a bloodline successor in the film.

The inane concept was presented to Warner executives by both Peters and Lemkin, who appeared effusive about the Christ motif and its considerable toy potential. Warner, which was in the process of launching a chain of retail stores devoted to studio properties like Looney Tunes and the DC universe, commissioned a full draft. But the finished screenplay was so snide in its regard for the titular character that Warner deemed it too reminiscent of the *Batman* sequel—hardly a ringing endorsement. Lemkin was dismissed from any further participation in the project. Later, he would profess great amusement over his attempt to antagonize the religious right with his clumsy allegory.

Peters's next recruit was Gregory Poirier, a screenwriter whose resume of B-movies didn't seem to suggest any particular aptitude for the Superman franchise. Poirier was even chuckled about in some circles for being a reformed writer for the adult film industry, in which he'd penned cursory motivations for performers under the subtle pen name Hugh Jorgan. His frequent collaborator was a director dubbed John T. Bone, for whom he wrote over forty sexually explicit titles. (The feat was likely left off his resume when he later found employment at Disney.)

Poirier's take, while less mocking than Lemkin's, was still irreverent and flirting with sacrilege: his *Superman Reborn* features a morose Man of Steel discussing his problems with a shrink, while comics villains Braniac, Silver Banshee, and Parasite provide the opposition. Facing off against his foes, Superman utilizes martial arts and sports a black rubber suit that Peters obviously ported over from Batman; Doomsday appears, oozing liquid Kryptonite, the better to fell the hero. In a bit of corporate synergy, Batman appears during Superman's "funeral" to pay his respects.

In the ethereal afterlife, Superman is counseled by both his fathers, the Kryptonian Jor-El and Earth's Jonathan Kent. Distressed his destiny hasn't been properly fulfilled, Superman awakens in the spaceship of friend Cadmus. Now powerless, he borrows Cadmus's superpowered suit to replicate his normal abilities. (In deference to Peters, the suit doesn't allow him to fly.) Myriad battles with the villains ensue, until Superman's impotence is resolved. By the climax, both Lois and Jimmy Olsen are aware of his secret identity.

Poirier's story isn't bashful about the more absurd conventions of comics. Parasite dubs himself Mayor of Metropolis; Braniac demands Superman's body (so he can harvest his DNA) or else he'll flatten the city with his massive spaceship. Weakened, Superman undergoes extensive martial arts training to restore his constitution. The entire narrative is filled with stylistic references to contemporary films—everything from *Independence Day* to *The Karate Kid*—regardless of how badly they might clash with the Superman legend. Remarkably, Lemkin and Poirier omitted Lex Luthor, who had been present for virtually all of Superman's prior adaptations.

Superman's chats with his psychologist were indicative of Poirier's notion that Superman be more existential, more preoccupied with his place in the world than with salvaging collapsing bridges. Peters, who fancied himself an outcast, began to warm to the idea that an alien from Krypton would naturally feel segregated from Earth society. He championed the script, but Warner, believing that a thoughtful hero makes for a boring hero on toy shelves, vetoed Poirier's rendition. He was Peters's strike two.

If Superman was facing hard times under his current caretakers, his former liaisons to Hollywood weren't faring any better. Christopher Reeve, who had busied himself with a series of TV movies since the aborted attempt to make *Superman: The New Movie* under the Salkind regime, spent his increasing free time jumping horses. During one event in 1995, Reeve's hands became entangled in the bridle as the horse panicked, throwing him headfirst into the ground.

The incident left Reeve a quadriplegic and resurrected tabloid speculation that the role of Superman carried with it a curse. Alyn had failed to find work following his participation in the franchise; Reeves had either shot himself or been murdered; now Reeve would spend the rest of his life in a wheelchair, unable to breathe on his own.

The cloud continued forming over the comics entity: DC had moved three million issues of *Superman* #75 in 1993, but the oversaturation of "collectible" copies had finally reached its limit. By 1996, sales had declined 72 percent. No longer fueled by the rampant spending of ignorant "investors," one of every six comic book stores was closing its doors. Millions of copies of the 1991 reboot *X-Men* #1, once so hotly desired by fans and market watchers, sat in 25-cent bins. Even DC and Marvel's temporary truce, in which they pitted their classic characters against each other in fistfights voted on by readers, did little for morale. The boom was over.

Meanwhile, Jon Peters wasn't finding much momentum outside of his attempts to bring Superman back to screens. He had flirted with the idea of producing *Under Siege 2*, but conflicts with eccentric star Steven Segal almost resulted in violence. His reteaming of Woody Harrelson and Wesley Snipes, a pairing used to great effect in *White Men Can't Jump*, arrived with little fanfare in 1995's *Money Train*. The crime caper tanked at the box office.

Most ignoble of all, Warner's fringe contribution to the Superman mythology, 1997's *Steel*, was a certifiable disaster. In the comics, Steel had been one of the "replacements" for an absentee Superman following his presumed demise. The hero was really John Henry Irons, a hardworking weapons engineer who achieved mythic stature when he created a super-powered suit of armor in honor of his fallen mentor.

The towering character seemed the perfect role for basketball icon Shaquille O'Neal, who would go on to appear in a series of film roles designed to either mock or capitalize on his immense physical stature and fame. But O'Neal, an admitted Superman fan who sported an "S" tattoo on his massive arm, was granite on the screen. The film, which contained virtually no references to the Superman mythology, made an anemic $1.7 million domestically.

Superman's suffering legacy in the mid-1990s captured the attention of two men offering potential salvation: one would attempt to meld Peters's incoherent demands with a devout interpretation of the character, with decidedly mixed results. The other would excel by creating his own stylized rendering of the character's comic book roots.

Superman's success in media seemed predicated on a simple rule: involve as few human beings as possible.

—————

Bruce Timm's love of animation had secured him a job at Filmation for a good portion of the 1980s. Bored with his job at Kmart, the aspiring artist took an animation test at the studio on a whim; he flunked the first time, passed the second. The job led to comics work on Marvel's *Masters of the Universe* title, an offshoot of Filmation's small-screen success *He-Man*; by 1989, Timm found himself under the Warner banner. His work on *Tiny Toon Adventures* led to the chance to cocreate *Batman: The Animated Series* in 1992. The program, which was as moody and sour in tone as the title character himself, was renowned for its meticulous devotion to the source material.

Timm eventually received word from the high offices that a new Superman film was in preproduction. Mindful of Superman's cross-platform potential, the studio figured a new animated series would both serve as a primer for a new film and benefit from the renewed interest in the character the movie would inevitably spawn. Better yet, Warner was set to debut a new network under its own banner and would appreciate (i.e., demand) propri-etary children's programming for afternoon blocks of airtime.

Timm's *Superman: The Animated Series* premiered in 1996. The "Timmverse," as fans of the artist would come to call it, was notable pri-marily for its Fleischer-inspired designs. Both Batman and Superman were square-shouldered he-men. Metropolis, which had long been a facsimile of New York, was more the Metropolis of Fritz Lang's creation, a bustling city with advanced technology that would often present mortal danger for the Man of Steel. And as in Fleischer's depiction, Superman's powers had finite limits: he would sweat and struggle when moving heavy equipment; a bomb might cripple or kill him.

Batman's and Superman's adversaries, with origins and personas ripped from the comics pages, were faithful to the source material. Paul Dini's scripts were a far cry from the simpleminded pabulum offered for years by *Super Friends*. Batman would often get into bone-crunching battles with enemies; Superman would be confronted with any and all manner of technology and otherworldly threats, resulting in property-destroying climaxes. Both heroes were given opportunities to examine their relation-ships and resolve emotional crises, rare for cartoon crime fighters.

Tim Daly, who had spent several successful seasons as Joe Hackett on NBC's *Wings*, became the latest in a line of actors to assume the vocal inflections of Clark Kent and Superman. (Clark's meekness was dialed down considerably; he and Lois were rather fierce rivals at the *Daily Planet,* constantly seeking to trump each other.) Clancy Brown used a rumbling baritone to great effect as Lex Luthor. Virtually every supporting character in the *Superman* comics series made an appearance throughout the show's fifty-four-episode run. Warner, ever mindful of how their properties could complement one another, eventually packaged both *Batman* and *Superman* episodes into one adventure hour. The duo even shared screen time in a few episodes.

The series, which was marketed toward children and didn't have to worry about the costs of exploding planets in live action, had fewer obstacles in bringing Superman to life. The cartoon was not going to make or break Warner's coffers. A lavishly budgeted big-screen disaster, however, could send the company reeling for years.

While Peters was still smarting from the dismissal of Poirier, Warner was busy scouting talent on its own. Filmmaker Kevin Smith had caught its attention with his smart and self-effacing *Clerks* in 1994: the film, which was shot at the convenience store Smith toiled in at the time, was a talky ode to shiftless menial workers with little ambition beyond harassing customers and clocking out. Smith's dialogue, laced with enough profanity to literally embarrass his own mother, was hailed as the voice of a generation. He also happened to be a comics freak who had sold his beloved collection to help fund the film.

Smith's sophomore effort, 1995's *Mallrats,* was a studio effort that led to diminishing returns. He began making rounds as a pen-for-hire, polishing drafts and assisting in dialogue rewrites. In 1996, he was beckoned into Warner offices. Employees tendered a trio of projects they felt he would warm to. Smith glossed over treatments for an *Outer Limits* redux and a *Beetlejuice* sequel to zero in on Greg Poirier's draft of *Superman Reborn.* He took it home, read it, and began scowling.

"There was a scene in which Superman was visiting his analyst, and telling him he, Clark Kent, was indeed Superman, and the analyst opens his office door and says to his secretary, 'Mister Kent is gonna need a lot of appointments . . .' or something along those lines," Smith shuddered. "My impression of that was, 'This can be better.'"

The cloying self-doubt bothered Smith, who trooped back to Warner to voice his discontent. Superman, he said, isn't the angst-ridden mope of Poirier's imagination. He's a rather genial guy who may have some issues, but the stuff on the shrink's couch reeked of a teasing 1950s comics cover.

The executives nodded gravely, parting ways with Smith without a rebuttal. Day after day, the writer/director was called in to relate his grievances to an ascending hierarchy of Warner studio heads. Finally, the elite brass were convinced: Smith was well versed in comics lore and would aspire to render a faithful interpretation of the franchise. He was hired.

Provided Peters agreed.

———

Kevin Smith, the pragmatist, met Jon Peters, the subliterate, in the summer of 1996. The huddle took place at Peters's home in Los Angeles, which Smith would later take great delight during his college lectures in describing as something akin to Batman's Wayne Manor.

Peters, Smith recalled, insisted they would work together well because both "were from the streets." (Smith was a suburban New Jersey kid; Peters had been a hairdresser since his late teens.) He reiterated his disdain for the mores of Superman. He insisted the flying effects from the Reeve films were "crap"; Superman was not to fly. The character's traditional red and blue tights were deemed sexually ambiguous; they were to be worn for only the bare minimum of screen time. Smith was directed to utilize the silver and black tights featured in the "Death of Superman" arc, duds the hero sported following his sojourn in the afterlife.

A puzzled Smith retreated to New Jersey to begin outlining his story, which he then mimed for Peters a few weeks later. To circumvent the no-fly rule, Smith had Superman powerless for much of the story. When he did need to go airborne, it was more a blurring sonic boom effect than a man gliding. Peters enjoyed this, egging him on. But as soon as "Kal-El," Superman's Kryptonian name, escaped Smith's lips, Peters blurted out, "Who's Kal-El?"

Despite Peters's obliviousness to the story's finer points, Smith was given the go-ahead to write a full draft, which he delivered in the fall of 1996. Warner was ecstatic over the script, which seemed to deftly juggle the conflicting edicts handed down by Peters and the expectations of fandom. Still, there were notes. There were always notes. "This is about the toys," the studio admitted to Smith. A scene in which Lois and Clark have a talky exchange on the top of Mount Rushmore was deemed extraneous. Smith didn't flinch, insisting he would walk away if the scene were excised. They relented.

Peters also had suggestions. "Let's add a giant spider," the producer said. "And a dog for Luthor." Peters, who had screened Smith's lesbian comedy *Chasing Amy* recently, thought a homosexual robot would be the film's Chewbacca, comic relief with good merchandising potential. Smith stared at his collaborator blankly. By the time Peters was demanding Superman dodge the swiping paws of polar bears, Smith was digging for his car keys.

Kevin Smith's second draft of *Superman Lives* was delivered in early 1997; Warner executives liked it, in spite of themselves. The unfiltered Smith had joked in the press that execs were calling him up multiple times a day to harangue him about their star property. Smith would later recant, saying that he meant the chairs in Peters's company, not the actual studio. By way of support, radio host Howard Stern professed his love of the script on the air, igniting a smattering of watercooler talk about the project.

Smith's irreverence is in full march in the work, which—like the Lemkin and Poirier drafts—takes its cues from DC's "Death of Superman" saga. His sop to Peters's "robot sidekick" mandate is an obscure DC character named L-Ron, after reviled Scientology founder L. Ron Hubbard. Speeding toward Earth after getting a global transmission from Lex Luthor, the parasitic Brainiac finds himself in Metropolis. On a television soundstage somewhere in that city, Lois Lane and Luthor are debating the merits of "outlawing" Superman within city limits. (The dialogue ends with an enraged Lois pouncing on Luthor.)

Superman's first on-screen appearance in over a decade would be in opposition to a gang of high-tech thugs led by DC villain Deadshot.

Responding to the commotion, he appears as a blur of red, his costume described as "um . . . 90's style" by a miffed Smith. Luthor seethes with the kind of sardonic dialogue Smith had made his name on, threatening Superman's "pajama-clad ass" with legal warfare. The bald villain later teams with Brainiac to construct a device that blocks out the sun's nourishing rays, suffocating the Kryptonian's source of power.

Throughout, Smith takes particular delight in paying homage to DC's literary history. There are references to Gotham City and the Joker; Batman himself appears to offer condolences during Superman's televised funeral. L-Ron and Brainiac's spaceship, complete with alien zoo, seems rife with toy potential, as do Superman's costume changes. His fatal showdown with Doomsday is torn straight from the comics: it's a spectacular slugfest that shakes buildings and cracks pavement. Having expired, he's resuscitated by the Eradicator, a fail-safe android planted by Jor-El to intervene in the event of his death. Together, the duo race toward Metropolis to thwart Brianiac's attempt to destroy the Earth.

Smith even worked in Peters's demand for a giant spider by way of a "Thanagarian Snare Beast," a nod to the home planet of DC hero Hawkman. The climatic battle with the "cross between a squid and a spider" caps Superman's return to action.

The script was light on its feet and genuinely affectionate toward the Superman mythology. Smith's obligation to Peters's bizarre requests didn't seem to prevent him from capturing the kick of an operatic science fiction yarn, the kind of fantastic narrative Salkind had tried to sell Warner on years before.

Superman Lives was given a green light and slotted for a summer 1998 release, just a little over a year away. The rush was on primarily because Warner's other pillar, *Batman*, had finally exhausted its welcome in theaters. Director Joel Schumacher's second visit to Gotham was *Batman & Robin*, a garish, overcooked fiasco that resembled nothing so much as Technicolor vomit. George Clooney and Arnold Schwarzenegger floundered in what amounted to an inadvertent homage to the Adam West series. The franchise's pedigree helped it hobble to a $107 million gross stateside, but it was nonetheless a certifiable disappointment.

Fortunately, *Superman: The Animated Series* was well reviewed and performing admirably, though in an ominous bit of foreshadowing, another ancillary pursuit was not.

Superman: The Escape was a roller coaster in the works at Six Flags Magic Mountain in Southern California that promised to be as violently entertaining a theme park attraction as had ever been constructed: 4.5 *g* of acceleration would send panicked attendees soaring four hundred feet into the air before dropping them at one hundred miles per hour. The entire hellacious journey would take a total of thirty seconds. The ambitious design had been problematic from its inception, and its opening had been delayed for over a year. On the Internet, which was now expanding rapidly, coaster enthusiasts exchanged scuttle about the prototype bursting into flames.

The incident would later seem an apt metaphor for the hero's celluloid trip.

———

Peters began babbling to Smith about recruiting Sean Penn as the Man of Steel because he "had the eyes of a killer." By and large, Smith was content to let Peters and the studio handle the arduous task of casting. He did, however, petition for his friend Robert Rodriguez to assume the reins behind the camera.

"I got a call from Robert, who'd read my draft and really dug it," Smith recalled. "He said Warner Bros. was trying to get him to come on as director. I encouraged him to do it, but ultimately he opted to make a flick at Dimension instead, out of a sense of loyalty to Bob Weinstein." As the head of Dimension Films, the ornery Weinstein had indulged Rodriguez on the limited-appeal vampire splatter flick *From Dusk Till Dawn* and expected some form of reciprocation; Rodriguez decided to helm Dimension's *The Faculty*, the latest in the teen-horror-movie boom that had started with *Scream*.

With Rodriguez dropping out of contention, an internal push began in the studio's bowels to reenlist the man who had turned Batman from a pop art punch line into a billion-dollar franchise.

But while his bent observations on life were well suited to the oppressive Gotham City, Tim Burton did not seem at all appropriate for the neon landscape of Metropolis.

15

Grounded

I made the movie; we just forgot to film it.
—Tim Burton

Timothy William Burton was born in Burbank, California, in 1958, won a scholarship to the California Institute of the Arts at the age of nineteen, and set about forging a career in illustration and animation. At the age of twenty, he attended the San Diego Comic-Con to catch a promotional reel of *Superman: The Movie*. He walked away feeling the flying effects were clumsy.

The artist's views tended toward the dyspeptic; this inclination was in sharp contrast to the work he was asked to do for the Walt Disney Company. The painstaking investments he made in films like *The Fox and the Hound* were clinical and monotone. To sate his darker creative impulses, he made several short films—including *Vincent*, about his childhood idol, Vincent Price. Emboldened, he directed *Pee-wee's Big Adventure* in 1986 (some years before Pee-wee's other big adventure made headlines); *Beetlejuice* was a 1988 hit. And in a move that would guarantee his financial future, he was selected to helm 1989's *Batman* and its even more despondent sequel, 1992's *Batman Returns*.

In 1997, distanced from the *Batman* monolith that had made the director a commodity in mainstream Hollywood, Tim Burton's current

222

filmography was not overflowing with commercial successes. *Ed Wood*, a black-and-white portrait of the B-movie director, was critically hailed but screened in front of mostly empty seats. Mass indifference was fine for a modestly budgeted character study, but his 1996 follow-up *Mars Attacks!* was ignored at a much higher decibel. The Warner Bros. feature, based on the flimsy narrative of a series of trading cards from the 1960s, boasted costly CGI effects and an expensive, expansive cast: Jack Nicholson, Glenn Close, Michael J. Fox, and, for the seeming sheer hell of it, Tom Jones.

It was typical Burton irreverence: The invasion of sadistic creatures from Mars is met with consternation by the world's authorities. The spiteful little terrors, realized via computer imagery, spout *ackackack* babble as they decapitate or vaporize Burton's performers. Audiences looking for a space saga a la *Independence Day* were perplexed to find a sardonic riff on that genre. That's even if they showed up at all; *Mars Attacks!* which inched toward the $100 million budget mark with marketing costs included, grossed less than $38 million.

Burton had signed a long-term deal with the studio in 1994. But thanks to his resistance to continuing the *Batman* franchise in the kid-friendly tone preferred by executives, it was not paying dividends for the studio. Both parties agreed that it would be to Burton's benefit to adapt another pervasive brand; he briefly toyed with the idea of doing a film version of *Scooby-Doo*, the Hanna-Barbera cartoon series that had been playing continually for decades, presumably because the series' pseudohorrific tone would make for an appealing playground. The project never gelled.

Remembering the magic he had worked on *Batman*, the studio finally decided to forward their gestating revival of *Superman* for his perusal. The three screenwriters who had toiled on the project had largely seen the character as an avatar for toys and generously budgeted action sequences; Burton saw the Last Son of Krypton as the ultimate outsider—a lonely soul, lost in a sea of billions on another planet. Themes of alienation had informed much of his work as far back as *Vincent*.

What he was not interested in was a redundantly faithful account of Superman's standard-issue story beats. The studio execs nodded, insisting he would be granted carte blanche to develop his own take. (Provided it

Director Tim Burton arrives at the Los Angeles premiere of *Charlie and the Chocolate Factory* on July 10, 2005. Warner Bros. spent millions on the development of Burton's *Superman* film before pulling the plug in 1998.

(Michael Germana/Everett Collection)

was not too morose: the studio had gotten flak from McDonald's over his *Batman Returns* being "gross" and difficult to peddle in Happy Meals.) He also had reservations about Peters, with whom he had clashed repeatedly on *Batman*. Peters had constantly interjected confounding ideas, fatiguing Burton and his crew. Warner insisted the producer would be reined in.

In April 1997, an eager Burton agreed to a directorial deal worth $5 million. The sweetheart "pay-or-play" contract entitled him to his full salary even if the film never got made. It would be, in retrospect, an important stipulation.

Burton's enthusiasm didn't extend to Smith's script. After being formally contracted to do two drafts, the writer wasn't asked to do a third. He tried to arrange a meeting with Burton, whose office failed to return his phone calls. The shutout proved irritating to Warner executives, who had backed Smith's take and had assured him he would be working on the film for the duration. (They had even begun negotiating a licensing deal with Burger King, confident that the writer's vision was ready to go before cameras.) Ultimately, the director's *Batman* pedigree trumped any cachet Smith had earned with *Clerks*. "He wanted something more Tim Burton–y, I guess," Smith later mused. "Maybe he wanted to see Superman all in black. With scissors for hands."

What Burton wanted was a more substantial focus on Superman's alien immigrant status. Both he and the studio toyed with enlisting screenwriters David Koepp and Akiva Goldsman before settling on Wesley Strick, who had performed an uncredited rewrite of Burton's *Batman Returns*. Strick, who was instructed to play up Superman's solitary angst, was baffled by Smith's draft and complained that Luthor's plan to blot out the sun was a cartoonish scheme once cooked up by sadistic town fogy Mr. Burns on an episode of *The Simpsons*.

Strick replaced the Eradicator, Smith's Kryptonian guardian of Superman, with "K," a more ethereal protector that Strick felt kept the spotlight on the title character. Burton deemed it "too Tinkerbell," but not before toying with the idea of casting Jack Nicholson as the voice of the sprite. The writer also turned the dual Clark/Superman persona triplicate, proffering a weirdly behaved Kal-El as a distinct third element of the character's internal conflicts.

To Peters's delight, Burton held little nostalgia for the character's costume or standard powers. Director and producer thought he could teleport from place to place or possibly tool around in a souped-up vehicle, circumventing the cumbersome flying effects. The black costume sported in the "Death of Superman" series was preferred over the red boots; Burton, a gifted artist, made additions to the suit on table napkins, conceiving of odd accessories, tubes, and wires. The physical changes would be so dramatic that one could believe Clark and Superman were two separate entities. Burton openly spoke about having Superman appear translucent at one point, his organs in full view. His Superman was more Edward Scissorhands than Clark Kent, more H. R. Giger than Joe Shuster.

Burton's primary directive was to damp Superman's power levels and increase his reliance on myriad gadgets to challenge his adversaries. The director's goal was twofold: to offset his boredom with the character's deity status and to address Warner's concerns over his merchandising potential. (The Bat-paraphernalia wielded by Michael Keaton in Burton's last superhero jaunt had been the springboard for hundreds of millions' worth of plastic junk sold.) Fans cried sacrilege, though in a twisted way the director was being ultrafaithful: as originally developed by Siegel and Shuster, Superman couldn't fly. For his part, Peters loved the new gizmos.

Strick's script was heavy on the toy potential—it even featured the long-shelved Superman villain Toyman—but at a literal cost: the film as envisioned by the writer burst through the financial ceiling the studio had mandated. Worse, the collective threat of Lex Luthor, Doomsday, and Brainiac were remnants of the earlier drafts; the studio began to grow anxious at the idea of having a revolving door of adversaries clogging up the narrative. (*Batman & Robin* had been stuffed with so many elements of comics lore that the film, in addition to being insipid, was too busy juggling character arcs to ever put emphasis on any one of them.) And most problematically, Warner exec Terry Semel detested Strick's overall apathy toward Superman's classic mythology. Strick was dismissed; executives began calling up Kevin Smith and fretting about the film's increasing resemblance to a money pit.

Smith's tenure on the film would provide years' worth of anecdotal material for his college speaking engagements. He was particularly fond of depicting Peters as a complete lunatic with the maturity of a spastic child. He also taunted Burton by claiming the director's climax to his 2001 *Planet of the Apes* remake was lifted from a *Clerks* comic book, a statement made in jest that was taken seriously by *New York Post* gossip hounds. When asked for comment, Burton sniffed that he never read comics.

Burton had been motivated enough by Strick's draft to make multiple approaches to talent. His conversations with Jim Carrey were serious enough that he had Strick rewrite the part of Brainiac to better suit the malleable comedian's talents. He agreed on a handshake to entrust the part of Luthor to Tim Allen, an unusual choice considering that the *Home Improvement* star had never displayed a propensity for menace.

He did not, surprisingly, have to concern himself with finding his Superman. That had been accomplished two months before Burton officially stepped on board, though it was a choice that had his signature eccentricity written all over it.

Nicolas Cage was born Nicolas Coppola, nephew to *The Godfather* director Francis Ford Coppola. Fearing nepotism would eventually cast a shadow over his career, the young actor adopted "Cage" from one of his preferred comic book heroes, Marvel's urban tough Luke Cage.

The thirty-three-year-old was that rare Hollywood find, a "serious" actor who could alternate award-winning performances with pumped-up celebrations of testosterone. *The Rock* and *Con Air* had seen the wiry Cage go from character acting to creatine-fueled bravado. His eclectic mix of traits appealed to producers looking to cast a thoughtful Adonis.

Cage had dearly loved Superman from his youth, when he frequently donned a makeshift costume to emulate the character's exploits in the Reeves series and made his own comics from glue and construction paper. When he achieved financial success, he even purchased a copy of *Action Comics* #1 for a six-figure sum. And like Burton, he was drawn to the character's sense of loneliness. Tormented, conflicted malcontents were Cage's specialty: his turn as a terminally depressed drunk in 1995's *Leaving Las Vegas* won him an Oscar. His Superman, he told *Movieline*, would be a "beautiful freak," an alien searching for his place in the world. He even took snaps of himself in a prototype costume, then showed them to his son. The child apparently didn't share Burton's revisionist attitudes, asking where the red underwear was.

Though Cage's affection for the character was considerable, it didn't compel him to turn himself into a charity case. He would be paid $20 million to perform Superman. (The role was actually Cage's third choice in the production; he'd offered his services as either Luthor or Brainiac.) Cage's participation also initiated a seriously contentious battle between Warner Bros. and Paramount, who had contracted Cage for the lead in the Brian De Palma thriller *Snake Eyes*. That film was scheduled to begin shooting in the summer of 1997, and it would overlap with the planned start date for *Superman* in October 1997 by three weeks.

Cage's agent told Paramount that the *Snake Eyes* shoot must accommodate the actor's commitment to *Superman*; Paramount insisted they had an ironclad agreement and weren't about to shuffle their plans around for a rival studio. The pissing contest extended to the point that Warner was advised to start looking for a new Man of Steel. Eventually, Paramount, not eager to anger a marketable actor, agreed to move up the shooting of *Snake Eyes* by ten days. If Cage was needed for shooting after October, he would return once *Superman* was completed.

Though the director and his star found common ground in the idea of Superman as alien outsider, Cage wasn't overly found of Wesley Strick's template. Being well versed in DC Comics continuity, Cage pushed for more adherence to the source material. He considered it sacrilege to assume the role and never appear in the classic costume or fly. "I like the shape of the Coca-Cola bottle," he told *Cinescape*. "I think they should stay true to the Superman costume."

The screenplay was reassigned to Dan Gilroy, a writer who had a loose connection to the franchise's grandfather, Richard Donner. "I had sold a pitch called *Auto Pilot* to Dick Donner," remembered Gilroy. "I had also worked with [future Superman directorial prospect] Wolfgang Petersen on a script called *Endurance*. Lorenzo di Bonaventura and some of the executives at Warner Bros. knew who I was. I had a meeting up at Jon Peters's house with Tim and Lorenzo and the whole development team, and I gave them my take. I thought Wesley's script lacked emotion."

Warner, which had by now abandoned plans for a summer 1998 release, instead nudged Gilroy to produce a draft within the next few months. Gilroy chatted with Donner informally about the project, with the director wishing the studio the best. Jon Peters reiterated that the crux of the story must involve the death and resurrection of the Man of Steel. "Jon was very much in tune with the popularity of that particular comic book and what that did with the history, and he wanted to bring that to the screen," Gilroy said.

Initially, Peters's obsession with the comic seemed to contradict his rabid dislike of the inherent structure of the character's adventures. By the time Gilroy was crafting his script, however, that animosity seemed to have disappeared. "Jon never told me he couldn't fly, and he never told me he couldn't wear the suit. But I also never got the sense that the die-hard fans of the franchise were going to dictate the story."

Gilroy rarely heard from the studio, which left the creative team to their own devices. Under Burton's supervision, they began constructing sets spread across three or four soundstages at immense expense, sinking more than $20 million into the locales. The director began scouting Pittsburgh for Metropolis locations. The studio's blind confidence in Burton led it to cement an October 1998 start date for a summer 1999 release.

Conceptual artist Sylvain Despretz toiled on Burton's myriad scenarios that featured Superman in assorted attire, wielding a variety of gadgets. Word began to circulate on fan sites such as Ain't It Cool News that the director was preparing to diverge radically from previous visual interpretations. Message boards became hotbeds of profane exchanges; fans claimed that Burton and his minions weren't fit to be caretakers and that Cage was "too weird" to assume the mantle of their beloved superhero.

"Fans are not clued into reality," Despretz said, insisting love for the character isn't a prerequisite for his job. "Fans think that years of buying comics entitles them to speak with authority about comics characters and pass judgment on producers and directors who exploit these characters for the silver screen.

"This delusion is laughable. Fans seem obsessed with a sense of personal kinship with an imaginary character, which is at best a publishing product. If fans sat in a room and tried to come up with a film about their hero, nothing creative nor effective would ever come of it."

But the bustling art department endured greater difficulties than the wrath of indignant fans. Under the tyrannical supervision of Burton and Peters, they had to scramble to keep up with the director's constantly morphing ideas and his producer's belligerent demands. At one point, Peters demanded Superman don a jet pack, the better to sell an assortment of action figures. Other days, he would shepherd neighborhood children in to evaluate designs for their plaything potential. When Peters was feeling particularly virulent, he would threaten to wrestle production designer Rick Heinrichs to the ground.

Despretz would later grumble at the thought of his tenure on the film. "I am an ant to a guy like Peters," Despretz railed, "and it shouldn't come as a surprise that an ant like me was treated so poorly by someone who is paid a fortune to believe that he is a movie deity."

Gilroy recognized the character flaws in Peters but didn't share the antipathy of other crew members. "I liked Jon personally. I would work with him again. I know other people would probably give you a different version or view of what their working experience with him was, but I found him to be passionate and committed. He was definitely opinionated in the strongest creative sense. It was not a piece of business for Jon. It was something bigger. I always felt that with him."

———

Through the spring of 1998, *Superman Lives* was the subject of an increasingly dubious string of rumors and innuendo, filtered through the hysteric online fandom community: Burton had approached comically hyperactive pro wrestler Hulk Hogan to portray Doomsday; Burton hated Cage and wanted Ralph Fiennes to play Superman; Sandra Bullock was wanted for Lois Lane; Peters wanted to make ultimate fighter Vitor Belfort a star and planned for him to cameo in the film.

One of the few substantial news blurbs to survive fact-checking at the industry papers was Burton's dismissal of Tim Allen for Kevin Spacey, who possessed the acting chops and glowering stare to portray a more diabolical Lex Luthor. Burton also promised the role of Jimmy Olsen to African American comedian Chris Rock, further angering fans who felt the choice was based more on publicity value than suitability. While talks with Fiennes were never confirmed, privately Warner executives were beginning to share fan concern that Cage was an inappropriate choice to star in what they had planned on being a mammoth tent pole film.

Gilroy's draft of the screenplay was submitted for approval and budget estimates in the winter of 1998. His take, which attempted to blend the sometimes contradictory visions of the multiple scenarists to come before him, was liked but not loved. One particularly unpopular element was left over from Strick's draft: the melding of Lex Luthor and Brainiac to become "Lexiac," an all-purpose adversary for the Man of Steel.

"The whole point of the script was that in the Dick Donner version, Jor-El tells Kal-El everything in that ship as he's coming to Earth," Gilroy recalled. "When Kal-El grows up, he knows his whole story. What Tim wanted was that events on Krypton unfolded so quickly that Jor-El had no time to construct anything that would inform Kal-El or transmit the information he needed. So poor Kal-El lands on Earth and grows up and has no friggin' idea what his powers are or where they come from. Tim was very much into, as Tim always is, exploring the outsider in society.

"At the same time, he was tracking very closely in the script the commercial aspects. It had all the bells and whistles you would've needed. Tim was totally in tune with that."

What Burton had failed to track was the expense of such an exotic tale. When the calculator was set down, the budget was pushing $150 million.

Studio heads Bob Daly and Terry Semel reviewed their slate of releases from the preceding months. The news was not encouraging. Warner had suffered record lows thanks to a string of poorly performing films. Kevin Costner's *The Postman* was a self-indulgent mess, its postapocalyptic vision costing nearly $80 million against a meager gross of less than $18 million; *Batman & Robin* had suffocated that franchise's winning streak; undersea thriller *Sphere* had tanked. Another dozen films had failed to open to any considerable business. The studio's bottom line was in critical condition. Even the proposed Burger King deal, formulated in early 1997, had been designed to get some rapid cash flow into the studio.

Superman Lives may have been more the sum of its parts, but its risk-to-reward ratio was increasing. Fans who didn't embrace Cage argued they would buy a ticket two or three times over if the product delivered. The melting pot of conflicting visions was destined to complicate matters even further.

Warner execs had let *Batman* get away from them. They couldn't allow their other worldwide brand to be molested.

On a day in April 1998, Nicolas Cage was fitted for a sculpted rubber Superman costume. A black wig, trademark spit curl in place, hid his receding hairline. "He looked like Nicholas Cage dressed up like a cross between Edward Scissorhands and Superman," described a source close to the production, one of the few people to have caught a glimpse of the embargoed screen test. "He had jet-black stringy hair, like Burton's, and a shiny black body suit. No cape. Silver 'S.' It was ugly beyond belief. A human nightmare."

The "human nightmare" was hoisted in the air for the film's inaugural flying effects test. The footage made its way to Warner offices.

That same day, the company made its decision. *Superman Lives*, scheduled to go before the cameras in October 1998, was officially a title brimming with irony. The project was shelved.

Smith knew the proverbial *Titanic* was sinking during the filming of his 1998 comedy *Dogma*. Chris Rock, who was to portray Olsen and was also a member of Smith's cast, came to the set with a dismayed look on his face.

"One morning, Rock comes in and tells us, 'They've pulled the plug on Supes,'" Smith recalled. "The word was that the budget had ballooned to $200 million and the studio hated the script."

When Warner made the official announcement that the film would be postponed, it effectively left its proverbial armored truck unlocked: both Burton and Cage were to receive compensation for their efforts, regardless of the film's production status. Burton cashed his full $5 million salary; Cage wound up with a $2 million severance.

True to his reputation, Peters refused to go down without a fight. The project was surprisingly close to him, representing many of his feelings about his renegade status in the corporate world. He even offered to help offset production costs with his own money, a virtually unheard-of solution in Hollywood.

"Jon Peters was extremely passionate about the project," Gilroy insisted. "It seemed to transcend a normal film for him. He seemed to really grasp the potential of what that franchise could be and what it could mean to people. I think it meant a lot to him personally. He invested twenty-four hours a day of his time to make that movie right. I know he was bitterly disappointed when they pulled the plug."

Burton, Peters, and Gilroy rallied to try to condense their sprawling screenplay into something more economically appealing to the studio. "Jon had asked if I would stay on and do a couple more drafts to try and

Actor Nicolas Cage at a screening of *Windtalkers* in New York City on June 6, 2002. Cage was director Tim Burton's choice for the Man of Steel in the aborted 1998 production; the actor's screen test horrified executives.

(CJ Contino/Everett Collection)

see if we could get the budget down to a point where they would reconsider doing the film." After three or four months of rewrites, Gilroy's newest draft seemed to hold potential. "Those drafts actually kindled some new interest that summer. I remember getting a flurry of phone calls, looking like maybe it was going to get back on track.

"Then it just sort of fell by the wayside."

During the scramble, a disenfranchised Cage began to distance himself from story conferences. The delays had dampened his enthusiasm considerably. While his waning interest may have been convenient for a studio that had reservations about his participation, his departure would also leave the project without a leading man.

Gilroy's efforts had reignited interest in the film, but the studio was still unable to come to terms with Burton's increasing distance from Superman lore and the glaring question mark of allowing Cage to embody one of their most valued properties. In late 1998, unable to decide whether or not to sink their fortunes into a film they had little confidence in, the studio gave Burton his official walking papers. Cage, who had shared Burton's thematic desires, marched with him in solidarity—or disappointment. Gilroy followed.

In a move that seemed a melancholy postscript to his experiences, Cage sold off his entire comic book collection, including *Action Comics* #1, at auction in 2002. The entire lot went for $1.68 million. Cage told reporters that he was getting to a place where he "didn't really want to worship false icons" anymore.

Superman Lives was not the only casualty of Warner's shrinking pockets. Arnold Schwarzenegger's long-gestating epic *Crusade*, to be directed by Paul Verhoeven, was deemed too expensive to go forward. The Austrian's other pet project, an adaptation of Richard Matheson's novel *I Am Legend*, was also shelved.

Instead, the studio placed its support behind two expensive films from *Superman* alumni Peters and Burton. Peters produced *Wild Wild West*, a big-screen remake of Robert Conrad's 1960s sci-fi western series. Will Smith, who had proven his box office appeal with hits *Independence Day* and *Men in Black*, was given the lead role. (Smith would go on to star in his own version of *I Am Legend* in 2007.) Peters even worked in his beloved giant spider: Smith faces off against a mechanical arachnid in the film's finale.

The studio's nine-figure investment in Burton's career was deemed sensible when the director began production on *Sleepy Hollow*, a reimagining of Washington Irving's Headless Horseman tale. Johnny Depp starred as a skittish Ichabod Crane, a role he based in part on the feminine body language of Angela Lansbury.

Wild Wild West was released in the summer of 1999, replacing *Superman* as Warner's big summer gamble for that year; it was deemed a noisy, superficial mess. The film grossed $100 million, respectable by most standards—but not when $170 million had been spent on its creation. The studio had thought Smith's reunion with *Men in Black* director Barry Sonnenfeld would prove irresistible. Audiences resisted.

Sleepy Hollow grossed roughly the same amount in November 1999, with its budget a relatively more reasonable $80 million. While not a money drain, it wasn't immensely profitable either.

The would-be crew of *Superman Lives* watched as their film's replacements went up in flames. One sardonic crew member sent out cards inviting fellow staffers to Superman's "wake," to be held at the Hollywood Athletic Club in the fall of 1998, just when the film would've been wrapping.

Ultimately, what Tim Burton would have done with Superman's mythology, how he would've filtered it through his view of society as a decaying wonderland, would never be committed to film.

"Tim's one of those people who's always much more interested in the psychological reality of a character and how it impacts him or her. Tim sees it's a dark, fucked-up, really hard world to survive in," Gilroy said. "To him, that's where the drama is. It's not a stretch when you look at Tim's work to imagine what he would've done with Superman.

"He's going to do a movie about a character who comes from another planet. Everybody in the past has always focused on how much fun it is to fly, jump, bend steel, that stuff. Tim was interested in, thematically, what's the other side of that? When you're on another planet and you *know* you're from another planet?"

Those who assumed Burton's grim visions would've tainted Superman, believed Gilroy, were not at all correct. "I never saw it as dark material. Tim's films are dark, but they're also very uplifting. I didn't think Tim was going to take it and make a bleak film out of it, no. It was not bleak at all. It was very uplifting. And very human."

Undeterred by Superman's failure to launch, Warner began development of a new *Wonder Woman* television series. Her 1970s incarnation, featuring the curvaceous Lynda Carter, had been a kitsch hit. Deborah Joy LeVine, who had left *Lois & Clark* amid creative differences, was tapped to produce. Though an open casting call was held, the project never left the studio's offices.

Morbidly, the slighted ghosts of Jerry Siegel and Joe Shuster continued their crusade to be compensated for their contribution to the company's trove of assets. Siegel had passed away in 1996; Shuster in 1992. Joanne Siegel, Jerry's widow, filed a suit charging that she was entitled to half of all Superman proceeds. The strategy this time was to question the creative team's work-for-hire status in the late 1930s and capitalize on new legal provisions that gave the originator of the work the right to reclaim copyright when it came up for renewal.

Prior to officially signing their deal with National, Siegel and Shuster had composed *Action Comics* #1–6, making DC's (and thus, Warner's) right to ownership a convoluted mess. The Siegels claimed a 50 percent stake in the property and even began to circulate stories that they would produce their own *Superman* films.

In April 1999, Warner sent the Siegel estate a stern letter threatening legal action if such a claim were to be pursued. In an effort to circumvent a legal morass, the studio offered them a $250,000 settlement if they would rethink their stance. There was never a response.

In between legal exchanges, the studio remained adamant about restoring the sheen to Superman's emblem. The departure of both Burton and Cage relieved concerns that their askew perspectives would be harmful to the character's legacy; it freed the studio to pursue other caretakers. Between talent guarantees, script development, and completed sets, Warner had invested over $40 million into his resurrection.

They were past the point of no return. Superman would fly.

He had to.

The Phantom Zone

Stallville?
—*Entertainment Weekly* headline, 2003

Burton's departure may have seemed a blessing in disguise for studio executives reluctant to embrace his distorted vision of Superman, with its awkward body suits and radically altered mythology. Unfortunately, Dan Gilroy's script was tailored to a fault. The template he left behind was distinctly Burton's own, with all the bizarre idiosyncrasies the director had made his name on.

As such, Peters's attempts to entice a revolving door of directors—Brett Ratner, Michael Bay, and Martin Campbell among them—were met with disinterest. No one wanted to try to reverse-engineer Burton's particular, peculiar point of view to reconcile it with his or her own interpretation of Superman. Worse, Peters had displayed little concern for the classic conventions of the hero. To many, especially a surging online contingent of purists, he was a liability. Any goodwill the producer had earned with his *Batman* success had evaporated, but if fans held hope that the dismissal of Warner heads Bob Daly and Terry Semel would be a sign from the gods, they were disappointed. Their replacements, Alan Horn and Barry Meyer, were just as supportive of Peters as the old regime.

Ain't It Cool News, in particular, became a beacon for disgruntled fans who had been hearing secondhand what Peters and Burton had been conspiring to do to their beloved Superman mythology. Rumors and innuendo posted by the site's administrators bore a poster featuring a bearded, Streisand-era Peters with a red line drawn through him.

"SUPERMAN'S #1 Enemy," it read. "Can The Man Of Steel Survive Jon Peters?"

What Hollywood breaks, fandom can fix. Passion for genre franchises, from *Star Trek* to the *Alien* movies, often serves as fuel for amateur screenwriters frustrated by the studio system's filmmaking-by-committee approach. The Web is rife with thousands upon thousands of screenplays and treatments that purport to adhere to the rigid demands of a fantasy's particular "rules."

While most fan authors consider their stories to be simple diversions, circulated among fellow admirers of a given property, some attempt to have their material read by the license holders. Unsolicited sequels, prequels, or remakes of copyrighted material are widely considered the calling card of a rank amateur: since the writer can't be aware of the owner's plans for the franchise, submitting *Die Hard IX* to agents and studio readers is one of the surest ways to stall a developing writer's career in its tracks.

If Alex Ford was aware of the stigma, he didn't pay any heed to it. And unlike most wannabe franchise caretakers, the budding screenwriter actually had representation (though no realized credits). An ardent fan of DC's waning hero, Ford submitted to Warner—via his agent—his own grand scheme to resurrect Superman for modern audiences.

Titled *Superman: The Man of Steel*, Ford's script was scrupulously faithful to comic book precedent and fan demands. *Man of Steel* begins with a redundant recap of Kal-El's spectacular arrival on Earth and subsequent discovery by the Kents. Luthor remains his prototypical opposition, an industrial billionaire with an eye on dominating the political culture of

Metropolis. Privately, Clark's interests are split between abrasive colleague Lois and Smallville's comely Lana Lang, the latter of whom is privy to his double life.

In a nod to DC's seemingly inexhaustible "Death of Superman" template, Ford imagined Superman nearly expiring as the result of a nuclear plant meltdown, his weakening power levels (foreshadowed by a cold earlier in the script) unable to protect him. Also-ran villain Metallo, a cyborg powered by Kryptonite, provides fight sequence fodder. Presumptuously, Ford's end tag promises that "the Man of Steel will return in *Superman: The Man of Tomorrow*, featuring Bizarro."

Ford is clearly reverential toward the source material, though his script may be heavier on adoration than storytelling ability. The dialogue is labored, with Luthor and Superman trading trite barbs that might be more appropriate for his animated exploits. His conflicts are superficial: a walking bomb, a runaway monorail. "This looks like a job for Superman," the hero awkwardly intones at one point. Winking references to the mythology and even verbatim quotes from the Donner films are interspersed throughout. Wonder Woman, in her civilian guise, also appears.

Burton's departure had left such a void in the project that Warner broke every unwritten submission law and invited Ford in for a story conference. Lorenzo di Bonaventura listened as Ford pitched his plan for a series of six or seven films, each one featuring a new string of secondary DC characters. The writer even plotted to "kill" Superman, but not until the penultimate installment.

Ford's passion was contagious, and an enthused di Bonaventura forwarded the script and its franchise outline for Peters's perusal. The producer, who was still hell-bent on reconstructing the character in Batman's image, balked. This did little to appease online fans, who had begun circulating the leaked script and rallied behind its promise of mythological fidelity. Peters and Warner paid little heed: Ford was dismissed.

The studio wasn't the only one scrambling after Burton's exit. DC, which held equal responsibility for the character and his various media pursuits, made its own attempts to jump-start the film franchise. Jenette Kahn approached several comics scribes for their take on the material.

Writer/artist Keith Giffen was among them. The prolific Giffen had created DC's Lobo in 1983; the violent intergalactic bounty hunter spared no insult in his pursuit of alien fugitives. Giffen would outline a film in which Superman's stoic persona was mismatched with Lobo's space-thug mentality. It was an operatic version of *The Odd Couple*, only with more colliding planets.

Surprisingly, Lobo's presence was Warner's idea, not his own. "I was approached by Jenette on behalf of di Bonaventura and [new Warner president] Horn," Giffen recalled. "It was sort of a backdoor treatment because the *Superman* movie was floundering badly. It wasn't my idea to bring Lobo in. That was already on the table."

Warner had long wanted to adapt the sardonic Lobo for the big screen, but previous attempts had resulted in mixed reactions, particularly from his pencil-wielding patriarch. "A *Lobo* movie had been kicked around in development hell for years. They don't know what to do with it. Believe me, I've read some of the scripts and oh, my God, they're horrifying." But from the studio's perspective, introducing the obscure Lobo on the coattails of a brand as recognized as Superman would provide rear entry for the character's own series of films.

Giffen toiled on a treatment and dutifully handed it over to Kahn. "We worked on the parallels. They're both the sole survivors of planets for different reasons. Plus, here was a villain that could really, really give Superman a run for his money. No matter how big a plan Lex Luthor has, it always comes down to him facing a guy who could drop-kick our planet into the sun and smack around the chubby bald man."

The outline began its journey through the byzantine executive tunnels of the Warner empire. Giffen heard that they liked it, but he thought little of it for weeks. One morning, he awoke to discover the treatment had somehow slipped into the hands of the pseudojournalists of Ain't It Cool News. "I guess it worked out well for me, because the guy who reviewed it for AICN called it the single best superhero treatment he'd ever read.

"Which is why," Giffen added, "it'll never get made."

In the proposal offered by Giffen in the fall of 2000, the mercenary Lobo is hired by a galactic drug cartel to kill Superman so they can harvest a common mineral on Earth, which also happens to offer an outrageous high to select alien beings. Naturally, Superman opposes Lobo's wanton exploitation of his adopted home planet, not to mention the bounty on his head; page upon page of superpowered fisticuffs ensue. AICN webmaster Harry Knowles had what appeared to be one of his self-described "geekgasms" over the story, and pleaded with Warner to "SEW JON PETERS' MOUTH SHUT WITH MOTHBALLS INSIDE!!!" lest he raise any opposition to it.

Warner didn't need the impassioned diatribe; they liked the script. Ultimately, however, they decided that Superman's scuffles with Lobo would cost a prohibitive amount of money. (Ironically, Giffen had been directed to "not think about budget" when approached.) Eventually, the writer was given the courtesy of an official "no" from the studio.

Giffen was disappointed—and apprehensive about Warner's alternative, revisionist plans. "Why would you want to take the single most recognizable pop culture figure and remove everything that's familiar?" he told Kahn. "You can go to Zaire, you can go to any country on Earth, you can drive deep into the heart of the Amazon, and say, 'Superman' and they'll go, 'Yeah, Clark Kent!' They know him. He's probably second only to Mickey Mouse in terms of cultural recognition."

Di Bonaventura kept multiple entries in contention for the Superman sweepstakes. William Wisher was afforded an opportunity to draft a new script using some of Gilroy's elements and the newest genre influence, Warner's own *The Matrix*. That film, written and directed by the Wachowski brothers, was a surprise hit in the spring of 1999. Keanu Reeves starred as a computer programmer destined to become the messiah for a band of rebels in an artificial intelligence–dominated virtual reality. The directors and their effects specialists had pioneered "bullet time," a method of slowing down and panning over action scenes that allowed for three-dimensional eye candy. Wisher was instructed to "*Matrix* up" Superman, making his flight patterns more viscerally thrilling for an audience armed with fresh expectations.

Wisher's outline never leaked from the studio's offices; what is known is that his efforts were acknowledged by Oliver Stone, who signaled his interest in directing. The politically conscious director had helmed *JFK* and *Wall Street*, presenting cynical views of abused power and government deception. He seemed an unlikely candidate for a tale about the world's most self-effacing patriot. Nothing came of the idea.

The studio then consulted with animation director Ralph Zondag, who had orchestrated the all-computer-generated film *Dinosaur*. Zondag's pedigree in animation led some to believe the studio, frustrated by the immense expense of replicating Superman's aerial feats in live action, may have been contemplating the idea of an all-CGI film. Robert Rodriguez was again contacted, but he had prior obligations to Dimension, which had just started unspooling what would become his insanely profitable *Spy Kids* franchise.

At one point, radio host "Mancow" Muller told listeners that Russell Crowe had announced during a concert for his rock band that he would portray Superman. The rumor mill then churned out that Peters had offered the cranky Australian actor $30 million for the role. If true, it was a transient offer. His name never came up again.

Rumor also had it that Nicolas Cage was still in contention, despite his putrid screen test. Finally, the actor made a formal announcement in the summer of 2000 that he would no longer be anticipating a start date.

Shortly thereafter, Paul Attanasio became the latest screenwriter to flail about in the character's lore: his *Superman Destruction* script was handed over in April 2001 to mixed reviews. Attanasio, a former film critic for the *Washington Post* and an Oscar nominee for both *Quiz Show* and *Donnie Brasco*, was rumored to have ignored past scripts, though it apparently didn't do him much good—apart from an increased bank account balance. For writing his *Superman* take and the script that would become 2006's *The Good German*, he received $3.5 million.

The revolving door of creative talent on *Superman V* continued spinning, so fast and so incessantly that it briefly snagged Tim Burton for a second time. The director had boosted Warner's sagging profile in the summer of 2001 when his remake of *Planet of the Apes* made a respectable $180 million. Impressed by Burton's return to form, the studio offered him his choice of casting.

But the moment had passed. Burton had received his full salary on the film and had expended too much energy on its aborted launch three years prior. He had nothing to offer Warner, which he believed was far too paranoid in its handling of *Superman* to ever make its progression onto the screen a practical notion.

———

Superman's media profile was weakened by the absence of a theater presence but not completely demolished. The multimedia ventures of the Warner empire made sure of it.

In 1998, *Seinfeld* was preparing to end its tenure on NBC. The show, which had long used Superman lore as fodder for exchanges or even entire narratives, had become television's most adored program. In January, six months before the show's finale, Jerry Seinfeld entered into an endorsement deal with American Express. Immediately, he approached Warner with the idea of using Superman as his foil in a commercial.

The superhero would appear as a cartoon alongside a live-action Seinfeld; Patrick Warburton, who portrayed perpetually dim lummox Puddy on *Seinfeld*, was hired to voice the character's umpteenth animated incarnation. The comedian also enlisted Jack Larson for a walk-on spot; when Larson arrived on set, Seinfeld interrogated him about the George Reeves series and requested an autographed photo. Though diluted somewhat by the marketing overtones, the commercial plays like an adoring vignette, with Seinfeld and Superman walking through New York and mutually musing about the various hardships of being a public figure. Warburton's laconic delivery morphed Superman from his stoic norm into a put-upon grumbler, defenseless when Lois attempts to purchase something and forgets her cash. (Fortunately, Jerry has his AmEx card.)

The union was agreeable enough to all parties, including consumers. Seinfeld and Superman would return in 2004 with two four-minute "webisodes" that allowed the comedian to peddle AmEx and further indulge his wish fulfillment. The encounters—including a road trip—were amiable enough. Barry Levinson directed both entries; Noel Neill pops up in one. The shorts were traded online with such velocity that AmEx recorded more than 250,000 e-mails, all the better to harass potential members with.

It wasn't Superman's first brush with online stardom. In 1998, acknowledging the growing influence of the Internet, Warner signed a deal with Brilliant Digital Entertainment to produce fifteen interactive Superman webisodes for its Entertaindom Web site; the seven-minute shorts utilized computer animation to offer short bursts of Superman in action. Brilliant signed similar licensing deals for television's *Xena* and even decrepit rock band KISS.

The developer's Multipath Adventures of Superman echoed the Choose Your Own Adventure children's books of the 1970s–90s. Visitors to the site could navigate a crudely rendered Man of Steel through a gauntlet of familiar opposition: the threat of the addled Bizarro, the city-smashing fury of Metallo. The shorts, fifty-seven in all, were given no press and stand as a little-seen addition to the character's animated legacy. Brilliant released only the first series of five episodes, "Menace of Metallo," on CD-ROM to quiet fanfare in 1999.

A less respectable interactive offering came courtesy of Nintendo's third-generation game console, the Nintendo 64. *Superman 64* promised players the ability to guide a high-powered Man of Steel through a virtual Metropolis suffering at the hands of Lex Luthor. Gamers found the controls unresponsive, the tasks repetitive: in some levels, Superman could do little more than fly through rings like a circus performer, subservient to the whims of his nemesis. The game was so poorly constructed that it became a running joke in the industry. Even Nintendo's official magazine, *Nintendo Power*, which held every right to spin propaganda in its favor, dubbed the third-party license the worst Nintendo game ever.

(It was, relatively speaking, an innocuous dent in the reputation of Superman spin-off properties. More glaring was an accident on the roller coaster Superman: Ride of Steel at Six Flags New England. The ride injured twenty-two attendees in 2001 when two cars collided. Broken noses and facial lacerations followed.)

A more positive contribution to Superman's body of work debuted in the fall of 2001, and came courtesy of the inimitable Bruce Timm. Partnered with Paul Dini, he developed the all-star *Super Friends* redux *Justice League* for the Kids' WB!

Warner had become so fiercely protective of its properties that at first they balked at the idea of sinking most of DC's most popular characters into a single series. Why allow characters to "jam," the studio reasoned, when individual mythologies could exist independently of one another, allowing for multiple sources of revenue?

But by 2001, both Batman and Superman seemed to have exhausted their potential as separate properties in children's programming. *Superman: The Animated Series* had ended in 2000; Batman had evolved into *Batman Beyond*, a radical future shock developed by Timm that had an ancient Bruce Wayne guiding new Batman Terry McGinnis through a more dangerous Gotham. And the remainder of DC's squad wasn't getting much in the way of game time.

Like Timm's previous efforts, *Justice League* took its subject matter seriously. After a three-part origin tale that explained how the various heroes united, the action was initiated at the Watchtower, a mammoth floating space station that acted as the world's sentinel. Predictably, the leader of the group was Superman, sporting Timm's trademark barrel chest. Tim Daly, who had voiced the character in *Superman: The Animated Series*, was unavailable to continue. George Newbern stepped in, unaware of either his predecessor or the fans' allegiance to his performance. "I just went in thinking I was the first guy," he recalled.

"The way they've done this series as opposed to other animated things I've done is not cartoony at all," Newbern said. "They strive for realism and natural-sounding voices as much as possible. With that direction, it's sort of been a challenge to make him as strong and as grounded as he needs to be and still be Superman. Early morning is better for me. My register's a little lower then."

Gone were the network-mandated pacifist leanings of the Super Friends. In *Justice League*, Superman and company throttled villains, fighting their way out of situations with clenched teeth and flying knuckles.

The Man of Steel's powers retained their Fleischer-era limits. "Our Superman can drown," explained series director Dan Riba. "He doesn't breathe underwater; he doesn't breathe in space. He needs air. It's something we established on the old show. It was sort of required we give him a scuba suit for one reason or another, and a spacesuit." Not surprisingly, the apparatuses mandated by such vulnerabilities made for ample toy potential.

Most stories in the first two seasons were composed of two-part episodes that explored each league member's heritage: Green Lantern stands trial for his life; Wonder Woman returns to Paradise Island and confronts an invading threat. By the third season, the unending fear among animated producers that audiences would grow bored manifested itself in a title change—to *Justice League Unlimited*—and an end to multipart narratives.

No hero or villain was too arcane for producers, who combed DC's archives to find niche characters that would delight fans. The Atom, the Question, Black Canary, and others chipped in on a regular basis, most making their first appearance in animated form. DC, said Bruce Timm, was surprisingly cooperative in granting rights to their library, though some more obscure choices, like the Phantom Stranger or Spectre, were deemed off-limits. "Some of these characters, even though they're supposed to be technically owned outright by DC, have equity issues, creator rights, partial co-ownership," Timm said of the red tape. "It's tricky. A lot of it has to do with them being optioned for TV series or movies."

Superman's rogue's gallery haunted him through several episodes of the series. Lex Luthor cropped up in several installments; Darkseid begged the league to help him combat Brainiac on his home planet. In a nod to the seeming inexhaustibility of the concept, Superman appears to be slain in the episode "Hereafter," victim of B-list villain Toyman. In another, he challenges his knockoff Captain Marvel, after Marvel naively endorses Luthor's presidential campaign. In one alternate-reality tale, Superman actually murders Luthor, prompting the team from "our" reality to keep tabs on the actions of their own Man of Steel. And in a device lifted from the comics pages, Batman actually maintains a supply of Kryptonite in case his ally goes rogue.

As in his solo series, Superman was given ample opportunity to become introspective. In one episode, he spends the holidays at the Kent farm with his alien friend Martian Manhunter. Clark is in his element, gleefully running down the stairs to light the Christmas tree. In another, his nightmares reveal fears that his powers may inadvertently hurt Lois Lane or Jimmy Olsen.

"Stan Lee coined, 'With great power comes great responsibility,'" observed that episode's director, Butch Lukic. "Basically, Superman becomes God at some point. He has to have certain worries or concerns over abuse of his power. As people, we'd be concerned over the same thing. You're with your girlfriend and all of a sudden your heat vision comes on by accident. I think it gives more humanity to the character."

(Ironically, a component of earlier film drafts that had fans incensed—the melding of Lex Luthor and Brainiac to become "Lexiac"—was used by Timm and Dini to celebrated effect in a fourth-season episode, "Panic in the Sky." Either fans had come to expect more fantastic elements from the cartoon series or they were more receptive to deviations from the canon if they weren't spearheaded by Jon Peters.)

Unlike live action, animated properties don't usually see profits from first-run airings; income comes from secondary pursuits like merchandising. *Justice League* racked up almost one hundred episodes, a near eternity for a cartoon. At the same time, the film studios were beginning to embrace even obscure comics characters with greater frequency than "original" properties, figuring that their multi-million-dollar investments must feature a proven commodity from some form of media, no matter how arcane. With its roster being raided by feature producers looking for the next big thing, the *League* was disbanded in 2006.

But DC and Warner continued to pursue the burgeoning market for niche offerings—on DVD shelves. In 2007, they adapted the "Death of Superman" narrative as a feature-length animated film, *Superman: Doomsday*, finally transferring the comics concept to another medium in its totality. Adam Baldwin (no relation to Alec) became the latest baritone to assume the role.

———

The DVD, a questionable format in 1997, was by 2001 a bountiful saving grace for studios. Thousands upon thousands of titles that had been sold to networks and exhaustively reproduced on VHS now had a new shelf life; film libraries that had lain dormant could now be polished, repackaged, and sold all over again.

The appeal of DVD's predecessor, Laserdisc, had largely been limited to serious film aficionados. The twelve-inch discs were cumbersome, the task of flipping them over to finish a film a burdensome demerit for casual viewers. DVD's compact disc–sized physicality and greater storage capacity made it a rightful successor to the tired VHS medium. DVDs offered superior picture and sound despite a more affordable price point than VHS, which had long adhered to a perplexing $80 retail sticker.

Warner had been an early proponent of the format, using the considerable influence of Warner Home Video to market it to both consumers and retailers. But because of hesitance on the part of customers, studios would often stagger large-scale releases. Warner was no exception, waiting until 2001 to issue one of its hallmark franchises on the new discs.

To stir up interest among those who were satisfied with their videocassettes, the studio collected scraps of deleted footage from *Superman: The Movie* and intended to release it as a three-hour epic. Richard Donner, who had by now built up substantial relations with Warner, voiced his disapproval. Instead, fans were offered a 151-minute edit that featured the more spectacular snippets left on the cutting room floor. Among them were Superman's gauntlet of fire, ice, and bullets and the excised cameos by Kirk Alyn and Noel Neill.

The *Superman* box set—which included standard-issue versions of the three sequels—was warmly received by fans. The lone voice of dissent was British film outfit Pueblo Film Licensing, which sued Warner Home Video in 2002. The plaintiffs claimed that they had purchased the rights to deleted scenes and documentary footage from Alexander Salkind years prior, and that the studio had no right to reinsert the frames without their consent.

Furthermore, they said, Warner had assured them it would not attempt to exploit *Superman III* without permission. The lawsuit, which claimed $20 million in damages, was settled out of court in December 2002.

Warner refused to comment on any money paid, though tampering with the source material of another film landed them in further hot water in 2002, when William Friedkin and William Peter Blatty, the director and writer of *The Exorcist*, sued Warner Home Video for issuing an "expanded" cut of their film without offering any cut of the revenue. Again, the studio avoided a court case with an undisclosed settlement.

———

Jon Peters's film project had drifted in the River Styx of Hollywood for virtually the entire life span of both *Lois & Clark* and *Superman: The Animated Series*. The two shows had been designed as mere supplements to the real meat—an expensive feature film—but they had instead carried Superman's torch. And with the movie still mired in conflicting visions and guarded pockets, it seemed only natural for Warner to contemplate another television venture for its perennial hero.

But unlike the creators of prior Superman series, handlers on the new show embraced a mentality of which Peters would surely approve: "no tights, no flights."

17

Superboy Redux

Clark has more issues than *Rolling Stone*.

—Chloe Sullivan on Clark Kent, *Smallville*

By 2000, both of Warner's treasured fictional icons—which had played a considerable role in supporting the company through three decades—had been put on theatrical ice. *Batman & Robin* was deemed blasphemously stupid by fans; the Superman film project had failed to inspire anything other than seven years of turmoil and a rumored $40 million in debt.

The studio knew both franchises were still viable, however, a fact that played heavily into evolving plans for its upstart media outlet. The WB Televison Network had debuted in 1995, populating the schedule with labored "ethnic" sitcoms. It wasn't until later in the decade that the channel improved its fortunes by programming with an eye toward young adults.

Shows like *Dawson's Creek* and *Felicity*, which put the spotlight on angst-doused teenagers, gobbled up the coveted demographic, making the network an increasingly popular destination for anyone under the age of thirty-five. Ratings for such programs were incomparable to those of Big Three network shows, but the spending habits of the junior soap opera fans who did watch justified advertisers' investments.

In 1999, writer/director Tim McCanlies, who had penned Warner's animated *The Iron Giant* with Brad Bird (the titular character proclaimed a desire to be like Superman, not the mindless weapon he was designed to be), approached the studio with an idea for a prequel series for its Batman property. The Dark Knight hadn't been seen in live-action television since the Adam West permutation.

McCanlies pitched a series dubbed *Bruce Wayne*, about the haunted orphan's formative years before his debut as a costumed vigilante. As sketched in a series bible by McCanlies, *Wayne* would take young Bruce on assorted treks across the globe, during which he'd soak up the information and lessons that would inform his mental and physical abilities. His butler, Alfred, would provide a framing narrative, as though the aging confidant were writing his memoirs—a story device that wouldn't have seemed appropriate coming from the ornery, private Wayne himself.

Warner's TV executives viewed the series as a hip antidote to the flailing *Batman* film saga, as well as an opportunity to merge a recognizable brand with the WB's trademark teen-drama sensibility. But their feature film counterparts, particularly Lorenzo di Bonaventura, weren't as thrilled. Batman, di Bonaventura believed, could still draw hundreds of millions in box office revenue with the proper care and guidance. Darren Aronofsky, who had directed the independent success *Pi*, was in talks with the studio to perform CPR on the theatrical property; he was toying with a premise similar to *Wayne*, in which a budding Dark Knight would take to the rooftops in his first year of adventuring. (The outline wasn't exclusive to either party; writer/artist Frank Miller had scripted *Batman: Year One* for DC in 1987.)

Internal posturing at Warner turned *Bruce Wayne* from a can't-miss proposition into a combustible source of irritation. The situation was perplexing to the show's supporters; with the appropriate plans in place, both the film and TV incarnations could have fed off each other. Di Bonaventura disagreed, arguing that a premise offered on free television was not going to prove enticing to filmgoers spending upward of $40 on a night out at the movies.

By 2000, the series bible had been relegated to studio vaults. But one particular passage held lingering interest. In it, McCanlies provided a synopsis of an episode in which Wayne crosses paths with a young Clark Kent during a high school journalists' convention in Gotham City. McCanlies never mentions Kent by name, but his mannerisms and (hinted) abilities are a dead giveaway.

Peter Roth, then president of Warner Bros. Television, was dismayed to see the concept he had championed quashed. Roth had been with CBS when *Super Friends* was a solid performer in its Saturday morning block. As far back as 1979, he had inquired about doing a Superboy television series, believing it would be a smash during the early-evening family hours; the Salkinds, who had jurisdiction over the property, weren't interested. Faced with *Bruce Wayne*'s demise, Roth approached Tollin/Robbins Productions, the proposed production company for the series, and suggested they focus on the young Clark Kent instead.

The idea was agreeable to all parties—except the writer who had originated it. McCanlies, who disagreed with Warner's teen-soap approach, wasn't invited to be part of the proceedings. To replace him, Roth brought in two writers, Alfred Gough and Miles Millar, who had once pitched a *Lois Lane* series to the network; that treatment was notable in that it ignored Clark Kent entirely. Roth had enjoyed it, but Warner Bros. Television was free to play with Clark himself if it so chose.

To appease McCanlies, Warner granted him rights to royalties from the show. Despite not having any active hand in the production, he was set to receive a handsome salary for that very Hollywood feat of not being employed.

"Smallville," the episode title for the Kent guest appearance on *Bruce Wayne*, soon became the working title for the series. The FOX network was intrigued enough by the premise to make a substantial bid for the show, but Warner's desire to boost its own network's profile canceled out the competition. Not that it lowballed producers; the WB paid a record rate for a debuting drama when it ordered thirteen episodes to premiere in the fall of 2001.

Gough and Millar immediately distanced themselves from previous adaptations with one crucial mandate. Unlike the Salkinds' Superboy, Clark Kent would never be seen in costume, nor would he ever take to the sky. (The prohibition of those trademark elements echoed Jon Peters's own controversial sentiments, though the disappointment of hard-core fans would likely be blunted by the diminished expectations of television.) Instead, Clark—a high school freshman—would experience adolescence by way of his maturing powers. A rise in libido, for example, would provoke the emergence of his heat vision. Throughout the course of the show, various abilities would be discovered, future peers (and enemies) encountered. By the series' end, Clark would be ready to leave Smallville and take flight as his more famous alter ego.

The most dramatic alteration of the character's accepted lore was to introduce Lex Luthor as a childhood pal of Kent's. Their early friendship had its roots in DC's *Superboy* comics of the 1950s, but the device had been ignored in virtually all of the character's media depictions. (Luthor had attended Shuster U with Clark in *Superboy*, but the two were already contentious.)

By placing Luthor in Smallville, producers afforded themselves the ultimate turn of the screw: while Lex and Clark would seem close, viewers would know of their eventual fates. This awareness would cast an ominous shadow over their friendship, a tragic tactic that George Lucas used to good effect in his *Star Wars* prequels through the decaying bond between Obi-Wan Kenobi and the future Darth Vader.

Casting the new millennium's Superman, in contrast to past searches, would prove comparatively easy. The prospective hero didn't need to concern himself with looking agreeable in tights or having Reeve's wirework intuition. One auditionee, Brandon Routh, was nixed, a decision that would prove ironic in a few short years; eventually, Jensen Ackles (*Days of Our Lives*) became the current generation's Jon Voight, ready to step in if no one else emerged as a more credible Kent.

Millar and Gough eventually settled on Tom Welling, a twenty-four-year-old model who had sporadic acting experience in episodic television. Welling initially turned down the part, fearing the series would descend

Actor Tom Welling at the premiere of *Ocean's Twelve* in Los Angeles on December 8, 2004. Welling's *Smallville* proved to be a consistent performer for the fledgling WB network through the majority of the decade.

(John Hayes/Everett Collection)

into camp. He relented after seeing the pilot script, which took a reverential, serious approach to the fantastic proceedings, echoing Donner's chant of "verisimilitude" from decades earlier.

Michael Rosenbaum had been bandied about for the role of district attorney (and future villain Two-Face) Harvey Dent on *Bruce Wayne*. The twenty-nine-year-old performer had appeared on the WB's unfortunately titled sitcom *Zoe, Duncan, Jack & Jane*. He was offered the role of Lex—but only under the condition that his shaved head wasn't misshapen or otherwise distracting. (A bald cap was attempted and deemed too phony.) Rosenbaum spent a few nervous minutes getting his locks shorn off before learning that his cranium was well suited for maturing villainy.

Since young Clark would be a student, he would live with his adoptive parents on the Kent family farm, where, presumably, he would use his powers to bale hay with greater efficiency. That meant substantial supporting roles for Jonathan and Martha Kent. Jon Schneider (*The Dukes of Hazzard*) was cast as his father, Cynthia Ettinger as his mother.

Production on *Smallville* commenced in the spring of 2001 in Vancouver, British Columbia, Canada, an increasingly popular destination for television series due to its favorable exchange rate and cheaper labor. Canadian Kristin Kreuk was cast as love interest Lana Lang, while Sam Jones III assumed the role of Clark's best friend, Pete Ross. Allison Mack was Chloe Sullivan, an ambitious young journalist who seemed to fill the absent Lane's role of being an overly curious damsel in distress and promised to further complicate his love life.

The pilot was screened in front of a test audience composed primarily of females, most of whom responded positively despite having no idea the show was about the future Superman. The news was encouraging to the WB, which had pegged the series as a "hip" revamp of the dusty mythology.

Producers were less enthused about Ettinger, who didn't seem to hit the appropriate notes as Martha Kent. The actor's youthful good looks distracted from the character's role as a wise matriarch. In an odd bit of serendipity, Annette O'Toole was approached to be her replacement. Millar and Gough had no idea she had portrayed Lana in *Superman III*, a rather biting comment on that sequel's legacy. The scenes with Ettinger were reshot.

Smallville premiered in October 2001 to the WB's best ratings for a debuting series ever with 8.4 million viewers. The numbers were still anemic when compared to the ratings of established networks, but the WB was ecstatic. They ordered a full season.

Promotional materials for the show depicted Clark bound to a cross in the fields of Smallville, a red "S" painted on his chest to make a superficial connection to his future. (The scene was from the pilot, the result of Clark's persecution by raucous jocks.) The pose was purposely messianic, signaling that *Smallville* might provide more substantial subtext than many WB viewers were accustomed to. It was also eerily reminiscent of the hate crime inflicted on Matthew Shepard, a gay college student, in 1998. Shepard was beaten and tied to a fence in a rural area; he later died of his injuries. Producers denied that the similarities were intentional.

The promise of more literate storytelling initially held little water. In its first season, *Smallville* quickly became dependent on a conceit fans dubbed "freak of the week syndrome." In Gough and Millar's scenario, the rocket blast that spirits young Kal-El to Earth brings with it a catastrophic meteor shower that blankets the town in Kryptonite. The noxious mineral not only incapacitates Clark as in the comics but also endows the humans who are exposed to it with strange and dangerous abilities. Thus the writers could create an endless supply of superpowered adversaries for Kent to contend with, most of them socially introverted outcasts with family or self-esteem issues. The device already seemed strained by episode 2, when a crush of Lana's morphs into a bug-man who can secrete webbing.

Producers also purposely flaunted Kreuk's sex appeal. In one episode, while suffering from a personality-altering affliction, she pounces on a meek Clark, appearing (via a body double) in nothing but her underwear. The hedonistic display was set to popular music, furthering Warner's synergistic agenda. The studio scored the show to bands signed to its labels, and viewers would be notified at the end of an episode who the performer was—the better to locate the album in record stores.

Where *Smallville* thrived, and where Superman fans found most of their sustenance, was in the doomed friendship between Clark and Lex, whom he had saved from a car crash in the pilot. The two would share their conflicting ideals and exchange verbal cues that elicited knowing smirks from even casual students of Superman lore. "Our friendship is gonna be the stuff of legend," Lex would intone.

———

Season two of *Smallville* reaped the benefits of experience: producers, heeding fans' growing dissatisfaction with the "meteor freak" crutch, began delving more deeply into Clark's aspiring-hero status. Best friend Pete becomes privy to his secret, a fact that puts him into harm's way more often than not. Clark discovers that his Kryptonian father Jor-El is alive, if only in spirit, with nefarious intentions to remove him from the Kents' influence. Terence Stamp, who had portrayed General Zod to great effect in *Superman II*, provided the voice of Jor-El after refusing on-camera participation in the show.

Most notably, Christopher Reeve made the first of two appearances as Dr. Virgil Swann, an astronomer who apprises Clark of his Kryptonian heritage. Reeve had also been approached to be a "creative consultant" on Jon Peters's feature film project; although nothing ever came of Peters's offer, the producer cited Reeve's efforts to return to normalcy following his accident as an "inspiration."

Reeve, who had indeed become an avatar for human courage through his highly publicized struggle with paralysis, had cheated the odds on several occasions. In the days following his accident, he had to be repeatedly talked out of suicide; drugs had prompted an allergic reaction that closed up his throat. Finally, after yet another bout with sepsis, he fell into a coma and never awakened. Reeve died on October 10, 2004. His own physician would later suggest the death had been brought on by a reaction to the antibiotic he was given.

(His tenure as Superman didn't end there, however. In 2007, artist Gary Frank assumed art duties on *Action Comics*. His Man of Steel is an admitted, loving homage to Reeve.)

Like many teen-angst shows of the day, *Smallville* garnered an increasingly rabid and vocal fan following. Appreciation Web sites began popping up, most of them slavish in their devotion to both the series' lore and its attractive male and female leads. Warner fueled their word-of-mouth support by creating faux news clippings from Chloe Sullivan and posting them online; in later seasons, viewers would be allowed to read Lex Luthor's e-mail. (Naturally, his service of choice was America Online, a popular destination among AOL Time Warner subsidiaries.)

By the middle of season two, *Smallville* had attracted 23 percent more viewers than at the same time the previous year, becoming the WB's most popular program. (Despite the ratings spike, rumors began to circulate that Warner wished to cancel the series to fuel more interest in its feature film franchise, which was becoming more tangible under new craftsmen. Neither the studio nor the network ever made an official comment on the matter.)

Fans seemed to take particular delight in the exchanges between Clark and Lex, with the more sexually charged among them discerning homoerotic subtext behind their brotherly bond. Online fans would post "slash" fiction that detailed the duo's remarkable nocturnal appetites for each other.

Rosenbaum wasn't quick to dissuade them, telling *Entertainment Weekly* in 2003, "I love it. In fact, if there's a line where I look at Clark and I say [with intense gaze], 'If you need me, I'm there,' we laugh our asses off. It takes us 10 takes to get it out. Let the audience think what they want to think."

For the less slash-inclined, Warner rolled out a series of young adult novels that added to the *Smallville* universe; the books were de facto mysteries in the Nancy Drew vein, with Clark, Lana, and Chloe investigating all manner of suspect activity in the meteorite-plagued burg. Inevitably, DC itself reclaimed the new incarnation, offering a monthly *Smallville* comic that adhered to the alternate continuity set by the series. *Smallville: The Official Magazine* kept viewers up-to-date on upcoming episodes and the eating habits of its cast, *Tiger Beat* style.

The sole merchandising angle that wasn't fully exploited was the toy market, which was largely barren of *Smallville* paraphernalia. Sans costumes and elaborate props, a jean-and-shirt-clad Clark Kent made for a poor action figure. Under its DC Direct banner, Warner released a skimpy line of figures intended only for the comics store market. (They would revisit the line in 2007, when the series had begun to make better use of the expansive comics mythology.)

As the show finished its second season and entered its third, producers began to rely increasingly on warped-psyche story hooks. Clark's exposure to red Kryptonite turns him from an amiable farm boy into a leather-jacket-clad lothario; a new flame of Lana's influences her behavior; an e-mail virus prompts Chloe's friends to attack her. (The only one who seemed to be exempt from the various psychological attacks was guest star Perry White, portrayed by O'Toole's real-life husband Michael McKean.) Actor Sam Jones III was dissatisfied with his lack of screen time and asked to be written out. The character of Pete was removed from the series, having moved away when the pressure of knowing Clark's secret became too much to bear.

Smallville's popularity in its initial three seasons helped the WB report its first-ever profits in 2003. The network tried twice to duplicate its success; both shows failed to capture a similarly devoted audience. *Tarzan* put a teenage spin on a different franchise; the series premiered to dismal ratings in 2003 and didn't last the season. The year before, the production company behind *Smallville* had explored another corner of DC continuity with *Birds of Prey*, which followed a trio of female crime fighters in Gotham that included former Batgirl Barbara Gordon. Tollin/Robbins even managed to navigate the legal morass and present glimpses of both Batman and the Joker in the premiere episode. But indifferent viewers seemed to have affinity only for the Man of Steel's unexplored years. *Prey* was canceled in 2003.

———

In an effort to offset the doldrums of Clark's senior year, Millar and Gough temporarily broke their own "rule" and allowed Clark to fly in the fourth season premiere. The show's success also coerced DC into finally relaxing its stringent hold on its characters. *Smallville* became the setting for chance encounters with embryonic versions of the Flash, Aquaman, and even 1950s kitsch holdover Krypto the Superdog.

Aquaman had become a recurring joke on the HBO series *Entourage* when fictitious movie star Vincent Chase suited up for a big-budget James Cameron feature. But the character's *Smallville* appearance so impressed executives that they ordered a pilot for *Mercy Reef*, a series about the oceanic hero's tadpole years. Despite a cast overhaul, it failed to resonate with the network and wasn't picked up. In an effort to scrape some revenue from the expensive pilot, Warner offered it to fans online as a $2 download.

Smallville's casting stunts were often the result of labored weekly meetings between Warner's film and television arms, with both sides being made aware of what the other planned to do. Producers had long desired to have Bruce Wayne appear on the show, both for its cool factor with audiences and as a nod to McCanlies's original concept. DC and Warner, close to settling on a deal with Christopher Nolan for his *Batman Begins* reboot of the film franchise, repeatedly nixed the deal.

Stretching matters was the arrival of Lois Lane. As interpreted by Millar and Gough and portrayed by Erica Durance, Lois was a self-sufficient army brat who didn't yet share cousin Chloe's love of the incriminating written word. Lois and Clark could barely hide their contempt for each other, a seeming cover for their hidden attraction.

Clark was pulled in the opposite direction by the perpetually trembling chin of Lana Lang, who adored her school beau but resented his persistent secrecy. Clark and Lana would consummate their relationship the following year, finally stoking the overly smothered libido of the main character, who had been surrounded by beautiful and willing admirers for five seasons. The delayed gratification was a purposeful strategy on the part of producers, who were painfully aware of how the rapid progress of Lois and Clark's relationship had turned their ABC series into a ratings corpse.

Durance's sardonic take on Lane divided fans, who either found her lovely or obnoxious but rarely anything in between. In 2006, the actor's admission of hosting "naked parties" was so enticing to radio host Howard Stern that he clamored for more details, then allowed his staff to bombard her with rude insults for not being more forthcoming. She left the show in tears.

Another Lois Lane, Margot Kidder, appeared as the assistant to Reeve's Dr. Virgil Swann, furthering the series' connections with the Donner films. In light of her publicized battles with mental illness, Gough had made certain she was emotionally stable before flying her to Vancouver. Following Reeve's passing, Kidder was asked to come on the show and, in a bit of meta morbidity, talk about Dr. Swann's death. She refused, declaring it "exploitive," and never returned to the show.

Clark graduates high school at the end of season four; season five begins with his discovery of the Fortress of Solitude, his polar refuge from the world and his means of communicating with his Kryptonian father. His relationship with Lex becomes increasingly hostile, with Luthor displaying a growing distaste for observation of the law. Lex's fortune allows him to purchase both things and individuals: running for office in the fifth season against Jonathan Kent, he enters into a smear campaign. The stress of the race fells the elder Kent, who dies of a heart attack in his son's arms, a melancholy concession to the classic Superman mythology.

The fifth season's growing investment in Superman lore proved crucial to its survival: the WB had placed it up against the *Survivor* juggernaut on CBS, where both Millar and Gough freely admitted they expected to be killed. Elements like the *Daily Planet* setting and the introduction of Brainiac and General Zod (who, true to the show's MO, possessed the body of Luthor) helped it average 5.3 million viewers weekly, a highly credible number for a show on a fringe network up against such formidable competition.

The show's primary players—including Welling and Rosenbaum—were contracted through seven seasons. Entering the fifth, Rosenbaum expressed some degree of disenchantment over the role, claiming that Luthor's machinations would eventually grow redundant if they weren't expedited. The good-humored actor informed the press that his family had told him he looked like an "idiot" with a shaved head; once, he had emerged from another room to find that one of his friends had stuck a Lex Luthor action figure in Rosenbaum's likeness directly up his rear end.

Welling was less apt to fidget. Both he and producers figured that the absence of the costume might spare the actor much of the stigma that accompanied the role. Instead, Welling wore the primary colors of the character (blue and red) in shirts and jackets. Oddly, his Kent sports no glasses, making positive identification of Superman a seemingly easy task for Lois in later years.

The issue of whether a teenage Clark Kent would automatically be considered a variation on Siegel and Shuster's Superboy in the eyes of the law became a hot topic in 2004 when Siegel's widow and daughter resumed their fight against Warner Bros.

According to the lawsuit filed in federal court in Los Angeles, the revised copyright laws of 1976 allowed the heirs of the duo to reclaim the copyright to the character of Superboy when it came up for renewal, which happened early in the new millennium. Naturally, Warner opposed the claim, arguing that Siegel and Shuster had created Superboy on a work-for-hire basis, giving their employer exclusive rights to the character.

In a March 2006 ruling, the judge disagreed, pointing out that National had obtained Superboy's copyright during one of Siegel's earliest contract disputes in 1948—and that there is, clearly, little need to request a transfer of ownership to something one already possesses. It was a bittersweet victory for Joanne Siegel and Laura Siegel Larson, who had witnessed Jerry rail against the considerable legal might of Warner and its corporate predecessors for a good portion of the twentieth century. Owning a crucial component of the Superman empire meant the studio would be beholden to their estate, a submissive position that the studio had not been subject to since the Salkind years.

In addition, if *Smallville* was to be considered an adaptation of the Superboy mythology, then Warner had been effectively in violation of the Siegels' copyright claim. The studio balked, saying that the show's depiction of Clark Kent was based on a premise that predates the 1944 creation of Superman's juvenile counterpart. The rebuttal was tenuous at best: prior to Superboy, the only mentions of a preadult Man of Steel had been a handful of panels depicting him as a toddler en route to Earth. The judge's ruling made no decision regarding the series' provenance, preferring to leave that to a copyright infringement trial.

The seismic effect of the copyright transfer was felt in the summer of 2006, when Warner's latest animated series, *Legion of Super Heroes*, underwent a substantial change in narrative. The series, which depicts a group of futuristic DC heroes who spiral back in time to enlist the help of Superboy, was immediately deemed a lightning rod for legal difficulties. Though he looks fourteen, the Superboy of the show was rechristened Superman. And in the comics, a new incarnation of Superboy (a clone of Clark Kent, not his junior self) was an unfortunate casualty of DC's *Infinite Crisis* crossover event. Editors maintained it was because of the demands of the story.

Despite the legal victory, Siegel's heirs had little opportunity to circulate their own Superboy comics or features: while they owned the copyright to the character, Warner still has the trademark on the name Superboy as well as the rights to his familiar costume, which is virtually identical to that of his older self.

But the possible profit participation for the Siegels was considerable: reruns of *Smallville* were sold to the ABC Family cable network in 2004 and into syndication in the fall of 2005 for a minimum of $400,000 an episode.

Like most court cases, however, it's more a marathon than a sprint: in late July 2007, Warner nabbed a crucial victory when Judge Stephen Larson ruled that the Siegels had failed to prove that Superboy was an original concept and not merely a variation on the Warner-owned Superman mythology. He voided the previous ruling that had awarded the Siegels control of the character.

It's a decision that essentially winds the court clock back to zero, with both parties again forced to prove their hold on the hero. Unless a closed-door resolution is reached, the Siegels and Warner seem destined to snipe at one another, like pencil-and-ink Hatfields and McCoys, long into the future.

———

Smallville's sixth and likely penultimate season premiered in the fall of 2006, sending Clark into the Phantom Zone while General Zod wreaked havoc back home. Having long exhausted the "freak of the week" conceit, the show was orchestrating comic book story lines with near-operatic intensity. Clark and Zod have a tree-smashing battle in a forest; defeated, Zod's spirit (which resembles the bearded visage of Terence Stamp from *Superman II*) leaves a confused Luthor to his own devices. Now employed at the *Daily Planet*, Chloe encounters Jimmy Olsen, who had been referenced in a previous episode as taking her virginity. Known for its frenetic openers, the series pulled in 5.04 million viewers for the episode, consistent with prior seasons. Fan interest was kept at an even keel throughout the year with bombastic narrative stunts (a smitten Lana marries Lex, Chloe develops superpowers) and a Bizarro-themed finale.

The season was broadcast on the CW network, the result of a merger between the WB and fellow upstart UPN. Divided, both networks had garnered decent demographic ratings but were never able to successfully gain a foothold among audiences or the media as the coveted "fifth network." The union was, in essence, a signal of defeat. Pooling resources and creating a slightly more substantial schedule might relieve the public's general apathy. Possibly as a good luck charm, the CW's bumper ads and network identification screens were tinted Kryptonite green.

Regardless of its future beyond the 2007–08 season, *Smallville* has already earned a place in the Superman pantheon by becoming the longest-running televised adaptation of the story in its seventy-year history. Ironically, Welling has logged more screen time than any previous Man of Steel without ever once having to don the iconic tights of the hero.

It's possible *Smallville's* eventual finale might force the issue, sending Clark Kent into new journeys as an adult with a familiar blue disguise. Regardless, the series can make a serious claim to being the most well-constructed, faithful, and competent take on the character to date—not to mention the lone project that inspired virtually none of the trademark chaos the character was known to elicit behind the camera.

Such labels were not likely to be placed on what Warner's feature division was brewing.

Fear of Flying

We were going to build a fucking planet! That makes it worthwhile to make a
Superman movie!
—Brett Ratner

To find the antithesis of the bleak landscapes of Tim Burton, one need look
no further than the filmography of Joseph "McG" McGinty Nichol, which
is as full of radiant color as Burton's is canvassed in black.

Like several Hollywood impresarios of the late 1990s and early new
millennium, the director had cut his teeth on short-form music videos, the
rapid cuts and staccato narratives of which informed his feature work. His
big-screen debut was the profitable remake of Aaron Spelling's *Charlie's
Angels* TV series; the film married McG's attention-deficit style with the
substantial hormonal appeal of Drew Barrymore, Cameron Diaz, and
Lucy Liu. The girl-power action-comedy cost an excessive $100 million
to produce but brought in more than double that in worldwide box office
revenue for Columbia Pictures. It was a noisy calling card that made the
rookie helmer one of the hottest "gets" in town.

Jon Peters—who had long been accused of allowing the latest hit films
to influence his creative desires—was agog over *Angels* in 2000. In 2002,
with di Bonaventura's blessing, the producer brought on McG to direct the
comatose *Superman V*.

McG shared Tim Burton's passion for the project but not his distinctive vision. He designed a series of elaborate pamphlets for Warner executives that highlighted what he wanted to do to the franchise, all in the vein of the pop confections for which he was becoming known. Superman, McG believed, called for a sensory assault on audiences conditioned by MTV and video games. The "Clark as messiah" motif was too opaque, too grim. McG wanted—promised—a roller-coaster ride. Challenging Peters's standing orders, the director asserted that his Superman would fly. He may have had to sacrifice the character's trademark cape as a compromise; in prototype suits crafted at Stan Winston Studios, the black-rubber molds weren't accompanied by the flourish.

Despite the efforts of more than a half-dozen screenwriters, no script was circulating that complemented McG's creative slant. Instead, he pitched writer J. J. Abrams to the studio. Abrams had created ABC's convoluted spy thriller *Alias*, as well as the modest WB success *Felicity*; like McG, he was being hailed as one of the industry's freshest and most inventive young talents. The scribe had broken in during his college years, when he penned the Jim Belushi vehicle *Taking Care of Business*.

Abrams and McG were given a finite amount of time to get the project gestating. The years of stalled activity on *Superman* had made Warner impatient, demanding. The studio's doldrums had extended through the 2001 summer movie season, which produced few hits worth boasting about. To add to the pressure, McG was committed to a *Charlie's Angels* sequel for Columbia. Abrams had a mere four weeks to invest in a rough draft.

Warner's jockeying for a new tent pole franchise led them down two wildly disparate paths. While Abrams and McG were busy orchestrating their solo version of the Superman story, the studio was considering the marriage of DC's two most iconic heroes into a single feature. The competing production would be titled *Batman vs. Superman*. To the studio's way of thinking, it was the cure for two ailing properties.

That one creative contingent would eventually be informed they had completely wasted their time was apparently a secondary concern.

Hyperkinetic director McG on the set of *Charlie's Angels: Full Throttle* in 2003. McG took over directing duties on the Superman sequel not once but twice—in 2002 and again the following year.

(© Columbia/Everett Collection)

Wolfgang Petersen had spent much of his directorial career awash; his *Das Boot* was hailed as a foreign-import masterpiece in the early 1980s, his *The Perfect Storm* a triumph of latter-day CGI effects work. His instincts were commercial without being pandering: both *Air Force One* and *In the Line of Fire* were regarded as literate actioners.

Petersen was one of the many names circulated in the Superman sweepstakes at the turn of the century. When di Bonaventura approached him to tackle the misbegotten franchise, Petersen suggested they bring Batman on board.

Superman and Batman had appeared in tandem countless times in their animated adventures, as well as in the comics. *World's Finest*, a long-running DC title, made the team-up its exclusive business. But high-profile franchises were rarely amalgamated in theaters, since executives would be aghast at the idea of diluting their individual profit margins. For instance, fans loved the Peter Briggs spec script that conjoined the *Alien* and *Predator* monster-movie series, but the screenplay collected dust for a decade before Twentieth Century Fox finally agreed to compromise the two wheezing properties. Jon Peters had even proposed a Batman/Superman team-up to Warner years earlier, but at the time *Batman's* sequels were still strong earners, and the idea was never pursued.

Petersen's timing was much better. By the beginning of the new millennium, the two heroes' box office prospects had atrophied; Warner had been frantically trying to resurrect Batman, but proposed projects detailing his formative years weren't yet camera-ready. With a single film, the studio might ignite interest that could then be diverted into separate theatrical pursuits.

Di Bonaventura sanctioned the idea and left Petersen to develop a script with Andrew Kevin Walker, the author of the popular thriller *Se7en*. Petersen's mandate was simple: the two heroes would initially be at odds, then encounter a common threat that would require their collective abilities. Walker labored on a script through mid-2002 and delivered a draft that spring to the rabid glee of Warner execs, who had virtually exhausted their resources in finding a bankable Superman property.

Walker's script pitted Superman's genial disposition against Batman's lumbering menace and relative lack of faith in humanity. Batman was, in fact, an absentee hero: Bruce Wayne had given up the guise five years prior to settle into domestic life following the offscreen murder of Robin. To set the two at odds, the screenwriter proposed that Wayne's new bride be killed at the hands of the Joker; because Superman advocates the killer's imprisonment, Batman rejects the Man of Steel for his sickening devotion to the letter of the law. (Michael Keaton's Dark Knight had watched the Joker fall to his death in Tim Burton's *Batman*. To salvage the popular villain, Walker had Lex Luthor create his clone.)

For much of the script, the two men chart separate courses. Batman follows the trail of his wife's killer, while Superman pursues his own leads in Smallville, where he's tempted to retire to small-town life and reunite with childhood sweetheart Lana Lang. During the climactic confrontation, Batman opposes Superman wearing Kryptonite-laced battle armor. (The Caped Crusader also makes use of a jet pack and a new Batmobile to quench the studio's ceaseless thirst for toy inspirations.) Luthor even pops up in an exoskeleton that grants him abilities comparable to those of his otherworldly nemesis.

Walker had obviously viewed the Fleischer reels of the 1940s; during one key sequence, an army of oversized robots that Luthor constructed begin to wreak havoc at a World's Fair, then in Gotham City itself. The scene, proposed in his early treatment, never made it into the circulated draft.

Walker's Joker was especially vicious, his Batman morose beyond belief. To modify some of his particularly morbid injections, Warner hired Akiva Goldsman, who had raised the ire of comics fans as the writer of *Batman & Robin*. Goldsman added trite, stilted dialogue that seemed to undermine the film's more mature themes. Nonetheless, the screenplay he delivered to Warner was accepted; the studio issued Petersen an official green light in the summer of 2002. The trades buzzed with the news, swapping rumors as to which actors would assume the mantles of the dueling icons.

Jude Law, a British actor with delicate features and a trim build, was an early, unlikely choice for Superman. Law had been a huge comics fan from adolescence and even sported a tattoo that paid homage to the graphic novel *Watchmen*, a serious, seminal exploration of the genre. Law's pen was poised over the contract, but he reneged when it was made clear that he would have little to no influence over the direction any possible sequels might take. Colin Farrell, who had no such reservations, was the studio's choice for Batman. Frequent Burton collaborator Johnny Depp was also scribbled down, though for which part—he seemed capable of both—is unclear.

Petersen knew of the McG/Abrams Superman project and realized that either his production or theirs would necessarily fall by the wayside. Di Bonaventura assured him *Batman vs. Superman* would be going ahead first.

At virtually the same time Warner announced the team-up film, Abrams turned in his expedited draft to executives. Abrams and McG had petitioned for a trilogy, with the first film setting the stage for later installments. It was clear the writer had not observed the canonical conventions of the character, a fact that delighted both Peters and a studio eager to produce something other than a facsimile of the Donner films.

In Abrams's draft, Krypton had not exploded. More egregiously, Lex Luthor had been demoted from billionaire industrialist to CIA agent, directed to keep tabs on alleged extraterrestrial activity. Lex himself would later be revealed as a Kryptonian.

The set pieces were heavily derivative of the *Matrix* franchise, which had been Warner's salvation during its lean years. Superman opposes rival Ty-Zor in an aerial martial arts battle; another scene has the Man of Steel submerge himself in a Kryptonite dunk tank in order to save Lois, now a peer from college. Abrams even hints that *Daily Planet* coffee fetcher Jimmy Olsen is gay.

Superman's origins are glossed over, though his preadolescent self does manage to save Martha Kent from being raped, a gross concession to more jaded times. His suit, hidden under his formal reporter's attire in most versions of the tale, now springs from a canister.

Warner was faced with an unexpected blessing: they had two salable Superman templates to choose from. Di Bonaventura, believing the Batman and Superman franchises could benefit from each other's presence on the same reel, was backing Petersen's vision. In his estimation, Petersen was the more focused and competent of the two directors; McG's *Superman* was too insubstantial to meet the audience's expectations. Warner president Alan Horn sided with McG and Abrams's revisionist take, believing that Batman could fend for himself under different management in a separate relaunch.

Di Bonaventura tried to appease Abrams by saying that production on *Batman vs. Superman* wouldn't prohibit the studio from eventually making his *Superman*, but Abrams balked, arguing that a team-up film seemed premature until both characters had been reestablished. Furthermore, he and McG were ready to move forward immediately. To their benefit, so was Warner: Sony's *Spider-Man* had just been released, shattering box office records and reigniting Hollywood's superhero boom. Suddenly, all the major studios had conference tables full of comic books.

In an effort to promote diplomacy, Horn circulated both scripts among executives and solicited their advice. He even petitioned divisions like marketing and merchandising to choose the more promising product.

The vote was nearly unanimous in Abrams's favor. The green light for *Batman vs. Superman* turned red; Abrams's *Superman* was approved to go forward in August 2002. Horn phoned Jon Peters to tell him his pet project remained on track. Peters began weeping, the emotional investment too much to contain. A disappointed Petersen's consolation prize was a "go" sign for his expensive epic *Troy*.

Di Bonaventura felt bullied. The maneuver had been the latest in a string of conflicts between him and Horn, who had been promoted to president over di Bonaventura in 1999. Since then the overlooked executive had helped Warner into more fiscally rewarding waters with the *Matrix* and *Harry Potter* behemoths, and the latest slight rankled. Di Bonaventura held clandestine meetings with honchos at corporate parent AOL Time

Warner in which he expressed dissatisfaction over Horn's strategy. Horn, he said, was favoring an immense slate of films that threatened to overwhelm the studio's bottom line; di Bonaventura wanted the company to be more selective about its output.

The corporate honchos were not sympathetic. In an unlikely coincidence, di Bonaventura suddenly resigned from his studio position in September 2002.

———

By 2002, webmaster Harry Knowles and his squad of militant geeks at Ain't It Cool News were wielding a surprising amount of influence over the studios. Using a network of industry contacts, Knowles would review scripts of films in development and pass judgment on their worthiness. Projects that received Knowles's blessings were often received enthusiastically by their respective studios; likewise, scripts that he dubbed blasphemous to either their originating property or to fans' intellect were a source of consternation for execs.

Knowles's tastes ran famously erratic: he admitted to crying during the maudlin noisemaker *Armageddon* (written by Abrams) and once decreed the *Godzilla* remake to be a modern classic. (In both cases, Knowles had been feted by studios, shipped to premieres and granted set access.) In most instances, Knowles's reporting was ungrammatical Scrabble-vomit text that meandered from his early-morning activities to what frame of mind he was in during the screening. Other reviewers and tipsters would contribute to his site under code names like "Moriarty" and "Quint," establishing a raucous network of anonymous critics.

Knowles had been following the myriad Superman projects since the site's inception in 1996, railing against the noxious tastes of Peters and imploring the studio to commit to a faithful rendering of the beloved character. Peters was seen as the Darth Vader of Warner's evil empire—a philosophy that fueled Moriarty's incendiary review of Abrams's *Superman* script in the fall of 2002.

Abrams's creative liberties were dissected in detail, everything from making Luthor a Kryptonian menace to allowing Superman's home planet to thrive. (Abrams planned future films that would revolve around epic battles for supremacy on the alien world.) Moriarty chastised Warner for not having any respect for the mythology or its fans and stopped just short of calling for a public lynching of all involved.

AICN's "Talk Backers," users who post their own reactions to columns on the site, agreed nearly unanimously with Moriarty's assessment. Their numbers troubled the studio: though "geeks" made up a small fraction of theatrical audiences, their fanaticism was loud, their repeat business favorable to the bottom line. Some particularly resentful critics set up an Internet petition, accruing thousands of signatures in protest of Abrams's retooling.

At Warner's behest, Abrams phoned Knowles to try to calm the revolt. He explained that the script was still a work in progress and that the small window he'd been given to craft a first draft hadn't allowed him to frame a layered interpretation of the character. Knowles claimed to be satisfied, and many of the naysayers followed suit. Abrams's *Superman*—to which a subtitle was never publicly attached—was set to enter preproduction in the fall of 2002.

The hue and cry did claim one casualty: McG, who finally succumbed to pressure to begin production on Columbia's *Charlie's Angels* sequel. He vowed to return to the project after photography on that film was completed, but Warner, eager to build on the project's momentum, wasn't prepared to wait.

The studio approached Bryan Singer, who had helmed Twentieth Century Fox's enormously successful *X-Men* film and was just finishing work on its sequel, but his conventional interpretation of the character didn't gel with Abrams's. Talks were initiated with Michael Mann, Steven Soderbergh, and David Fincher. Eventually, Warner entered into a deal with Brett Ratner, an explosive personality who had turned Jackie Chan into a U.S. box office attraction with New Line Cinema's *Rush Hour* franchise. Because he was contractually committed to a third *Rush* picture, he had to seek the blessing of New Line to accept; it was granted. The excitable Ratner sent out Christmas cards with his face plastered over Superman's body.

The news drew mixed reaction from fans. Many felt that Ratner, like McG, was interested more in visual tricks than any narrative substance. The director was also the subject of myriad rumors about his private life, particularly about his dalliances with women. The most sensational: drug smuggler Jason Sylk alleged that as a teenager, Ratner had selected fifteen-year-old Rebecca Gayheart from a lineup of models with carnal intentions.

The director had even talked his way into film school, where he secured financing for a student film from Steven Spielberg's Amblin Entertainment. He used the check to pick up girls.

———

Fans who were resistant to the way the project was shaping up found further reason to complain when reports began circulating over who would portray the Man of Steel.

Ratner's deadline to cast the role was January 2003 in order to meet an April start date. He initially considered *Smallville*'s Tom Welling, who had audience awareness in his favor. Welling met with Ratner, but several issues damaged the actor's chances. To allot room in his schedule for a feature, his series would have to be either canceled or placed on hiatus. What's more, Welling's presence might turn off audiences who felt that a television actor was undeserving of their box office dollars. Warner never warmed to the idea; the studio thought that *Smallville* could coexist comfortably with a feature film and that there was little reason to cross-pollinate the two.

As the search continued, Ratner was stymied by Superman's reputation for miring actors in typecasting. Warner intensified such concerns when it insisted that whoever Ratner cast must commit to the planned sequels up front—studio execs were unwilling to gamble a huge property on an actor who could hold them hostage financially if the first one was a hit.

Director Brett Ratner arrives for the Producers Guild of America Awards at the Universal City Hilton in Los Angeles on January 22, 2006. Ratner made an unsuccessful attempt to mount a *Superman* sequel in 2003, clashing with producer Jon Peters.

(Michael Germana/Everett Collection)

The director spent months courting Josh Hartnett, with whom he had been blunt: he cautioned Hartnett that taking the role meant making a ten-year pledge to the franchise. In the end, the actor refused to be a prop in Ratner's spectacle, even for compensation that could've totaled $100 million over three films. He turned down the role a total of four times before the studio got the message. Warner was irritated by Ratner's inability to secure Hartnett, who had submitted a screen test that wowed executives.

Ratner moved on to Paul Walker, whose surfer looks didn't seem well suited to Superman. The actor was working with Richard Donner on *Timeline*, and he approached the director for advice. Donner told him to avoid doing it purely for financial reasons. Walker, who envisioned an eclectic career, refused the offer, even though the salary would've effectively set up his family for life. "I don't think I want to die as Superman," he told reporters.

Jude Law toyed with the idea of flying over to Los Angeles for a screen test, but commitments in London forced him to pass. Victor Webster, a dark-haired actor who had appeared in Marvel's faux-X-Men syndicated series *Mutant X*, also entered into talks; in interviews, he complimented Ratner and Abrams on producing "a very serious action-drama."

In Ratner's most egregious flirtation with fan resentment, he submitted Ashton Kutcher for a screen test. The lanky, goonish actor had been a supporting player on Fox's *That '70s Show* and was seen as little more than the current generation's Fonzie. Ratner liked his reel, but the studio wavered. Kutcher later admitted to *Details* magazine that even he found the idea preposterous. "Could anybody fucking take me seriously as Superman?" he asked. "Let's be honest about that."

Ratner's search—in his mind, at least—ended with Matthew Bomer, a relative unknown who was currently toiling in the daytime soap opera *Guiding Light*. All of the requisite pieces were in place: he looked the part, he carried no baggage with audiences, and his thirst for success emboldened him to take the chance he'd be typecast.

Warner execs weren't as enthused. Like Alex Salkind before them, they insisted on having a recognizable actor in the role. They were left with only one viable name: Brendan Fraser. Fraser possessed the physicality but had concentrated primarily on comedic roles. Some of them—including Dudley Do-Right and George of the Jungle—openly parodied the concept of the alpha male Boy Scout. The dance continued: Ratner wanted Bomer; Warner wanted Ratner to secure a popular performer.

By now, hitting the planned April 2003 start date would be impossible. Rumors began circulating that the frustrated studio was petitioning Michael Bay to take over the directorial reins. It was a dubious comfort to protective fans: in a generation full of viscerally tuned, emotionally empty orchestrators of film, Bay was the most bombastic of all, with enough smash cuts in his movies to prompt seizures. Roger Ebert once called his *Armageddon* a two-hour film trailer.

Ratner refused to confirm the hypothetical betrayal, noting that he and Bay shared the same agency and that there was little chance their management would pit two coveted earners against each other.

By March 2003, Ratner had made little progress. He had only one confirmed player, Anthony Hopkins, who had promised Ratner he would play Jor-El without bothering to see a script. (Hopkins had grown to like the director during the filming of the third Hannibal Lecter movie, *Red Dragon*.) Meanwhile, the studio was recoiling from the estimated price tag of Abrams's script—as much as $225 million. A stubborn Ratner insisted the expenditure would be worth it: he planned to create an entire planet for the screen, along with other revolutionary effects work.

Jon Peters, who had seen his labors go unrewarded for nearly a decade, gnashed his teeth at Ratner's intractable management style. Left to their own devices, two stubborn people rarely function well in an enclosed space; during one exchange, Peters tried firing Ratner's casting director. The power play landed Peters and Ratner in a shouting match, during which Ratner allegedly brandished an armed bodyguard in order to quell the situation.

Ratner denied the story later, saying that he wouldn't need a bodyguard if he had to handle someone. But the internal struggles became a mutual headache for him and the studio. When Ratner's option on the film expired in mid-March, he departed the project.

Harry Knowles continued to champion the Abrams script but praised Ratner's exit, claiming that the director had called him on several occasions to get remedial lessons in Superman lore. Ratner would later label Knowles a "hypocrite," regretting the hours he had spent on the phone with the genre buff. "I . . . flew [Knowles] and his fat fucking father to fucking LA . . . for the premiere of *Money Talks*," Ratner huffed. "The first fucking time Harry Knowles was in LA." The calls in question, he said, were to offer Knowles a consultant position on the film, not to school himself on Superman trivia. Ratner lamented the loss of what he considered a friendship.

In bizarre role reversal, it was the Hollywood mogul who bemoaned the fact that the fan wouldn't return his phone calls.

The degree to which Abrams's script had been revised as a result of fan revolt is unknown; Alan Horn assured fans that Luthor would indeed be a human, not a Kryptonian, and that other, more dramatic alterations would be taken under careful advisement before shooting began.

When exactly that would be was still in question. The film had been slotted for a summer 2004 release, and Warner was now scrambling to replace it with another summer "event" property. To the studio's misfortune, the haste compelled it to back the ill-advised *Catwoman* feature starring Halle Berry. Loosely based on the thieving escapades of Batman's archvillainess, the film was a campy disappointment. (During its development, news had spread that Warner also planned to revive the Wonder Twins from the numbingly insipid *Super Friends* series. After *Catwoman*'s collapse, nothing else was ever said about the nostalgic bid.) Bizarrely, the studio even flirted with a *Supergirl* remake with Akiva Goldsman producing, a recipe that seemed prematurely optimistic about the primary franchise's success.

After Ratner's exit, the studio courted M. Night Shyamalan, a writer/ director who had proved to be the single most bankable commodity for Disney since Mickey Mouse. His *The Sixth Sense* had become the sleeper hit of the era, grossing more than $600 million worldwide. His follow-up, *Unbreakable*, was a meditation on how inheriting the powers of a super- hero might influence the life of a common man. Though it received mixed reviews, Shyamalan's name helped it to sizable profits.

Warner asked if he was interested in directing the story of a real super- hero. Shyamalan was, but only if he could write the screenplay as well. The studio was too invested in Abrams's long-term plans to consider it, and the two parted ways.

The fruitless development had dragged on for so long that McG had finished shooting and editing his *Charlie's Angels* sequel. The film was only a modest hit, grossing a sum comparable to its swollen budget, but Warner still viewed McG as the "it" handler for its most valued property. He resumed duties on *Superman*, which he cloyingly redubbed *FlyBy*, in September 2003.

With McG's return came renewed rumors that the studio was heav- ily behind Kutcher for the title role. But in a report that trumped even that bit of questionable casting, fan sites buzzed with news that Warner had instead offered the role to singer Justin Timberlake in the hopes that his substantial teen following might help offset any fears about the film underperforming. Timberlake was looking to get into film and would later receive warm notices in supporting roles, but he carried all the wrong kinds of baggage for the role. The singer, as self-aware as Kutcher, refused to entertain the idea.

The concept of stunt casting didn't end with Superman. The studio encouraged McG to cast Beyoncé Knowles as Lois Lane, believing the

African American singer's presence would immediately signal to people that *FlyBy* would be a reimagining of the Superman myth and not a redundant addition to existing continuity. The director preferred Selma Blair, who was an ardent fan of Lois and openly spoke of her desire to participate.

Through McG's dual development periods, Jake Gyllenhaal had been a recurring thought to take on the cape. The youthful actor's name had been bandied about for both Batman and Superman during Wolfgang Petersen's development of the team-up film; Gyllenhaal had even been approached to take over for Tobey Maguire when the *Spider-Man* star wrenched his back and his participation in the first sequel was questionable. Despite the trifecta of possibilities, Gyllenhaal never assumed any of the superhero roles.

Keanu Reeves was also considered, his name hauntingly similar to those of ill-fated Supermen gone by. The actor had flown as Neo in the *Matrix* series, but that character had given him enough of a messianic workout for his career, and he declined.

An equally improbable coincidence was the slight smashup between Jon Peters and Gerard Christopher, the sophomore Superboy from the Salkinds' TV series. Having left his BMW on the street while he ran into a Starbucks, Christopher emerged to find Peters's vehicle crunching the nose of his own, which had just come out of the shop.

"He jumped out of the car like a little tough guy, like he was going to beat me up," Christopher recalled. Peters, upon seeing the sizable Christopher, calmed down and gave him a business card, insisting his office would pay for damages.

"I don't care who you are," the actor said. "Give me your license and insurance information. You backed into my car."

Peters finally relented, and then attempted to mollify Christopher by mentioning that he was producing a new Superman film and there might be something in it for him. Peters never called.

Like Ilya Salkind, McG wanted to supplement a little-known feature player with an expensive supporting cast: Shia LaBeouf, the young actor who was tapped for Jimmy Olsen, told *USA Today* that McG's latest wish list included Scarlett Johansson for Lois Lane and Johnny Depp for Lex Luthor.

Casting struggles were accompanied by conflicts over location shoot-ing. McG wanted to film Metropolis's exterior scenes in New York City, citing concerns over "authenticity." In actuality, the director suffered from the ever-ironic fear of flying and didn't want to acquiesce to Warner's man-date that he shoot the film in Australia, which would shave $25 million or more off the budget and provide valuable tax incentives. Traveling over a body of water was of particular concern to McG, a necessity if the studio insisted on an overseas shoot. And they did; Warner had already booked soundstages there.

McG's agent, Patrick Whitesell, tried to quell studio fears by assuring them McG would resolve his apprehensions. In June 2004, he was sched-uled to board a plane for Australia to scout locations.

When the plane took off, McG was not on the passenger manifest.

———

McGinty had succumbed to his phobias. In a slapdash attempt to salvage his position on the film, he created a presentation for executives that out-lined how it could be shot affordably in Canada. His cajoling had little effect; the studio needed to cut whatever costs they could from the film's immense expense, especially in light of the tens of millions that had been sunk into previous, aborted productions. McG was sent off. In a move in step with his insubstantial style, he was said to have signed on to direct *Hot Wheels: The Movie*.

The parting was spun as largely amicable, though McG stuck to his story that New York would've been the more authentic locale. "When I flew to New York to scout, I became enamored with our greatest American city," his statement read. "It was clear to me that this was Metropolis. As a filmmaker, I felt it was inappropriate to try to capture the heart of America on another continent."

Bay's name resurfaced, perhaps in part because a mysterious "S" emblem appeared on his Web site around the time of McG's departure. It was pulled days later; Bay claimed that one of his fans had added it without his knowledge. In the end, it was speculated that Bay was using the rumor to coerce DreamWorks into increasing the budget for his current project, *The Island*, lest he jump ship.

Abrams, who had long coveted a feature directing chair, petitioned Warner to let him helm his own script. The studio was not receptive, believing that the last thing the cursed production needed was a novice overseeing more than $200 million worth of the studio's assets. (Paramount disagreed, snagging Abrams to helm the pricey *Mission: Impossible III* in 2005.)

By 2004, the various incarnations—*Superman V, Superman Reborn, Superman Lives, FlyBy*—had cost the studio an estimated $65 million in development costs. The bloated budget and time line were put to shame by fans who, fed up with the system's clogged machinations, were using economical production tools to create their own live-action adaptations.

Sandy Collora, who apprenticed at Stan Winston Studios, made a stir in 2003 when he circulated *Batman: Dead End*, a short film that featured a grim Dark Knight smacking around the Joker. In a frenetic development, the hero is also forced to stare down extraterrestrial terrors from the *Alien* and *Predator* film franchises. (Collora had access to Winston's library of rubber monster suits.) It was a parade of copyright infringement, though Collora avoided litigation by distributing it for free.

In 2004, shortly after McG departed *FlyBy*, Collora released *World's Finest*, a "teaser" to a nonexistent feature that had Batman and Superman teaming up. Another short, John Fiorella's *Grayson*, featured Batman's ward avenging his demise; Superman makes an appearance. The films' impressive production values belie the minimalist resources of their makers.

Superman's screen time in the two fan films clocked in at several minutes each. It was more footage of the Man of Steel than Warner had managed in eleven years.

Takeoff

I call it the industry of Superman. . . . It's powerful stuff.
—Bryan Singer

The actor Brandon Routh, a failed auditionee for *Smallville* in 2000, stood in front of the camera, shirt unbuttoned, hands pulling at the lining to reveal a familiar "S" emblem underneath. His glasses were oversized, his rigid, cleft jaw straight out of Joe Shuster's imagination.

Routh relaxed his pose. Sometime later, he was awarded the honor: first place at the Lucky Strike bowling alley's 2003 Halloween costume party. Located in Hollywood, the retro-tinged lanes are a popular go-to joint for industry power players looking to faux-slum it in blue-collar ambience. Routh worked there as a bartender, the cliched employment of any struggling actor. His resume had been spotty, consisting primarily of guest appearances on episodic television. He lived with his sister.

The Norwalk, Iowa, native was also apparently devoutly religious: when he was released from the cast of *One Life to Live* in 2002, he posted a message on his Web site that warned producers, "You may get far in this world . . . but this world is not the world that matters." He added, "I will leave God to judge those who have wronged me."

The Halloween costume was inspired by Routh's first agent, who had signed him with the comment that "if there's another Superman movie, you're going to get it." Routh was tall, trim, and bore a passing resemblance to the definitive screen superman, Christopher Reeve. Still, Routh didn't take the possibility too seriously. He'd tested for the role of young Kent in *Smallville*, and he'd videotaped an audition for McG's film after meeting J. J. Abrams's assistant at the bowling alley, but when nothing came of either attempt, his agent's suggestion began to seem highly unlikely.

Even so, the costume had netted him some compensation: as first prize winner at the party, Routh received $100.

———

In June 2004, Alan Horn sat down with Bryan Singer expecting to hear details of Singer's proposed remake of *Logan's Run* for the studio. (The 1976 sci-fi film details a society that euthanizes anyone over the age of thirty, an apt metaphor for the very Hollywood habit of dismissing mature tastes.)

Eventually, talk turned to the studio's Achilles' heel, its meandering crusade to get Superman back into theaters. Singer listened as Horn went through the laundry list of obstacles: wrong script, ballooning budget, wrong cast, impetuous producers, and lethargic directors.

Singer processed the information and volleyed his gut reaction: the problems had stemmed from Warner's insistence that the Superman legend be revised. It's America's modern myth, Singer argued. Richard Donner had set a perfect template for the character's screen presence. There was no reason to improve on the wheel.

Singer left the meeting with an agreement that he would return armed with a more concrete pitch. Some days later, he did, with a story hashed out on a trip to Hawaii with writers Dan Harris and Michael Dougherty. (The screenwriting partners had authored *X2*, his 2003 sequel to *X-Men*.) The trio's efforts were based on a vague premise Singer had been toying with for some time—that a new Superman film should begin with Superman "missing" from the American consciousness. Singer had broached that idea with Richard Donner during a press tour for *X2*, which Donner's wife, Lauren Shuler-Donner, had produced; Donner had nodded in approval.

Singer had then brought it up to Harris and Dougherty when McG took his leave from the project. He strayed when he felt the studio wanted either a Batman/Superman team-up or a remake of the original.

But now, a more lenient Horn was willing to listen. The film, Singer argued, should be analogous to Superman's real-world hiatus from the screen. The studio's fear that he would no longer be relevant in a jaded culture should be mirrored in the story itself, as the Man of Steel returns from a long absence to find that society has grown ambivalent about his heroics. Singer and his writers had played around with various conceits, the most sensational of which involved Superman coming back to a middle-aged Lois Lane. In the final pitch, Superman has spent five years in outer space, voyaging to and from the ruins of Krypton; when he returns, he finds that Lane has moved on without him, even birthed a child. She's also won a Pulitzer Prize for her editorial "Why the World Doesn't Need Superman."

Singer's film would pick up where Donner's work on the first two movies had left off, vaguely referencing the original films' story points (while ignoring the inferior sequels) and even duplicating the production design on Superman's Fortress of Solitude. Singer's Superman would fly. He would wear the classic costume. He would be humble and just and noble.

Horn was intrigued. The director's pedigree was undeniable: he had sifted through the convoluted world of the X-Men to create two hugely profitable films for Fox, with a third on the way. Unlike McG and Ratner, Singer was in the superhero business. Horn liked him, and liked his pitch. Best of all, Singer appealed to the exec's bottom line with the magic word: "trilogy."

The president announced in July 2004 that Warner Bros. would be going ahead with a fifth *Superman* film, with Bryan Singer at the helm.

Swear to God, Horn mused. This time we're not kidding.

Warner's gain was Fox's loss: they had fast-tracked *X-Men 3* for a summer 2006 release and would be forced to move forward without the franchise's screen author. Singer had been combative in negotiations on the third picture, demanding a greater percentage of the gross. When he left the production, Fox executives were so irate that they locked the doors leading to his on-lot office. Trades and fan sites began to take particular delight in pitting the two behemoth studio tent poles against each other; the story would only get richer as time went on.

Singer lamented the missed opportunity. In his version of the X-Men story, the persecution of mutants had been a thinly veiled metaphor for the plight of homosexuals, a story the openly gay director took a custom interest in. But Superman was the crown jewel of all franchises, the grandfather of comics. It was not an offer that would likely repeat itself.

Before officially committing, Singer had again approached Richard Donner, this time seeking his formal blessing. The director had never been consulted by anyone at Warner, a fact that raised no small degree of resentment. But now here was Singer, hat in hand, paying respect to a vision of the character Donner had helped define. Donner was flattered, and impressed with Singer's reverence for the source material, an emotion that had eluded the hollow aspirations of his predecessors. He told Singer to move forward. Singer also consulted with Miles Millar and Alfred Gough to make certain *Smallville* and the feature wouldn't confound viewers with any glaring contradictions.

Despite Singer's caution, Harris and Dougherty were allotted a scant four weeks to deliver a draft of their screenplay. Undeterred, the two went about the business of fleshing out Superman's reintroduction, his morphed relationship with Lois, the senses-shattering set pieces, and the Grand Guignol scheme of perpetual public nuisance Lex Luthor. (Their energy level was upped when Donner sent them a well-wishing fax, asserting that Superman "couldn't be in safer hands.")

McG's sole remaining contribution to the film was Brandon Routh's audition tape, which Singer had stumbled across during a marathon screening of previous prospects. Routh was boyishly charming without being juvenile; Singer thought he possessed a quiet strength. In August 2004, he called Routh in for an informal chat over lunch; the actor fumbled the cream and sugar and, consciously or not, fed into Singer's idea of Clark. The direc-

Director Bryan Singer orchestrates a shot on the Australian set of *Superman Returns*. Singer's hiring ended more than a decade of fruitless development on the sequel at Warner Bros.

(© Warner Bros./Everett Collection)

tor thanked him and sent him off. Routh didn't know it, but Singer had already made his decision.

The selection was known to select few besides Singer for months following the meeting—Routh himself didn't get a call until October. The veil of secrecy caused no small degree of strife for an online community anxious for a decisive announcement. Comics scribe Mark Millar entered into a bizarre bet with Harry Knowles that the next Superman would be James Caviezel, who had turned down the part of Cyclops in Singer's *X-Men* and portrayed the literal Messiah in Mel Gibson's *The Passion of the Christ* in 2004. Caviezel had openly lobbied for the role of Superman, professing a love for "iconic characters," but Singer disliked the on-the-nose parallels with the actor's previous project, which the media would surely flog to death. Knowles knew as much and agreed to take Millar's $1,000 bet.

(Earlier, Millar had gleefully orchestrated a hoax among Ain't It Cool readers by insisting Orson Welles had written a script for a Batman feature film in the 1940s. The possibility of such an iconic lost project prompted pages of debate.)

Singer ended the speculation in October 2004, announcing Routh's casting to the media only weeks after Christopher Reeve's passing. Singer also made it known that Burton's choice for Lex Luthor, Kevin Spacey, had agreed to return to the project. Spacey would relinquish his responsibilities as caretaker of London's legendary Old Vic Theater in order to spend several months in Australia, bald—and perhaps sharing Gene Hackman's mild contempt for the task at hand. "It's a fucking comic book for God's sake. It's not Othello," he told *Wizard* magazine in 2006.

Singer's television project *House* was just debuting, with British actor Hugh Laurie starring as physician Greg House. Laurie's turn as the cantankerous doctor convinced Singer that he would be perfect for Perry White, the prickly chief of the *Daily Planet*. Unfortunately, *House*'s early shooting schedule for its second season removed Laurie from contention. Singer turned to Frank Langella to fill in.

Singer's choice for Lois was Kate Bosworth, a porcelain-faced actor who had to dye her blond hair a darker shade for the role. (*Lost* star Evangeline Lilly had briefly been considered.) Passing up the chance to reconceive the Jimmy Olsen character—as black, gay, or absentee—he selected WASPy Shawn Ashmore, his Iceman from *X-Men*, to fill Olsen's shoes. A scheduling conflict put Sam Huntington into the role instead; interestingly, Shawn's twin brother Aaron would tackle Olsen in his *Smallville* incarnation two years later.

Dougherty and Harris's script initially involved the dual threat of Luthor and General Zod. Singer's sole choice for the latter role was Jude Law, who had been a candidate for the part of Superman under both McG and Petersen. Law declined the chance to explore the other side of the mythos's moral coin, and a deflated Singer excised Zod from the film.

In his most intriguing announcement, Singer revealed that he would be repurposing footage shot by Donner with Marlon Brando, allowing the deceased actor to reprise his role as Jor-El. The conceit, though gimmicky, would provide further connection to the earlier films. Brando's estate was granted a handsome royalty for the privilege.

Quickly, debate began to rage—more about Superman's attire than the actor inhabiting it.

The costumes of latter-day superhero epics like *X-Men* and *Daredevil* had released actors from the kind of training regimen Reeve had embarked on in the mid-1970s to tone his physique. Routh put on twenty pounds but relied on sophisticated body suits to provide muscle contour and definition; his underlining also acted as a girdle, burying any trace of a misshapen torso. Routh's youthful face, however, was altered only by the addition of blue contacts; his visage seemed more comparable to Superboy's than Superman's.

Singer disliked the idea of an oversized "S" dominating Routh's appearance; he preferred a smaller insignia, embossed and confined between his pectoral muscles. The yellow emblem on the cape had been wiped, deemed too redundant and self-congratulatory. Superman's brilliant red color scheme was dialed down to a muted magenta, a more somber color reminiscent of the tones of the Fleischer cartoons.

There had been much ado about Superman's codpiece, endless discussions between Singer and costume designers over its size, shape, and protrusiveness. Despite events in *Superman II*, Superman was largely asexual.

Once those crucial discussions were finalized, Singer and Warner released the first images of Routh in the suit in early 2005. Message boards were ablaze with compliments and criticisms: The "S" is too small, the colors too smothered; Routh looks too young. A comparatively vocal minority praised its "retro," iconic look. Fans booted up photo-editing software and satisfied themselves by enlarging his chest insignia, lengthening his cape, lightening the colors. An exasperated Singer shook his head at the dissection of the most excruciating minutiae of the images. He would change little, if anything.

In spring 2005, for the sheer symmetry of it, Warner flew a banner during the Cannes Film Festival announcing that *Superman Returns* would be coming the following summer. Perhaps the studio considered it good luck to continue the Salkinds' tradition.

Officially, Jon Peters was still working on the film, but he was nowhere near the dominant force he had been on the earlier projects. Singer and his writers had formulated their approach without his input; though his credit would remain on the film, his revisionist ideals wouldn't make it to the screen. But Peters did make one integral contribution: his relentlessness in keeping the film afloat, forcing it to have a pulse, had paved the way for Singer's admission into the sweepstakes.

Superman Returns star Brandon Routh at the press conference for the unveiling of his wax figure at Madame Tussauds in Times Square on June 27, 2006.

(William D. Bird/Everett Collection)

Filming for *Returns* began in February 2005 in Sydney, Australia, the studio's long-desired destination for the expensive project. Singer had projected a budget north of $200 million; his financiers, aware of the millions already invested, didn't flinch. The budget didn't include marketing costs or the hemorrhaged cash from the previous failed starts. All in, Warner put themselves on the chopping block for $300 million, minus the 12.5 percent Federal Tax Offset "rebate" on the cost of principal photography in Sydney.

Even in the face of Routh's good health, the oft-rumored "curse of Superman" refused to expire. A crew filming supplemental material for the inevitable DVD release met with a series of misfortunes: a producer was mugged and suffered broken ribs; an editor on the project fell through a closed window, puncturing his lung; a cameraman fell down a flight of stairs and lost part of his little finger.

Midway through shooting, Routh received a letter of encouragement from Christopher Reeve's widow, Dana Reeve, a generous display of sentiment from a woman facing her own battle with lung cancer. "Go forward," Reeve implored Routh. She passed away in March 2006.

The blessing was fuel for the actor, who had spent months strung up on wires and working long days in an effort to reignite the character's status as a box office attraction. Warner's eight-zero investment hinged on Routh's presence as the Man of Steel, a considerable weight on the rookie performer's shoulders.

Singer, too, was feeling the strain. At one point he suspended shooting for three weeks—at considerable expense—to "clear his head." He told the press that the film was an "awesome responsibility." His appreciation of the art-vs.-commerce dichotomy was informed on the one hand by his love for the character and on the other by recent news that the studio had laid off over two hundred employees. The risk was as sizable as the reward—if Jon Peters had been right, if contemporary audiences were too frayed to accept the moral rigidity of Superman, he would effectively cripple both his career and a studio's fiscal year.

Comic books remained the hot commodity in Hollywood, but their scenarios had become far grimmer. *Sin City*, a lavish adaptation of Frank Miller's graphic novels, was a black-and-white orgy of violence. Warner's own *Batman Begins* was a dark, moody homage to the character's vigilante roots; far from assuming the role, Adam West would've been an early casualty in the current climate of Gotham City. Another DC property, *Constantine*, featured its antihero descending into literal hell, puffing on cigarettes all the while. Save for Batman, none of the heroes even bothered with tights.

Warner, though confident in Singer's abilities, was perhaps fretful over the same concerns Peters had long voiced—and was certainly active in hedging its wager. The studio had entered into an arrangement with Legendary Pictures to cofinance twenty-five pictures over five years, starting with the expensive *Batman Begins*. The two companies agreed to split the investment on *Superman Returns* right down the middle. Warner would only take half the hit, literally or figuratively.

The nucleus of the demanding, easily irked fan community is still the San Diego Comic-Con. There filmmakers share the concentrated highlights of their upcoming genre films in hopes that fans will spread ecstatic praise and raise the profile of their expensive projects.

Singer was no exception. During the July 2005 convention, he broke from shooting *Superman Returns* and attended a panel discussion of Warner's most anticipated 2006 release. Singer, who had built up a considerable amount of goodwill with *X-Men* and its sequel, battled jet lag and the intimidating sea of expectant attendees to deliver a monologue on his vision of the Superman character. He later showed five minutes of footage for the crowd, who yelped their approval.

He almost made it off the podium without a scratch.

"Clark is Jor-El. . . ." he began. "No, wait. *Kal*-El. Kal-El." The gaffe prompted a chorus of good-natured heckling. The director also irked Warner executives by wearing the movie's massive budget like a badge of honor; the studio feared the figure would make expectations unmanageable and scrambled to downplay the expenditures.

Warner also concerned itself with the ancillary product that the film would anchor—and the myriad ways in which consumers would be assaulted with the brand. The studio signed a multi-million-dollar deal with Burger King: gluttonous customers at the drive-through would be subject to Superman banners, Superman toys, and Superman food packaging. Frito-Lay would offer kiosks at grocery stores where customers could experience their own version of "super hearing," their crunching amplified by a tinny speaker. Soda drinkers could mimic "super strength" at Pepsi displays. The sugar-laden Cap'n Crunch would come packaged with bits that turned milk blue. Routh himself would appear in a "Got Milk?" ad campaign.

The marketing blast would in turn direct attention toward Warner's merchandising push. A Superman inflatable muscle suit from Mattel exploded with air-dense muscle at the touch of a button. A sixteen-inch Superman could be rocketed from a propulsion device to take temporary flight. More detailed models commanded $200 premiums from serious collectors willing to pay to capture Superman in mid-heroics, heaving the nose of a plane skyward or taking Lois for a flight around the *Planet*'s trademark globe.

While Singer had circumvented Peters's efforts to turn the film into an elongated toy commercial, he and his writers were sensitive to the studio's need for supplemental income. They outfitted Superman for his five-year outer space exodus in a jet-black leotard, giving Warner an excuse to market different action figures. It was the sole concession to the producer, who had never gotten his wish for giant spiders, homosexual robots, or an earthbound Superman.

That journey back to Krypton's ruins, where Kal-El comes to grips with the destruction of his heritage, was shot at great expense: $10 million was spent on sets and effects work. Singer eventually cut it out when he realized it didn't move the narrative forward. Also removed were references to September 11, which Singer ultimately found to be overwrought.

Filming for *Superman Returns*, uneventful as "event" pictures go, was completed in the fall of 2005. That left less than a year for optical effects to be completed and for Singer to edit together his footage. The marathon effort may have prompted Singer to become disconnected in the home stretch: sources close to the production maintain that his editing duties were compromised by excessive partying and bleary-eyed orchestration in the days following.

On soundstages a world away from Australia, another Superman production was being mounted, one as different in tone and content as was possible.

Paul Bernbaum, a screenwriter who cut his teeth on episodic television, had long admired the *Adventures of Superman* series with George Reeves. (In the early 1990s, he even purchased one of Reeves's original costumes for $43,000.) As Bernbaum grew older, he also grew more fascinated with the actor's lurid private affairs. In 2002, he wrote a spec script that explored Reeves's life and untimely death. Focus Features—then USA Films—purchased it shortly after it hit the open market; Kyle MacLachlan (*Twin Peaks*) lobbied for the role of Reeves.

"He did a screen test," recalled Bernbaum. "Early on, [directors] Michael and Mark Polish were attached to the script. Kyle is somebody that they wanted to use. But by the time something gets to film, so many things happen. The script went from USA to Miramax, then back to USA. The Polish brothers weren't attached to it anymore, and it just didn't happen with Kyle." The new regime cast Adrien Brody as a fictionalized ver-

Actor Ben Affleck appears as doomed TV personality George Reeves in the 2006 feature *Hollywoodland.*

(© Focus Features/Everett Collection)

sion of the investigator hired by Reeves's mother to search for the truth behind his death; Ben Affleck signed to play Reeves soon after.

In order to accommodate the murky suspicions surrounding Reeves's fate, Bernbaum scripted multiple scenarios regarding what happened the night of the actor's death, giving each viewer the option of selecting the explanation that makes the most sense to him or her.

"They were all drunk, George was drunk, he was on pain medication, and he'd apparently canceled the wedding two days beforehand," said Bernbaum. "I could definitely see a fight going on between him and Leonore Lemmon. She was not a meek little woman. I don't think she killed him, but accidentally, that's a possibility." The writer added, however, that "if I had to make a decision, I would say he shot himself."

Before filming began, Affleck consulted with Jack Larson on his friendship with Reeves. "I have the best goodwill in the world toward Ben, whom I spent a day with," Larson recalled. "I understand he's terrific as George. I just hope they don't accuse Toni Mannix of this bizarre murder."

Larson's peer Noel Neill was less enthused, dismissing the film as a "horror movie."

"Ben Affleck is portraying George Reeves, which is a laugh," she scoffed. "I talked to the writer and he said he had written a part for me, but I guess people were cut out for whatever reason. That was fine with me." (Both Neill and Larson appear in *Superman Returns*, Neill as a dying heiress taken financial advantage of by Luthor, Larson as a barkeep.)

Initially, Warner was unwilling to let the rival studio use any of its trademarked material, which meant Affleck would be forced to parade around in a costume devoid of the Superman emblem. The studio later relented, but censored any sight of the trademark in promotional spots. The film's original title, *Truth, Justice, and the American Way*, was scuttled due to similar issues.

Hollywoodland was released in September 2006, some months after Bryan Singer's spectacle hit theaters. Affleck, whose career had been tee-tering since a series of misfires—most notably the critically reviled *Gigli*—received generally good notices for his portrayal of Reeves's tortured psyche. His film did only modest business.

Relative to the expenditure, so did its bigger brother.

On the heels of a multimedia blitz, *Superman Returns* bowed in nearly four thousand theaters on June 28, 2006, two days earlier than Warner had orig-inally planned. Audiences had been primed for the character's comeback with ceaseless television spots and his visage adorning everything from bath towels to soft drinks. A&E had even aired an edited version of a Superman documentary produced by Singer, essentially a two-hour commercial for the film. (Kevin Spacey narrated, but only after prolonged prodding from Singer.) National Geographic broadcast a *Science of Superman* special that speculated on the Man of Steel's abilities in terms of real-world physics. (One disturbing revelation: Superman catching a falling Lois would likely result in her neck breaking.)

Routh's Superman even appeared on the cover of *The Advocate*, a popu-lar gay publication. Inside, an article debated the lithe, dark-haired super-hero's sexual preference and drew parallels between his secret identity and the public personas of closeted community members. Singer was puzzled, declaring the film "the most heterosexual" he'd ever directed. Amid the controversy, DC directed those so inclined to sample Batwoman, a charac-ter newly revealed as a lesbian.

Critics found nothing as terminally offensive in *Superman Returns* as in the anemic sequels of the 1980s; they did, however, find the film curi-ously morose. "This is a glum, lackluster movie," sighed Roger Ebert, who also took aim at Routh's middling performance. "Routh lacks charisma as Superman," he wrote. Ebert, like several critics, found it odd that Routh had few lines as Clark, and even fewer as Superman. He seemed to exist as a veritable action figure, all daring and little exposition.

Others found little pleasure in the overt messianic subtext; at one point, Superman appears to fall from the skies with his arms outstretched, a deafeningly obvious reference to Christ's crucifixion. Even the immortal "Death of Superman" angle is revisited briefly as the hero lies dying in a hospital, his supporters standing vigil outside its doors.

Some who had worked on abandoned versions of the Superman project were disenchanted by what eventually made it to the screen. "After all this time, they put out a movie and it goes nowhere," Keith Giffen moaned. "I don't like the film because of the implications. In [Donner's original] *Superman*, everyone spent a lot of time talking to this giant Marlon Brando head. It said, 'You're the last survivor of Krypton, good luck. It blew up.' So what's the linchpin of this movie? 'I think I'll go see if Krypton's there!' And I come back bummed because it's not? Go talk to Marlon Brando!"

Though Singer's adaptation doesn't match the more criminal attempts to repaint the character, it does commit to a single element of controversy by introducing Lois Lane's son, whose emerging powers imply he's the progeny of the newly returned hero. The continuity is confusing: If Singer is, as he states, hewing to the Donner template, one assumes the child is the result of Clark and Lois's union in *Superman II*. But if so, what of the moronic "super kiss" planted on Lane at the climax of that film? If she was robbed of her memory of the affair, an inexplicable pregnancy would be a rather rude intrusion. The idea is never explored.

Amid conflicting reactions, *Superman Returns* earned $21 million its opening day, placing it at a middling eigth on the list of all-time midweek openings. In contrast, *Spider-Man 2*, released two years prior, collected $40 million under similar circumstances.

By the end of its first seven-day stretch, Singer's film had earned $106 million. The numbers were solid but hardly encouraging. The movie was performing well, but it wasn't meeting the standards set by a $300 million investment and a marquee bleating the name of the most recognizable character in comics.

The news was humbling to the studio, which had seen its other major summer release, a noisy remake of *The Poseidon Adventure*, stumble. Singer expressed his ire early on, claiming that he "had certain issues" with Warner's marketing strategies, which appeared muted in comparison to Sony's *Spider-Man* efforts.

Most notably, the film lost the battle initiated in the trade papers between it and Fox's second *X-Men* sequel, which had opened a month earlier. Following Singer's departure, the director's chair had been filled by Matthew Vaughn, who departed just as quickly for unspecified "personal reasons." Desperate to make the planned release date, Fox called Brett Ratner.

Both fans and media had predicted that the hasty production and Ratner's questionable creative impulses would've doomed the franchise; instead, *X-Men: The Last Stand* blossomed into a $459 million global hit, compared to $391 million for *Superman Returns*. Domestically, the X-Men brought in $234 million to Superman's $200 million.

From a statistical standpoint, *Superman*'s IMAX take was more impressive: by its thirteenth week of release, the film had earned $30 million in just 128 theaters screening the 3-D experience. It was the first studio film to be shown in an enhanced version designed specifically for the oversized format, which submerges viewers in an intense audiovisual experience. (Only twenty minutes of the film is in 3-D.)

"'Superman Returns' will be profitable for us," Warner's Jeff Robinov told the *Hollywood Reporter*. "We would have liked it to have made more money, but it reintroduced the character in a great way and was a good launching pad for the next picture." Warner head Alan Horn told the *L.A. Times* that *Returns* "should have done $500 million worldwide"; it wound up making just over three-quarters of that amount.

The postmortem soon turned to the question of whether Warner would actually move forward with the franchise, one that it had battled for so long to revive. Early, Singer told reporters a sequel would arrive in 2009; industry types circulated rumors that Horn would insist the follow-up be brought in at a more reasonable $150 million. In October 2006, the studio formally announced that Singer would return as director and producer for the sequel, soon christened *The Man of Steel*. The film was set for a March 2008 shoot and summer 2009 release.

The news may have come as a surprise to commentators who presumed Warner had egg on its face over the first film's pedestrian returns. But most stories on the matter refused to consider the film's success as a device for the merchandising: *Superman Returns* paraphernalia accounted for a large portion of Mattel's second-quarter profits in 2006. Warner shared the company's good fortune in licensing revenues.

Singer insisted a sequel would provide more of the action that fans had lamented the absence of in his inaugural flight, with more science fiction whiz-bang and possibly an appearance by nemesis Zod.

Wolfgang Petersen continued to support a *World's Finest* team-up film. (Routh was less enthused, telling *Wizard* in 2006 that the two heroes "should never be at war.") Warner's own ideas made Petersen's plan seem almost quaint in comparison: in early 2007, studio executives began informal talks to bring their *Justice League* property into live action, discussing the possibility of having Superman anchor the squad of lesser-known heroes. The inaugural screenwriters were Kieran and Michele Mulroney; vaunted for their script-doctoring abilities on big-budget eye candy like *Mr. & Mrs. Smith*, the husband-and-wife team had no original credits on their resume.

Immediately, fans began to wonder whether or not Warner's next big franchise would fall into the same creative doldrums as its predecessors.

———

At the premiere of *Superman Returns* at Grauman's Chinese Theater in Los Angeles, Tom Mankiewicz and Richard Donner settled into their seats.

Mankiewicz turned to his friend and collaborator: "Boyo, if I told you twenty-eight years ago that thirty years from now we're going to be sitting in a theater in Westwood for the opening of a *Superman* movie—"

Donner interrupted him. "I would've had you removed for a mental exam."

The lights went down. The curtains parted. And despite Hollywood's most concentrated efforts to the contrary, Superman flew again.

Epilogue

Following his infiltration of the Klan, **Stetson Kennedy** went on to write several books, including *Southern Exposure* and *I Rode with the Ku Klux Klan*. Now in his nineties, he remains one of the most valuable sources of information on the racial prejudice of twentieth-century America.

Bud Collyer was just as successful on television as in radio: he hosted *Beat the Clock* for eleven years and *To Tell the Truth* for twelve. He died of a circulatory ailment on September 8, 1969, at the age of sixty-one.

Max Fleischer continued to dabble in animation until his death from congestive heart failure in 1972 at the age of eighty-nine. During his latter days, he had resided in the Motion Picture & Television Country House, a rest home for industry retirees.

Kirk Alyn made occasional appearances on episodic television through the 1960s; in the 1970s, he enjoyed the nostalgic attention of conventiongoers, making frequent appearances at shows paying tribute to his best-known role. He died from natural causes in 1999. He was eighty-eight.

Following her tenure on *Adventures of Superman*, **Noel Neill** quit acting to focus on her family. Now in her late eighties, she still makes appearances at conventions.

Adventures of Superman producer **Robert Maxwell** supervised children's fare like *Lassie* and the TV adaptation of *National Velvet* through the 1960s. He died February 3, 1971.

Jack Larson went on to produce several films with professional and personal partner James Bridges, including *Urban Cowboy* and *Bright Lights, Big City*. Now in his late seventies, he resides in California.

After the George Reeves series ended, producer **Whitney Ellsworth** went on to consult for TV's *Batman* before retiring to attend to his painting. He died at the age of seventy-one in September 1980.

With Chuck Harter, **Bob Holiday** wrote a book on his experiences with stage heroics, *Superman on Broadway*. Now in his seventies, he owns Bob Holiday Homes in Hawley, Pennsylvania.

Margot Kidder has worked only sporadically since the 1990s, appearing in several episodes of ABC's *Brothers & Sisters*. A native of Canada, she became a U.S. citizen in 2005.

Marlon Brando made intermittent appearances in features, which climaxed with his supporting role in 2001's *The Score* alongside Robert De Niro. He died of pulmonary fibrosis on July 1, 2004, at the age of eighty.

Gene Hackman entered the 1990s as one of film's more respected actors, known for infusing populist entertainment with carefully crafted performances. He won a Best Supporting Actor Oscar for 1992's *Unforgiven*.

Jack O'Halloran found work as heavies in episodes of 1980s television series including *Murder, She Wrote* and *Hunter*. Offscreen since the 1994 feature film *The Flintstones*, he now works in the software industry.

Richard Donner orchestrated some of the more indelible examples of 1980s cinema, including not only the *Lethal Weapon* films but also *The Goonies*. His *16 Blocks*, starring Bruce Willis as a beleaguered cop, did modest business for Warner in 2006.

Richard Lester abandoned directing after the tragedy involving actor Roy Kinnear during the shooting of *The Return of the Musketeers*. In the 1990s, director Steven Soderbergh interviewed him for a book about Lester's career; transcripts of their extensive conversations compose the bulk of 1999's *Getting Away with It*.

Richard Pryor was diagnosed with multiple sclerosis in 1986; the disease slowly curtailed his presence at the box office. He passed away at the age of sixty-five on December 10, 2005.

In the early 1990s, **Helen Slater** voiced Talia al Ghul in several episodes of *Batman: The Animated Series*. In 2007, she agreed to appear as Supergirl's aunt in season seven of *Smallville*.

After misfires like *Honor Bound*, **Jeannot Szwarc** stepped away from helming theatrical features; he returned to directing episodic television in the late 1990s. His credits include episodes of *Boston Legal*, *Without a Trace*, and *Smallville*.

In 1979, **Tom Mankiewicz** cowrote and directed the pilot for the long-running TV detective drama *Hart to Hart*, and went on to helm several episodes. In 1985, he reunited with Richard Donner, helping to script the fantasy epic *Ladyhawke*. His first feature directing effort, 1987's *Dragnet*, was a big-screen homage to the Jack Webb procedural series of the 1950s and '60s.

Ilya Salkind founded the Ilya Salkind Company in 2003. The company produced *Young Alexander the Great* and has planned a film version of the legend of the Abominable Snowman. In 2005, Salkind announced his intention to film a bio picture on the lives of Jerry Siegel and Joe Shuster.

After splitting from friend Ilya, **Pierre Spengler** found rejuvenated success as the producer of direct-to-video movies, including several Jean-Claude Van Damme vehicles and the *Pumpkinhead* horror franchise.

John Haymes Newton found recurring work as a guest star in various TV dramas, including *Nash Bridges* and *ER*. He's also appeared in several episodes of *Desperate Housewives*.

Gerard Christopher made several appearances in dramas like *Silk Stalkings* and *Melrose Place*. He is now involved in real estate.

Dean Cain continued to appear in made-for-TV movie roles, the most notable of which was his turn as convicted murderer Scott Peterson in *The Perfect Husband*. In 2007, he agreed to a guest appearance as the villainous Dr. Curtis Knox on *Smallville*.

Teri Hatcher assumed another high-profile role by appearing as a Bond girl in 1997's *Tomorrow Never Dies*. In 2004, she became the focus of media scrutiny thanks to her "comeback" vehicle, the hit ABC ensemble drama *Desperate Housewives*. The role earned her a Golden Globe for Best Actress in a Musical or Comedy in 2005.

In 2004, **Kevin Smith** scripted a screen version of lesser-known super-hero tale *The Green Hornet* with intentions to direct. He later withdrew, citing pressure over being responsible for a major studio release and unease over interpreting iconic characters in light of his *Superman* debacle. He instead concentrated his efforts on his own New Jersey–based mythology, the View Askewniverse, releasing *Clerks II* in 2006.

Tim Burton teamed with frequent collaborator Johnny Depp for *Charlie and the Chocolate Factory* in 2005 and *Sweeney Todd* in 2007. In a mirror of his *Superman* experience, his involved efforts to dramatize the life of weird-news archivist Robert Ripley were scuttled when Paramount refused to sign off on the exorbitant budget.

Nicolas Cage alternated box office successes (*National Treasure*) with misses (*Matchstick Men*). In early 2007, the comics aficionado finally assumed the guise of a four-color hero, Marvel's vengeful spirit Ghost Rider. The film was a box office success. In 2005, he named his second child Kal-El.

Jon Peters received his executive producer credit on *Superman Returns*. He made headlines in summer 2006 when he sued to evict ex-wife Christine Forsyth-Peters from his property in Los Angeles. The two had been divorced since 1993; Forsyth-Peters maintained that their postdissolution difficulties stemmed from stress over the *Superman* feature.

McG followed up his *Charlie's Angels* sequel with *We Are Marshall*, a docudrama examining the aftermath of the plane crash in 1970 that claimed the lives of thirty-seven members of the Marshall University football team.

Following his success with *X-Men: The Last Stand*, **Brett Ratner** released his third *Rush Hour* film in summer 2007. Despite middling reviews, it made $49 million its opening weekend.

As a teen idol, **Tom Welling** made the obligatory appearance in a horror movie, 2005's *The Fog*. He also appeared in two *Cheaper by the Dozen* films, portraying the second-eldest member of Steve Martin's clan. He was contracted to appear through seven seasons of *Smallville*.

Bryan Singer promised to get "all *Wrath of Khan*" on the *Superman Returns* sequel slotted for a summer 2009 release. He continued to executive-produce the medical drama *House* on the Fox network and directed Tom Cruise in the World War II thriller *Valkyrie*.

Following the premiere of *Superman Returns*, **Brandon Routh** introduced his wax doppelganger at Madame Tussauds wax museum and voiced a character in an episode of the animated series *The Batman*. His follow-up film, *Life Is Hot in Cracktown*, had the actor portraying a drug addict.

Following his return to the screen in 2006's *Superman Returns*, **Superman** married longtime flame Lois Lane during a public ceremony held in the fortuitously named Metropolis, Illinois; he continues to negotiate his contract for future sequels.

Though said to be generally agreeable to work with, he remains adamant that no green M&Ms be placed in his trailer.

Source Notes

Chapter 1: Test Patterns

Cabarga, Leslie. Telephone interview by author. July 19, 2006.

Kennedy, Stetson. Telephone interview by author. October 2, 2006.

Neill, Noel. Telephone interview by author. September 20, 2006.

Pointer, Ray. Telephone interview by author. July 26, 2006.

Bracker, Milton. "Turnstiles at Fair Click Record Tune." *New York Times*, July 4, 1940.

Cabarga, Leslie. *The Fleischer Story*. Rev. ed. New York: Da Capo, 1988.

Elliot, Jeff. "Kirk Alyn: Superman Remembers." *Starlog*, March 1979.

Fleischer, Richard. *Out of the Inkwell*. Lexington: University Press of Kentucky, 2005.

Grossman, Gary H. *Superman: Serial to Cereal*. New York: Popular Library, 1976.

Maltin, Leonard. *Of Mice and Magic*. New York: Plume, 1987.

Scapperotti, Dan. "Able to Soar Higher Than Any Bird." *Comics Scene*, February 1990.

TIME. Americana. March 28, 1949.

———. "Are Comics Fascist?" October 22, 1945.

———. "Cliff-Hangers." May 31, 1948.

———. "Comic Culture." December 18, 1944.

———. "Jungle Sam." December 1, 1952.

———. Miscellany. August 10, 1942.

————. The New Pictures. July 6, 1942.

————. "Not So Funny." October 4, 1948.

————. "Superman Adopted." May 31, 1948.

————. "Superman in the Flesh." September 14, 1942.

————. "Superman's Dilemma." April 13, 1942.

Tollin, Anthony. CD booklet for *Superman on Radio*. Schiller Park, IL: Radio Spirits, 1997.

Chapter 2: The Monkey Suit

Larson, Jack. Telephone interview by author. July 17, 2006.

Neill, Noel. Telephone interview by author. September 20, 2006.

Bifulco, Michael J. *Superman on Television*. 10th anniversary ed. Grand Rapids, Mich.: Michael Bifulco Publishing, 1998.

Brian's Page. "The Mainstream Scene Database." www.brianspage.com/database.html (accessed August 29, 2007).

Grossman, Gary H. *Superman: Serial to Cereal*. New York: Popular Library, 1976.

Kashner, Sam, and Nancy Schoenberger. *Hollywood Kryptonite*. New York: St. Martin's Press, 1996.

LeBell, Gene. *The Godfather of Grappling*. Santa Monica, CA: Gene LeBell Enterprises, 2004.

Mandell, Paul. "TV's Superman Remembered." Pts. 1, 2, and 3. *Starlog*, October 1983, November 1983, December 1983.

Schwartz, Julius, with Brian M. Thomsen. *Man of Two Worlds*. New York: HarperCollins, 2000.

Swires, Steve. "Superman's Pal Jack Larson." *Starlog*, June 1988.

Weaver, Tom. "Phyllis Coates." *Starlog*, February 1989.

Wilson, Patricia Ellsworth. "Ellsworth at the Grand Canyon: Present at the Creation of Superman and the Mole-Men." *The Adventures Continue* 14 (Summer 1997).

Chapter 3: Purgatory

Holiday, Bob. Telephone interview by author. July 31, 2006.

Larson, Jack. Telephone interview by author. July 17, 2006.

Lupus, Peter. Telephone interview by author. October 17, 2006.

Harter, Chuck. *Superboy & Superpup: The Lost Videos*. Hollywood, Calif.: Cult Movies, 1993.

Holiday, Bob, and Chuck Harter. *Superman on Broadway*. 2003.

Stephens, Lynn. "Able to Bend Playbill in His Bare Hands." *Comics Scene*, February 1990.

TIME. "Paper Cutups." April 9, 1966.

Chapter 4: Flights of Fancy

Mankiewicz, Tom. Telephone interview by author. August 21, 2006.

Salkind, Ilya. Telephone interview by author. February 7, 2006.

Bosworth, Patricia. *Marlon Brando*. New York: Viking, 2001.

Brando, Marlon, with Robert Lindsey. *Songs My Mother Taught Me*. New York: Random House, 1994.

Casting Society of America, "'Lethal Weapon' director/producer and 'Heroes' casting executive to be honored at Casting Society of America's 23rd Annual Artios Awards." Press release, August 2, 2007.

Donner, Richard. Interview by Kenneth Plume. IGN Entertainment, May 1, 2001, http://movies.ign.com/articles/057/057536p1.html.

———. "Richard Donner on Superman." Inverview by Don Shay. *Cinefantastique*, Summer 1979.

Gerani, Gary. "Bringing the Comics to the Screen." *Starlog*, November 1976.

Harmetz, Aljean. "The Life and Exceedingly Hard Times of Superman." *New York Times*, June 14, 1981.

Hunter, Allan. *Gene Hackman*. New York: St. Martin's Press, 1987.

Manso, Peter. *Brando: The Biography*. New York: Hyperion, 1994.

TIME. "Here Comes Superman!!!" November 27, 1978.

———. "Paperback Godfather." August 28, 1978.

———. People. April 14, 1975.

Chapter 5: Cape Fears

Mankiewicz, Tom. Telephone interview by author. August 21, 2006.

O'Halloran, Jack. Telephone interview by author. August 17, 2006.

Salkind, Ilya. Telephone interview by author. February 7, 2006.

Goldman, William. *Adventures in the Screen Trade*. 2nd rev. ed. London: Abacus, 1996.

Kidder, Margot. "One-on-One with Margot Kidder." Interview by Barry Freiman. Superman Homepage, February 8, 2005, www.supermanhomepage.com/movies/movies.php?topic=interview-expo-kidder.

McMurran. Kristin. "It's Stardom, Not Flying, That Christopher Reeve Fears." *People*, January 8, 1979.

Prowse, David. *Straight from the Force's Mouth*. Filament Publishing, 2006.

Reeve, Christopher. *Still Me*. New York: Random House, 1999.

Starlog. "Chris Reeve to Play Superman." June 1977.

Chapter 6: Metropolis Now

Adams, Neal. Telephone interview by author. October 4, 2006.

Mankiewicz, Tom. Telephone interview by author. August 21, 2006.

O'Halloran, Jack. Telephone interview by author. August 17, 2006.

Salkind, Ilya. Telephone interview by author. February 7, 2006.

Dorfman, Kent. "Superman: Ready for Takeoff." *Starlog*, February 1979.

Meyers, Richard. "Ilya Salkind." *Starlog*, January 1978.

———. "The Man of Steel Has Got to Fly." *Starlog*, August 1978.

———. "Superman the Movie" *Starlog*, March 1979.

Petrou, David Michael. *The Making of Superman the Movie*. New York: Warner Books, 1978.

Siegel, Jerry. "Superman Originator Puts 'Curse' on Superman Movie." Press release, October 1975. In "Jerry Siegel's 1975 Press Release," http://homepage.mac.com/mikecatron/.Pictures/SiegelPR1975wm.pdf.

Starlog. "Superman Film Takes Flight." October 1977.

TIME. "Onward and Upward with the New Superman." August 1, 1977.

Chapter 7: Reel Steel

Mankiewicz, Tom. Telephone interview by author. August 21, 2006.

O'Halloran, Jack. Telephone interview by author. August 17, 2006.

Salkind, Ilya. Telephone interview by author. February 7, 2006.

Barthel, Joan. "Christopher Reeve: A Surprising, Super Man." *Cosmopolitan*, March 1983.

Clarke, Frederick S. Sense of Wonder. *Cinefantastique*, Summer 1979.

Donner, Richard. "Richard Donner on Superman." Inverview by Don Shay. *Cinefantastique*, Summer 1979.

Ebert, Roger. Review of *Superman: The Movie. Chicago Sun-Times*, December 15, 1978.

Fyrbourne, Richard. "The Man Behind Superman: Richard Donner." *Starlog*, January 1979.

Kael, Pauline. "The Package." Review of *Superman: The Movie. The New Yorker*, January 1, 1979.

Reeve, Christopher. Interview by Brian McKernan. *Omni*, March 1983.

———. Quoted in untitled *Superman II* article by Dave Pine. *Time Out*, April 1981.

Starlog. "Hollywood Hotline." December 1981.

———. "Record Price for Superman Comic." August 1980.

———. "Super-Money Mystery." November 1980.

———. "Superbman—The Other Movie." November 1980.

———. "Superman II Movie Magazine." June 1981.

———. "Superman II Progress Report." June 1979.

———. "Superman Lands in Top Secret Base." July 1980.

TIME. "Man and Superman." January 5, 1976.

Chapter 8: Dicked

Mankiewicz, Tom. Telephone interview by author. August 21, 2006.

O'Halloran, Jack. Telephone interview by author. August 17, 2006.

Salkind, Ilya. Telephone interview by author. February 7, 2006.

Burns, James. "Sarah Douglas." *Starlog*, June 1981.

Crawley, Tony. "Superman II Sequel Chaos." *Starburst*, April 1979.

Dickholtz, Daniel. "Steel Dreams." *Starlog Yearbook*, 1998.

Donner, Richard. Quoted in "Able to Change the Course of Mighty Movies" by Edward Gross. *Comics Scene*, February 1990.

Greenberg, Robert. "Superman II: The Adventure Continues." *Starlog*, May 1981.

Gross, Edward. "Able to Change the Course of Mighty Movies." *Comics Scene*, February 1990.

Kidder, Margot. Interview by Fred Topel. About.com, November 27, 2006, http://movies.about.com/od/directorinterviews/a/donner112706_2.htm.

Lester, Peter. "Tell Us It Ain't So, Superman!" *People*, August 24, 1981.

Lester, Richard. Interview by Steven Soderbergh. In *Getting Away with It*. London: Faber and Faber, 1999.

Maltin, Leonard. *Leonard Maltin's Movie Guide*. 2007 ed. New York: Plume, 2006.

Munn, Mike. "The Making of Superman II." *Starburst*, March 1981.

Reeve, Christopher. Quoted in untitled *Superman II* article by Dave Pine. *Time Out*, April 1981.

Starlog. From Around the SF World . . . May 1980.

———. "Star Wars, Empire . . . Going Once, Going Twice." January 1982.

———. "Superman II Ready for Flight." July 1979.

TIME. People. April 14, 1975.

Yule, Andrew. *The Man Who Framed the Beatles*. New York: Donald Fine, 1994.

Chapter 9: Pryor Motives

Salkind, Ilya. Telephone interview by author. February 7, 2006.

Best of Starlog Volume 4. "Final World on Greatest American Hero Lawsuit." 1983.

Boyer, Da Marie, and Patrick Daniel O'Neill. "David and Leslie Newman: Super-Screenwriters." *Starlog*, August 1983.

Ebert, Roger. Review of *Superman III*. *Chicago Sun-Times*, June 17, 1983.

Garrett, James. Quoted in *The Man Who Framed the Beatles* by Andrew Yule. New York: Donald Fine, 1994.

Greenberger, Robert. "Annette O'Toole: The New Woman in Superman's Life." *Starlog*, July 1983.

———. "Cary Bates: 17 Years with the Man of Steel." *Comics Scene*, September 1983.

———. "Superman III." *Starlog*, February 1983.

Hunter, Allan. *Gene Hackman*. New York: St. Martin's Press, 1987.

Kidder, Margot. Quoted in "Tell Us It Ain't So, Superman!" by Peter Lester. *People*, August 24, 1981.

Pryor, Richard, with Todd Gold. *Pryor Convictions*. New York: Pantheon, 1995.

Reeve, Christopher. Interview by Brian McKernan. *Omni*, March 1983.

———. Interview by Brian McKernan. Transcript. March 1983. CapedWonder.com, www.capedwonder.com/newwebsite/pages/articles.htm.

———. Quoted in "Tell Us It Ain't So, Superman!" by Peter Lester. *People*, August 24, 1981.

Starlog. "Are You Ready for Superman III?" September 1981.

———. Log Entries. October 1983.

———. "Pryor Would Love Role in Superman III." October 1981.

———. Star-Studded News. June 1982.

———. "Superman III Takes Flight." December 1982.

Chapter 10: Girl Power

Salkind, Ilya. Telephone interview by author. February 7, 2006.

Szwarc, Jeannot. Telephone interview by author. November 5, 2006.

Bosco, Scott Michael. "Ilya Salkind Interview." *Digital Cinema*, April 2000.

———. "Jeannot Szwarc Interview." *Digital Cinema*, November 1999.

Dunaway, Faye. *Looking for Gatsby*. New York: Simon & Schuster, 1995.

Ebert, Roger. Review of *Supergirl*. *Chicago Sun-Times*, January 1, 1984.

Johnson, Kim Howard. "Derek Meddings: The Man Who Creates the Magic for Supergirl." *Starlog*, June 1984.

O'Neill, Patrick Daniel. "Helen Slater: Learning to Fly as Supergirl." *Starlog*, December 1984.

Pirani, Adam. "Jeannot Szwarc: Filming the Fantasy of Supergirl." *Starlog*, January 1985.

Starlog. "Supergirl Soars This Summer." May 1984.

Chapter 11: Nuclear Disaster

Mankiewicz, Tom. Telephone interview by author. August 21, 2006.

Salkind, Ilya. Telephone interview by author. February 7, 2006.

Wolfman, Marv. E-mail interview by author. July 13, 2006.

Broeske, Pat. "Man of Steal?" *Los Angeles Times*, April 26, 1987.

D'Angelo, Carr. "It's a Bird, It's a Plane, It's Superman IV." *Comics Scene* 3, no. 12 (1987).

Delugach, Al. "Cannon's Bid as Major Studio." *Los Angeles Times*, August 24, 1986.

Easton, Nina. "Superman Lawsuit Trial Date Set." *Los Angeles Times*, February 1, 1990.

Ebert, Roger. *Two Weeks in the Midday Sun: A Cannes Notebook*. Kansas City: Andrews and McMeel, 1987.

Friendly, David. "They're Lowering Their Sites at Cannon Films." *Los Angeles Times*, January 15, 1987.

Gross, Edward. *Superman IV* retrospective. Cinescape.com, April 28, 2000, www.mania.com/20867.html.

Hackworth, CB. "Son of Krypton, Son of Cannon." *Starlog*, July 1986.

Johnson, Kim Howard. "Lois Lane's Last Headline." *Starlog*, July 1987.

———. "Unmasking of Superman." *Starlog*, August 1987.

McAsh, Iain. "Christopher Reeve Flies High." *Film Review*, July 1987.

———. "Pillow Talk." *Film Review*, July 1987.

Mills, Bart. "Mighty Superman IV to Rescue." *Los Angeles Times*, January 2, 1987.

Nickson, Chris. *Superhero: A Biography of Christopher Reeve*. New York: St. Martin's Press, 1999.

Plesset, Ross. "Time Tunnel: Superman IV." *Dreamwatch*, July 2006.

Pyun, Albert. Interview by Nicanor Loreti. *La Cosa Cine Fantastico*, July 2005.

Reeve, Christopher. Interview by Brian McKernan. *Omni*, March 1983.

Warren, Bill. "The Animated Adventures of Superman." *Comics Scene* 3, no. 16 (1988).

Chapter 12: Escape the Cape

Christopher, Gerard. Telephone interview by author. October 11, 2006.

Salkind, Ilya. Telephone interview by author. February 7, 2006.

Blaising, Matthew, et al. "Superboy Star Reveals How He Flies." *San Francisco Examiner*, August 18, 1989.

Brady, David. "Alexander and Ilya Salkind's new Superboy is perhaps worst comic adaptation to date." *Los Angeles Times*, November 13, 1988.

Brennan, Judy. "Family Feud in Wake of Columbus Movies." *Los Angeles Times*, November 24, 1993.

Buckley, Steve. "'Original' Superman Story Doesn't Fly." *Boston Herald*, January 1, 1997.

Gross, Edward. "John Haymes Newton: Boy of Steel." *Comics Scene* 4, no. 17 (1989).

Mangels, Andy. "Superman: The Man of Screen." *Wizard Superman Tribute Edition*, 1993.

Timpone, Anthony. "The Adventures of Superboy." *Starlog*, February 1989.

Willman, David. "Columbus Sails Right Past Bankruptcy." *Los Angeles Times*, May 6, 1992.

Chapter 13: Krypton by Moonlight

Christopher, Gerard. Telephone interview by author. October 11, 2006.

Zabel, Bryce. Telephone interview by author. October 9, 2006.

Cain, Dean. Quoted in "Raising Cain" by Mark A. Perigard. *Boston Herald*, March 25, 1997.

Cerone, Daniel. "Superman Undergoing Planetary Shift." *Los Angeles Times*, September 17, 1994.

Flint, Joe, and Dan Snierson. "Clark Canned." *Entertainment Weekly*, May 30, 1997.

Jacobs, A. J. "Citizen Cain." *Entertainment Weekly*, February 16, 1996.

Los Angeles Times. Untitled *Lois & Clark* article. July 12, 1994.

Mangels, Andy. "Hollywood Heroes." *Hero Illustrated*, January 1994.

Nakayama, William. "Dean Cain: Humanizing Superman." *GoldSea Asian American Daily*, n.d.

Scheider, Roy. Quoted in "That Man in a Cape Is Still Flying" by John J. O'Conner. *New York Times*, April 9, 1995.

Weinstein, Steve. "Done In by Low Ratings." *Los Angeles Times*, June 14, 1997.

Chapter 14: Down, Down and Astray

Gilroy, Dan. Telephone interview by author. September 20, 2006.

Smith, Kevin. E-mail interview by author. February 9, 2006.

Braden, Scott. "Superman Lives?" *Riot*, December 1997.

Griffin, Nancy, and Kim Masters. *Hit and Run: How Jon Peters and Peter Guber Took Sony for a Ride in Hollywood*. New York: Simon & Schuster, 1996.

Gross, Edward. "Super Mess." *Cinescape*, May/June 1998.

———. "Superman Lives: The Development Hell of an Unmade Film." Cinescape.com, May 5, 2000, www.mania.com/20991.html.

———. "Superman Reborn." *Cinescape*, June 1995.

Lamken, Brian Saner. "The Ever-Lovin' Blue-Eyed Timm." *Comicology*, Spring 2000.

Lee, Andy. "Superman Re-Animated." *Fan*, April 1996.

Romano, Lois. "Riding Accident Paralyzes Actor Christopher Reeve." *Washington Post*, June 1, 1995.

Schaefer, Stephen. "'Radio Flyer' Grounded?" *Entertainment Weekly*, September 13, 1991.

Wharton, David. "Superman Ride Still Grounded." *Los Angeles Times*, August 17, 1996.

Chapter 15: Grounded

Despretz, Sylvain. E-mail interview by author. July 13, 2006.

Gilroy, Dan. Telephone interview by author. September 20, 2006.

Smith, Kevin. E-mail interview by author. February 9, 2006.

Ascher-Walsh, Rebecca. "Cape Fear." *Entertainment Weekly*, May 29, 1998.

Burton, Tim. *Burton on Burton*. Edited by Mark Salisbury. London: Faber and Faber, 2000.

Busch, Anita. "Cage Heat." *Premiere*, August 1997.

Cage, Nicolas. Quoted in "Nicolas Cage Is Rocking, Rolling, Adapting" by Ann Oldenburg. *USA Today*, December 2, 2002.

———. Quoted in "Superman Lives, Part 3" by Edward Gross. *Cinecape*, May 19, 2000.

Chang, Kenneth. "Splat! Comic Books No Longer Reaping Big Sales in a Single Bound." *Los Angeles Times*, March 2, 1996.

Grobel, Lawrence. "The Good Times of Nicolas Cage." *Movieline*, June 1998.

Gross, Edward. "Superman Lives: The Development Hell of an Unmade Film." Cinescape.com, May 5, 2000, www.mania.com/20991.html.

Hughes, David. *Greatest Sci-Fi Movies Never Made*. Chicago: A Cappella, 2001.

MacFarquhar, Larissa. "Stranger in Paradise." *Premiere*, June 1997.

McDonald, Heidi. "Inside the Superboy Copyright Decision." *Publisher's Weekly*, April 11, 2006.

Nashawaty, Chris. "A Head of Its Time." *Entertainment Weekly*, November 19, 1999.

Page Six. *New York Post*, August 7, 2001.

Shapiro, Mark. "Steel Reserve." *Starlog*, September 1997.

Spelling, Ian. "Steel Dreams." *Comics Scene*, May 2000.

Chapter 16: The Phantom Zone

Giffen, Keith. Telephone interview by author. July 22, 2006.

Lukic, Butch. Telephone interview by author. July 27, 2005.

Newbern, George. Telephone interview by author. July 28, 2005.

Riba, Dan. Telephone interview by author. July 27, 2005.

Timm, Bruce. Telephone interview by author. July 28, 2005.

Ain't It Cool News. "SUPERMAN LIVES Stuff . . ." January 21, 1999, www.aintitcool.com/node/2856.

Bronstad, Amanda. "Warner Bros. Sued Over Liberal Use of Superman Footage." *Los Angeles Business Journal*, July 15, 2002.

Deutschman, Alan. "Commercial Success." *Fast Company*, January 2005.

Knowles, Harry. "Confirmation on LOBO vs SUPERMAN Movie Development!!!" Ain't It Cool News, October 25, 2000, www.aintitcool.com/node/7288.

Nintendo Power. "Five Worst Games Ever." October 2005.

Chapter 17: Superboy Redux

Aurthur, Kate. "Young Male Viewers Boost 'Smallville.'" *New York Times*, May 20, 2006.

Jensen, Jeff. "Shows of Strength." *Entertainment Weekly*, November 23, 2001.

Levin, Gary. "Smallville Is Super for WB." *USA Today*, November 25, 2002.

McCanlies, Tim. Interview by Daniel Robert Epstein. UGO Networks, n.d.

McDonald, Heidi. "Inside the Superboy Copyright Decision." *Publisher's Weekly*, April 11, 2006.

McNary, Dave. "Super Snit in 'Smallville.'" *Variety*, April 4, 2006.

Moro, Eric. "All the Smallville Things . . ." *Cinescape*, February 2002.

———. "The Hero, the Villain." *Cinescape*, April 2003.

Rabinowitz, Naomi. "Lex Appeal." *Soap Opera Digest*, December 2001.

Rosenbaum, Michael. "Lex-Man." Interview by Brian Hiatt. *Entertainment Weekly*, May 19, 2003.

Rossen, Jake. "'Flash' Animation." *ToyFare*, November 2005.

Siegel and Larson v. Time Warner et al. Order granting defendants' motion for reconsideration. Case no. CV-04-8776-SGL (RZx) (U.S.D.C. Cent. Dist. Calif., July 27, 2007).

Chapter 18: Fear of Flying

Christopher, Gerard. Telephone interview by author. October 11, 2006.

Ebert, Roger. Review of *Armageddon*. *Chicago Sun-Times*, July 1, 1998.

Entertainment Weekly. "Plan of Steel." October 11, 2002.

Fierman, Daniel. "Stallville?" *Entertainment Weekly*, March 14, 2003.

Greenberg, James. "Never Say Die: Superman." *Premiere*, January 2002.

Hiatt, Brian. "Empty Suit." *Entertainment Weekly*, March 18, 2003.

Holson, Laura. "In This Superman Story, Executives Do the Fighting." *New York Times*, September 15, 2002.

———. "Warner Brothers' Chamber of Secrets." *New York Times*, September 7, 2003.

Knowles, Harry. "Harry Talks with JJ Abrams for a Couple of Hours About SUPERMAN." Ain't It Cool News, September 28, 2002, www.aintitcool.com/display.cgi?id=13404.

———. Quoted in Page Six. *New York Post*, March 7, 2003.

Kutcher, Ashton. Quoted in "Ashton Kutcher" by Andrew Goldman. *Details*, September 2006.

Masters, Kim. "A: Men of Steel. Q: What's Been Missing from the Attempt to Pull Off a Hugely Expensive New Version of Superman?" *Esquire*, July 1, 2003.

———. "Why Movies Are So Bad." *Esquire*, December 1, 2002.

McG [Joseph McGinty Nichol]. Quoted in "*Superman* Director McG Quits Project" by Stephen M. Silverman. *People*, July 12, 2004.

Moriarty [Drew McWeeny]. "Moriarty's Review of JJ ABRAMS SUPERMAN Script!!" Ain't It Cool News, September 23, 2002, www.aintitcool.com/display.cgi?id=13350.

Raftery, Brian. "Dynamic Duel." *Entertainment Weekly*, July 26, 2002.

Ratner, Brett. Interview by Devin Faraci. CHUD.com, July 30, 2006, www.chud.com/index.php?type=interviews&id=7251.

Susman, Gary. "Achilles Heel." *Entertainment Weekly*, August 13, 2002.

———. "Bye Bye Brett." *Entertainment Weekly*, March 20, 2003.

———. "Kent Wait." *Entertainment Weekly*, February 27, 2003.

———. "Man and Superman." *Entertainment Weekly*, March 14, 2003.

———. "McG Whiz." *Entertainment Weekly*, June 5, 2003.

———. "Super Friends." *Entertainment Weekly*, July 9, 2004.

——— "Tales from the Kryptonite." *Entertainment Weekly*, September 26, 2002.

———. "Throttled." *Entertainment Weekly*, July 12, 2004.

———. "Wolfgang Petersen to Direct Batman vs. Superman." *Entertainment Weekly*, July 9, 2002.

Tunison, Michael. "McG of Steel?" *Cinescape*, October 2002.

Walker, Paul. Quoted in "Paul Walker on Turning Down Superman." Superhero Hype, November 10, 2003, www.superherohype.com/superman/index.php?id=399.

Webster, Victor. Quoted in "Cape Fear: Who Should Be 'Superman'?" by Kate O'Hare. Zap2it, March 3, 2003.

Chapter 19: Takeoff

Bernbaum, Paul. Telephone interview by author. October 12, 2006.

Giffen, Keith. Telephone interview by author. July 22, 2006.

Larson, Jack. Telephone interview by author. July 17, 2006.

Mankiewicz, Tom. Telephone interview by author. August 21, 2006.

Neill, Noel. Telephone interview by author. September 20, 2006.

Bowles, Guy Scott. "Superman Torch Is Passed." *USA Today*, March 17, 2006.

Callaghan, Dylan. "A God with Feelings." Writers Guild of America West, n.d.

Caviezel, Jim. Interview by Robert Sanchez. IESB.net, October 12, 2004.

Duralde, Alonso. "How Gay Is Superman?" *The Advocate*, June 2, 2006.

Ebert, Roger. Review of *Superman Returns*. *Chicago Sun-Times*, June 27, 2006.

Eller, Claudia. "Picture This: Warner Bros. Having a Rare Down Year." *Los Angeles Times*, August 18, 2006.

Entertainment Weekly. "Superman: People of Steel." June 24, 2005.

———. Untitled Superman fact sheet. April 14, 2006.

Gajewski, Josh. "Homegrown Hero." *USA Weekend*, June 16, 2006.

Grove, Martin. "Singer Was Man of Steel in Making Superman." *Hollywood Reporter*, June 7, 2006.

Head, Steve. "*Superman Returns*: Casting the Man from Krypton." IGN Entertainment, April 12, 2006, http://movies.ign.com/articles/701/701420p1.html.

Jensen, Jeff. "Greatest American Hero?" *Entertainment Weekly*, June 23, 2006.

Knowles, Harry. "Believe It or Not—Orson Welles' BATMAN . . . the Mind Boggles . . ." Ain't It Cool News, September 26, 2003, www.aintitcool.com/display.cgi?id=16188.

———. "$1000 Bet Answered and Accepted Regarding Jesus & SUPERMAN!" Ain't It Cool News, September 2, 2004, www.aintitcool.com/?q=node/18264.

Reuters. "Bootlegging Returns with Superman Sequel." September 29, 2006.

Rich, Joshua. "Hero's Welcome." *Entertainment Weekly*, October 29, 2004.

Robinov, Jeff. Quoted in "Fox Got Bigger Hit, but WB Happy with Singer" by Anne Thompson. *Hollywood Reporter*, August 18, 2006.

Routh, Brandon. Interview by Mike Cotton. *Wizard*, August 2006.

———. Official Web site, n.d. Quoted in Brandon Routh bio. Superman Super Site, www.supermansupersite.com/routh.html.

Singer, Bryan. Quoted in "Fox Got Bigger Hit, but WB Happy with Singer" by Anne Thompson. *Hollywood Reporter*, August 18, 2006.

———. Quoted in "Greatest American Hero?" by Jeff Jensen. *Entertainment Weekly*, June 23, 2006.

———. Quoted in "Superman Torch Is Passed" by Guy Scott Bowles. *USA Today*, March 17, 2006.

Smith, Sean. "Steely Man." *Newsweek*, September 12, 2005.

Spacey, Kevin. Interview by Mike Cotton. *Wizard*, July 2006.

Swanson, Tim. "Super Troupers." *Premiere*, February 2006.

Telegraph. "From Zero to Superhero." June 30, 2006.

Thompson, Anne. "Fox Got Bigger Hit, but WB Happy with Singer." *Hollywood Reporter*, August 18, 2006.

Index